GOSPEL
HERE & NOW

GOSPEL HERE & NOW

YOUR LIFE IN THE STORY OF GOD

JOHN GRECO

Discovery House.
from Our Daily Bread Ministries

Gospel Here and Now: Your Life in the Story of God
© 2018 by John Greco

Discovery House is affiliated with Our Daily Bread Ministries, Grand Rapids, Michigan.

Requests for permission to quote from this book should be directed to: Permissions Department, Discovery House, P.O. Box 3566, Grand Rapids, MI 49501, or contact us by email at permissionsdept@dhp.org.

Interior design by Beth Shagene

Library of Congress Cataloging-in-Publication Data
Names: Greco, John, author.
Title: Gospel here and now : your life in the story of God / John Greco.
Description: Grand Rapids : Discovery House, 2018. | Includes bibliographical
    references.
Identifiers: LCCN 2017043896 | ISBN 9781627078542 (pbk.)
Subjects: LCSH: Bible—Meditations.
Classification: LCC BS491.5 .G728 2018 | DDC 242—dc23
LC record available at https://lccn.loc.gov/2017043896

Printed in the United States of America

First printing in 2018

For Jude

With your round cheeks and bright smile,
you, my son, are a ball of joy.
I love you and pray you will know the joy
of the Lord throughout your life.

Contents

THE GOSPEL HERE AND NOW

"Faith does not eliminate questions.
But faith knows where to take them."
—ELISABETH ELLIOT

Bigger Than a Story

ECCLESIASTES 1:1–11

I entered through the front doors of Christian Heritage School as I had done a thousand times before, but this September morning was different. When I arrived at my desk, it would face the back of the classroom rather than the front. I was now a teacher—at least part-time—at the small Christian school in Trumbull, Connecticut, I had attended years earlier as a student.

A few weeks prior, in what I thought would be a quickly forgotten email, I congratulated the school's new headmaster and offered to help in any way I could as he settled in to his role. To my surprise, he responded that same afternoon, asking if I would meet him for lunch the following day. Over sandwiches and chips at a local grill, he told me there was, in fact, something I could do to help the school: teach an introductory Bible course.

He explained that Bible courses were the most difficult for some of the high school's incoming transfer students. Unlike history, mathematics, or English, the Bible was often a strange and foreign world for young people new to formal Christian education. The headmaster wanted to provide a class that would cover the basics of the Bible, but he needed someone to teach it. The teaching schedules of the full-time faculty were already overloaded, so he was looking for someone with a biblical studies background to teach this course, four days a week. I jumped at the chance.

Since there was no set curriculum, my initial approach was to teach straight through the Bible, starting in Genesis and working my way to Revelation, highlighting important people and events over our two semesters together. The Bible is, after all, a story. That idea has become something of a cliché in recent years with the publication of many wonderful books and studies aimed at helping people read the Bible as a single, unified narrative with Jesus at the center. But, as I discovered during my first few weeks of class, sometimes telling the story is not enough.

On our first day together, I punted. I handed out the course syllabus, told my new students a little about myself, and asked them what they were hoping to learn over the course of our year together. There were only fifteen in the class, so I could spend a couple of minutes focused on each one. Their questions were good, and I left school that afternoon excited to jump into the creation account from Genesis the next day.

Over the next two weeks, however, I found myself continually falling behind in my lesson plans. Each class period would end before I could get to all my points, and I would start the next day trying to make up for the previous day's abrupt ending. Since I was a new teacher, the lion's share of the blame was probably mine, but I sensed there was more to my stumbling pace than that. Every day, the students asked a lot of questions—great, important questions—which would always find their way back to the gospel. Essentially, they wanted to know what difference the gospel should make in their lives. That's why we could never finish the class lessons I had planned.

These were kids who, for the most part, had grown up in church. They were being raised by Christian parents but had gotten the idea that the good news of Jesus Christ was nothing more than getting into heaven someday when they died. These high school students couldn't understand why we were spending so much time in Genesis, talking about Adam and Eve, Noah, and Abraham. No matter how many connections to Jesus I showed them in those early chapters of the Bible, they simply weren't interested. None of it mattered to their everyday lives.

And, in one sense, they were right.

If the Old Testament is only background for Jesus' mission, isn't it worth skipping over? By the same token, if Acts through

Revelation is just the history of the early church—interesting as it may be—isn't that merely a distraction from the gospel? The Bible may well be a unified story from start to finish, but if we can't see that the gospel is there on every page, it doesn't matter how well we know its people, places, and events—it's all just filler. Story is not enough.

In the Dark, Under the Sun

In the book of Ecclesiastes, King Solomon wrote, "What has been is what will be, and what has been done is what will be done, and there is nothing new under the sun" (1:9). It's not the kind of verse you often see on family Christmas cards. It's downright depressing, but it neatly sums up the theme of Ecclesiastes and, I realized much later, the feeling in my classroom.

Solomon wrote as a man looking for fulfillment in this world. He tried everything: acquiring knowledge (1:12–18), pursuing pleasure (2:1–11), living wisely (2:12–17), working hard (2:18–26). He had money, power, and more wives than he could count, but nothing seemed to bring lasting peace and contentment. He discovered what many people have discovered down through the ages into our day: this world is broken, and we are powerless to fix it. "What has been is what will be."

The key to understanding Solomon—and the difference the gospel makes to our lives here and now—lies in the phrase "under the sun." From where we live our lives, *under the sun,* everything does appear to be meaningless. "All is vanity," as Solomon wrote (Ecclesiastes 1:2). We live; we die. We come into this world with nothing, and we leave with nothing. There are joys, to be sure, but there is also suffering, and no one escapes it completely. From this vantage point, it seems Solomon is correct: "There is nothing better for a person than that he should eat and drink and find enjoyment in his toil" (2:24).

If the promise of the gospel is only that we go to heaven when we die, it doesn't change much here and now. That kind of promise makes the hopelessness we often feel in this life only temporary, but it doesn't remove the weight from our shoulders as we walk through this world.

Above the sun, however—now that's a different story. From heaven's perspective, this world may be broken, but it was not always so, and it will not always be so. In fact, because of the life, death, and resurrection of the Son of God, the brokenness of this world is being undone right now. Solomon, in his search, got a glimpse of this. He saw that, in the end, God's justice will prevail: "Fear God and keep his commandments, for this is the whole duty of man. For God will bring every deed into judgment, with every secret thing, whether good or evil" (Ecclesiastes 12:13–14). Solomon indeed discovered there is hope for this life when viewed from God's perspective, above the sun, but he didn't see the whole picture. Not quite. God's plan, as He works through human history, is not just to judge the world but to save it (John 3:17).

In the beginning, the world God created was good. But then, sin invaded. From the garden paradise where God placed our first parents, the disease of sin spread across time and space, corrupting and twisting everything in its path. Everlasting life, as tremendous as it is, does not begin to set all this right. What about the creation around us that waits for its redemption? What about the kingdom of darkness that opposes God and stalks all who have been created in His image? What about God's holy design for humanity, now shattered? The gospel is the cure for every strain of sin's disease. It's so much bigger than a ticket to heaven to hold until we die. That's the good news.

This book will take you on a journey through the Bible, but this trek will do more than simply retell God's story. We'll start with the gospel. More specifically, we'll start with six unique ways in which the death and resurrection of Jesus Christ is said to have changed our world for the better, and we'll trace those themes across biblical history.

Though there are other themes we could survey, I've chosen

six gospel promises that are repeated in different ways over and over again in Scripture. Each theme is given one week of focus, resulting in six weeks' worth of daily readings. The first four days of each week deal with the Old Testament. The fifth chapter is drawn from the Gospels—from the life and teachings of Jesus himself. And the sixth is from the book of Acts, one of the New Testament letters, or Revelation. In God's story, Christians are part of the New Testament community, so the last chapters of each week have special significance as we look at how the gospel affects our lives right here and right now.

The Bible is a story, but it's bigger than a story. It's *God's* story, so it can never really be contained between two leather-clad covers and placed on a shelf. God's story spills out into history and into the lives of His people. But it's difficult to see the roles we are to play if we don't understand what's already taken place. We must know what the gospel has accomplished and we must learn from those who have come and gone before us in this grand narrative.

That's what my high school Bible students really wanted to know: *What difference does the gospel make in my life today?* Looking around, here under the sun, it can be hard to tell. God's Word invites us to take another look, from the vantage point of heaven. And from that lofty place—with history stretched before us and the work of Christ evident across the ages—we will find the hope that Solomon sought all those years ago.

YOUR LIFE IN THE STORY OF GOD

The Bible is a story, but as the story of God, it's a huge, ongoing narrative that permeates every detail of our past, present, and future. The good news of Jesus Christ—the gospel—is more than a ticket to heaven; it's the power and presence of God in our lives here on earth. The gospel is the promise of better things even now, a preview of the day when God makes "all things new" (Revelation 21:5).

1. Why do you think so many people—from King Solomon to many of us today—struggle with feelings of futility? Why does life so often seem to be "vanity"?

2. How would you answer the question my students posed to me: "What difference does the gospel make in my life today?"

3. What areas of life would you most like to see the gospel affect? What kind of change do you long to see?

The Bigger-Than-a-Story Story

2 TIMOTHY 3:16–17

Several years before my stint as a teacher, I was a student at the same small Christian school in suburban Connecticut. During my junior year, I thought it might be fun to try out for our drama department's spring production, *The Music Man*. But while I was patiently waiting for my audition, watching other students perform for the director, a thought occurred to me: *I can't sing or dance.* I had no business trying out for a show like this. When it was finally my turn, I sang a few lines of "Jingle Bells" and admitted that it probably sounded terrible. The director shook her head politely, but I knew the truth.

The only part of my audition I enjoyed was reading from the script. And that must have been the part the director liked too. When the cast was announced, I discovered I had not one or even two but *three* separate speaking roles in the show. I had several costume changes, plenty of makeup to apply and remove and then reapply, and lots of lines to memorize—but I didn't have to sing, and the only dancing I had to attempt was a short waltz on a crowded stage at the end of the show. (The director put me and my dance partner in the back.)

The week before the show premiered, I had memorized my lines, perfected my delivery, and timed all my wardrobe and makeup changes down to the minute. I was ready to go. But then a classmate asked me what the show was about, and I realized that I didn't truly know. I had only skimmed the script for my own lines and showed up at rehearsals when it was time for my own scenes. Even during run-throughs of whole acts, when I wasn't onstage I was backstage, changing clothes or fussing with my fake mustache. I had never actually seen the entire show and decided it might make the experience of being in *The Music Man* a bit more enjoyable if I read the whole script. So, with just a few days to go, I sat down one night and did just that.

Knowing the musical from beginning to end made a difference. While my performances up to that point had been fine, when I understood where my roles and scenes fit into the larger story, my delivery somehow had more life. I could feel it, and my director could see it. After our first dress rehearsal, she asked me what I had done to improve my performance. "Just practice, I guess," I said. I was too embarrassed to admit I had just recently read the script for the first time.

Knowing the Whole Story

For many of us, our experience with the Bible is a lot like my experience with *The Music Man*. We know a few scenes, and we do our best to play the roles we've been given, but we would walk with renewed joy and purpose if we knew where we truly fit in the larger story—if we knew the entire script.

But that's not often the way the Bible is taught. A Sunday morning sermon will usually focus on one text or theme. A Bible study might walk participants through one book of the Bible or trace a topic of interest. And a through-the-Bible reading plan will get a faithful reader from the "In the beginning" of Genesis 1 through the final "Amen" of Revelation 22—but she would be like someone who has traveled across Europe by train, never getting off at a stop. Technically speaking, she saw Europe—but she didn't experience it. Not really anyway.

There is, however, a danger the other way too. Sometimes, in an attempt to find their place in God's story, people impose their own questions on the Bible rather than letting Scripture speak for itself. This can lead people to read false meanings into certain verses, or it can cause tremendous frustration because the answers these readers want to find are just not there.

God's Word makes this promise about itself: "All Scripture is God-breathed and is useful for teaching, rebuking, correcting and training in righteousness, so that the servant of God may be thoroughly equipped for every good work" (2 Timothy 3:16–17 NIV). There's no promise to address all our curious questions or provide a roadmap to a life of wealth and success. The Bible is a gift, given to help us know the God who loves us. As we dive into the story, we'll do well to remember that God is the main character. Whether we're reading about Moses or Samson or David or Barnabas, every chapter is about God.

Over the course of this book, we'll try to steer clear of both extremes. Our goal will be to trace six important biblical themes across the entire story of redemption, zeroing in on the people and events that illuminate those themes and point to Jesus Christ. Along the way, though, we'll do well to remember that this is God's story. We have a role to play, but that role is informed by the larger story—what has gone before, what is happening right now, and what will someday come. But so we're all on the same page, I offer the following summary of God's story from Genesis to Revelation.[1]

Genesis to Revelation: The Short Version

In the beginning, it was all about goodness. God made the heavens and the earth, and they were good. In fact, God made all things to reflect His own goodness. But sin twisted the goodness of creation—all that we can see and all that we can't. Every aspect of creation was affected. Nothing was left unbent.

Worse still is that *we* opened the door and invited sin in. Our first parents, Adam and Eve, were deceived and believed a lie about God's heart. As a result, they discovered what it was like to be separated from that good heart. Down through history, every child of Adam and Eve has experienced this brokenness firsthand. The situation, apart from God, is hopeless, for nothing broken can fix itself. But thankfully, our Maker does not want us to be apart from Him.

Through a man named Abraham, God created a nation to be a light to the world. Israel was to walk in God's ways and invite her neighbors to do the same. But Israel failed. Over and over again, the people disobeyed God, and instead of inviting others to know the true God, they chased after the false gods of the other nations. It would seem that God's plan had failed—but the plan never depended on the faithfulness of people. It rested on the faithfulness of God.

At just the right moment in history, God himself put on flesh and came to earth to be born to a virgin in Bethlehem. Jesus did what Israel never could: obey perfectly. Jesus did what the sacrifices of animals never could: pay for sin. And Jesus did what broken people never could: make a way back to the Father. Someday, He'll return to put an end to every evil thing and restore the unbroken goodness of God to all creation.

Until then, those who know Jesus have His perfect work— His life, death, and resurrection—credited to their accounts. God invites Jesus' followers to walk with Him, to play their parts in His story, and to be His representatives in the world. It's what Adam and Eve, and later the people of Israel, were supposed to do but never could. But it's possible here and now because of the gospel.

Genesis to Revelation: The Short, Short Version

No matter how familiar we are with the Bible and its story, we can all use a reminder of the central message. As we dig deeper into the six themes of the gospel, I hope you will remember that God, who is faithful to fulfill His promises, loves you.

But even more than that, I hope you'll see—from Genesis to Revelation—how big the gospel is, and how it can make a dramatic difference in your life right here and now. Your life is part of the story God is telling.

And now, let's start at the beginning once again . . .

YOUR LIFE IN THE STORY OF GOD

Knowing the whole story of the Bible, including the six themes I've identified as Creation, Relation, Salvation, Nation, Formation, and Restoration, will help us play our roles in the story more effectively. At base level, the Bible, from Genesis to Revelation, tells the story of a perfectly good God who loves His rebellious creation—including each of us—enough to give himself for its benefit.

1. Can you recall a time, like my experience with *The Music Man*, that you realized you were lacking a larger view of something? What happened?

2. What do you think of the assertion that God is the main character of every Bible story?

3. Is it easy or hard for you to believe that God loves you? Why?

CREATION
God Is Up to Something New

*"There is not one little blade of grass,
there is no color in this world that
is not intended to make men rejoice."*
—JOHN CALVIN

Love's Overflow

GENESIS 1–2

Before there existed a single blade of grass, a lone molecule of water, or enough oxygen to sustain a gasp, there was love. Before the first twinkle from the first star began its journey thousands of light years through the blackness of the cosmos to prick a hole in the nighttime sky, there was love. Before time began its relentless march and space—in apparent infinitude—unfolded across the galaxies, there was love.

There is a river called *history* that has wound its way to the very moment you are living right now, to the very instant that finds you reading these words. It is a river that has been polluted, almost from its source, so it can be difficult for those of us downstream to discern its true taste. But before that raging river began to flow, before innumerable tales of heroes and heartache splashed between its banks, there was love.

"In the beginning, God . . ." (Genesis 1:1). That is how every story would begin if we could trace "Once upon a time" back to its actual origin. Everything from Shakespeare's comedies to Hollywood blockbusters to the greatest true tales of days gone by, to your life and mine—they all start in that moment. They all start with God.

God is already center stage when the Bible opens. His presence is a given. He requires no introduction. He is eternal, so we can expect Him to be there "in the beginning," just as He was before the beginning, if we can even imagine such a concept. Throughout Genesis and the sixty-five books that follow, God reveals himself to us, but it's in these opening pages that we get our first glimpse at His heart.

Six times we read that creation was "good" (Genesis 1:4,

10, 12, 18, 21, 25), and when completed, "very good" (1:31). We're meant to remember God's goodness as we continue reading God's Word—and as we live in God's world. The indelible mark of goodness the Lord stamped on everything He made is now damaged by sin—but it is still there, unmistakable.

The sunset illuminating the sky in brilliant orange and purple reflects the beauty of its Creator. The mama bear tending her cubs is a tribute to the Father's fierce protection of His children. The dance of our solar system proclaims the Lord's delight in rhythm and order. Chrysanthemums in their splendor declare God's extravagant provision. And the puppy bounding through a meadow of tall grass echoes joy divine.

■ ■ ■

Human beings, more than any other created thing, were designed to display God's goodness. The Bible tells us that "God created man in his own image" (Genesis 1:27). No other creature is given this honor. While theologians down through the centuries have pondered all that it might mean to be created in God's image, at the most basic level it means we resemble our Maker in much the same way a child resembles her parents. Notice the similar language in Genesis 5:3, where we read, "When Adam had lived 130 years, he fathered a son *in his own likeness, after his image,* and named him Seth" (emphasis added; compare with 5:1).

We were created to be God's kids. Our lives were meant to be so full of goodness that it would be impossible for others not to see the resemblance we bear to our Dad.

But something went wrong.

Sin entered the world, and all of creation now groans under its burden. Creation is still good, of course, but that goodness is marred. Life goes on, but death stalks her as prey. Joy is matched by sorrow. Peace is shattered by war. Love is cornered by hate. Justice is quietly brushed aside by indifference.

We still bear the image of God, but that image has been

twisted by vice, and it often remains hidden behind the masks we wear to cover our shame. At our worst, we barely reveal an inkling of God at all. But the goodness of God's image in us is still there. It has not been completely obliterated, though there is no area of life free from sin's infection.

Left on our own, we are unable to live the lives for which God created us. But this is not news: deep within, we know this to be true. We feel it in the aches of our bones and the aches of our hearts. We taste it in tears born of suffering. We come face-to-face with it at funerals and in courtrooms. Every harsh word spoken or received is a reminder. We see it behind the police tape that surrounds a crime scene on the evening news and in the faces of children who go to bed hungry on the paid infomercial that follows.

But the good news is this: God doesn't leave us on our own, simply to die under the strain of sin's disease. God's story doesn't end in pain. He sent His Son to redeem creation—and that includes you and me. He is bending back into place the twisted goodness, making it new once again. And He is bringing full restoration to the image of God in every person who recognizes the "exact imprint" of the Father in the Son (Hebrews 1:3), who sees the "image of the invisible God" in Jesus (Colossians 1:15).

This is the gospel story. This is the gospel *here and now* in everyday life, experienced by those who bend a knee to Jesus as the rightful King of all creation.

The God Who Is Never Alone

God's love is central to the act of creation. But that's more than a nice thought to help us make sense of our world or get us to sleep at night. That love is written into the story. Genesis 1–2 allows us to revisit the world as it existed before humanity dove headlong into sin, to conjure in our imaginations a life in which we're free to walk through paradise with our Maker in perfect harmony with our surroundings. And it offers a deeper clue to God's heart for creation in an unlikely place—the Trinity.

Attempts to understand and describe the Trinity could fill libraries. The Trinity is like the sun, and our minds bear the same frailty as our eyes. The sun's rays are an immeasurable blessing; in fact, our lives could not exist without them. But staring at the sun can never help us understand our nearest star any better. Our eyes were simply not designed to take in the full brilliance of the sun. In the same way, our minds are too small to fully comprehend the Trinity. That's not to say that we can't benefit from diving deep into theological waters—it just means we will never master the Trinity. But isn't that what we should expect when we serve an infinite God?

Put rather simply (and to avoid building one of the libraries I mentioned), God is one, but He exists in three Persons—the Father, the Son, and the Holy Spirit. Each member of the Godhead has distinct personhood and a unique role, but the Father, Son, and Spirit are not "parts" of God. Each is fully divine, coequal, and coeternal. They are united in purpose and action. And, especially important for our purpose at this point in God's story, the Trinity enjoys perfect community.

The Father, Son, and Holy Spirit were present together at the beginning. Notice the first three verses of Genesis 1, which describe the universe's formation. We've already seen the Father's involvement: "In the beginning, God created the heavens and the earth" (v. 1). But the Spirit was there as well: "The Spirit of God was hovering over the face of the waters" (v. 2). The Son, was there, too, though we'll need some other passages of the Bible to confirm that. Genesis 1:3 reads, "And God *said* . . ." (emphasis added). God created everything by His Word, and that Word is Jesus Christ. The New Testament reveals this mystery: "In the beginning was the Word, and the Word was with God, and the Word was God. He was in the beginning with God. All things were made through him, and without him was not any thing made that was made" (John 1:1–3; compare with Colossians 1:16). So we are to see the very words that God speaks at the beginning of the universe as the activity of Jesus in creation.

Ancient people used myths to explain how the world around them came into being. These myths usually involved gods who created humans by accident or as an afterthought. In most of these accounts, humans exist only to serve the gods as slaves or to "feed" them by offering sacrifices. But the true God does not need anything. God's story begins with the true creation account, revealing that He made human beings the pinnacle of His creative activity. With great intentionality, God molded the first man out of the earth with His own hands and breathed into that man His own breath of life (Genesis 2:7).

I've heard it said that God created people so He would have someone to share in His love. Though this thought is somewhat kinder than the ancient creation myths, the bottom line is the same: human beings were made to fill up something lacking in God. But that's simply not true. Before the creation of a single atom—when there was only God, and God alone, for unending eons past—love was perfectly given and received within the Trinity. The highest level of vibrant community existed within God himself. Creation, then, came as an overflow of that love, not out of necessity. Though you and I were created with a need for God, God does not need us. But don't worry, the reality is far better: *He wants us.*

When my wife, Laurin, and I were first dating, she wrote and edited *YouthWalk*, a devotional magazine for teenagers. In the pages of that small, monthly volume, she helped readers understand God's love in new ways. Early in our relationship, Laurin gave me a stack of *YW*s to read, issues she was especially proud of. Over the next few weeks, I pored over them, knowing that the words on those pages, though written for teenagers, were a window into the heart of the woman I was falling in love with. As I was reading one morning before work, one line in particular grabbed my attention: "God started from scratch and had the ability to make us any way He wanted."[1] Have you ever thought about yourself like that? Up until that moment, I hadn't.

God, because He's God, had infinite possibilities before Him, and He chose to create *you*—with your personality, appearance, talents, intelligence, and everything else that makes you special. God has even given you the potential to grow and develop these qualities. Though, at times, you may have wanted to change the way you were made, God never has. He loves you just the way you are.

Why did God make you? Not because He needs you, but because He wants you. The thought of you makes Him happy. You, as part of His good creation, are an overflow of His love.

YOUR LIFE IN THE STORY OF GOD

Human beings are made in God's image, created to display His goodness in the world. But, twisted by sin, we're selfish and destructive and dying. Our only hope is in God, who through all eternity has demonstrated perfect love among the three members of the Trinity—Father, Son, and Holy Spirit. That love overflows to us, not because God *needs* anyone, but simply because He *wants* us.

1. What do you believe the phrase "made in the image of God" implies? How has sin affected God's image in humanity?

2. How does the Trinity model love for us? What can we learn from each member's role in creation?

3. Do you believe that "the thought of you makes [God] happy"? Why or why not?

DAY 4

Invitation to Create

EXODUS 31:1–11

With all the obnoxiousness expected of my thirteen years, I raised my hand in response to an obviously rhetorical question. My Bible teacher had been making the point that only God can truly create. As human beings, we can build, arrange, mix, match, innovate, and collect, but at the end of the day, we have no power to create something out of nothing.

From buildings to bombs to blankets, everything we make is constructed from something given to us by God. Even what we consider "man-made" materials have their origin in nature, at the beginning of whatever process brought them to their current state.

"Can any of you create something from nothing?" my teacher asked, expecting no response at all. But in the back of the room, I stretched my hand toward the ceiling.

"I can," I said.

My teacher, already a saint for dedicating his professional life to middle school students, indulged me. "What can you create from nothing?" he asked.

Taking his engagement as permission to demonstrate, I stood and walked to the blackboard at the front of the classroom. Picking up a piece of chalk, I got to work. Thirty seconds later, I dropped the chalk down on its shelf and stood back. "There," I said. "Something out of nothing."

I had drawn a crude cartoon character—a wolf with sunglasses, if I recall. He was one of a thousand doodles to which my childhood imagination had given life in the margins of my textbooks that semester.

The teacher smiled. He knew he had been beaten. My

drawing was more than the sum of the chalk I used to make it. Though not truly formed out of nothing, I had made something that hadn't existed before. In front of my classmates that day, I had performed an act of creation.

But this shouldn't surprise us. Is *A Tale of Two Cities* just ink and paper? The ceiling of the Sistine Chapel merely paint and plaster? "Amazing Grace" only notes on a page? When we create, we are imitating our Creator, and that has the potential to bring Him great joy.

"Every good gift and every perfect gift is from above," Jesus' half-brother James wrote (James 1:17). These good gifts include the things we make from existing materials and also the works that spring forth from our imagination, "for by [Christ] all things were created, in heaven and on earth, visible and invisible" (Colossians 1:16). There are no exclusions there, so my teacher's point is still a valid one: anything we create is done in partnership with God. Only He can create something out of nothing. "By faith we understand that the universe was created by the word of God, so that what is seen was not made out of things that are visible" (Hebrews 11:3). But God loves it when we join Him in creative work. God made all the raw materials of the earth, knowing there would be endless possibilities for new things. And then He gave us hands and minds, and set us loose to create.

Think of the smile on God's face the first time someone discovered percussion—banging sticks against a log as the first drum. Or when someone scribbled down the first alphabet, opening the doors of history, literature, and written communication to the world. Or the moment someone combined peanut butter and chocolate, and took a bite. What about the first electric light? Indoor plumbing? Jet engines? Each of these good gifts is only possible because God invites us to create with Him. And it's been this way from the beginning.

Back in the garden, God gave Adam the responsibility to name the animals (Genesis 2:19–20), allowing man's imagination to be forever imprinted on God's handiwork. He also told the first couple, "Be fruitful and multiply and fill the earth and subdue it, and have dominion over the fish of the sea and over the birds of the heavens and over every living thing that moves on the earth" (Genesis 1:28). Within that command is an implicit call to join God in the ongoing act of creation, to extend the borders of the garden outward until the whole earth is filled with God's glory (see Psalm 72:19; Isaiah 6:3).

But after the garden, human creativity became more complicated. Sin took its toll on every part of life. Now, not everything we make reflects the goodness of our Creator. While we still bear His image, and our work has the potential for great good, we're also fallen—so the products of culture are blemished by our sin.

Think of a movie that contains great truth but also glorifies premarital sex, or a song on the radio with a melody that lifts your soul but lyrics that mock God's Word. What about the food that our ingenuity has made inexpensive and abundant but at the cost of nutrition? Our sinfulness has the power to mangle God's good gifts into things He never intended. But the gospel has the power to redeem even this.

Bezalel and the Tabernacle

The book of Exodus records some of the most exciting episodes within God's story. It could be said that the stories of Moses were the gospel "there and then" for the Israelites. We see the gospel—God's redemption story—in the life of Moses. He points us to Jesus, who likewise saves all of us from slavery to sin.

Moses led God's people out of physical bondage in Egypt, away from the anger of Pharaoh, who had chased them into the desert. Through Moses, God parted the Red Sea, and His people escaped through the water just in time for the waves to crash down on Pharaoh's army. Once safe, the people camped at the base of Mount Sinai, where Moses received commandments from the Lord for them.

On the mountain, God also gave Moses instructions for a tabernacle to be used for worship and sacrifices. This special tent would be the place where God's presence resided with the people. Though it was to be portable, so the people could take it with them on their journey, the tabernacle would be the holiest place on the planet, the very spot where heaven and earth met. It is with this tabernacle in mind that God said to Moses:

"See, I have called by name Bezalel the son of Uri, son of Hur, of the tribe of Judah, and I have filled him with the Spirit of God, with ability and intelligence, with knowledge and all craftsmanship, to devise artistic designs, to work in gold, silver, and bronze, in cutting stones for setting, and in carving wood, to work in every craft" (EXODUS 31:2–5).

We often talk about a person being "inspired" to make something beautiful, but Bezalel's inspiration was literal. He was indwelt with the Spirit of God for a special construction project, long before God poured out His Spirit on all of His people (see Joel 2:28–29; Acts 2:1–41). Beyond this special filling, God gave Bezalel an assistant in Oholiab, and to both men He gave the ability to teach, so others could join them (Exodus 35:34). In all of these men, the Lord "put skill and intelligence to know how to do any work in the construction of the sanctuary" (Exodus 36:1).

God brought together a crew of builders, designers, artists, and craftsmen to make His tabernacle, and He put a man filled with His Spirit in charge of the project. But He didn't have to.

The author of Hebrews tells us the tabernacle on earth was but "a copy and shadow of what is in heaven" (8:5 NIV). This is perhaps why God told Moses, "Exactly as I show you concerning the pattern of the tabernacle, and of all its furniture, so you shall make it" (Exodus 25:9). The tabernacle was to be the most important construction project, and the most important work of art, ever undertaken in the history of the world. God could have simply spoken it into being. Or, like He'd done with the Ten Commandments on stone tablets, He could have carved the tabernacle out of raw materials with His own finger (Exodus 24:12; 31:18; 34:1; Deuteronomy 10:2). God didn't need to work through imperfect human beings to get the job done, but He chose to do so. He wanted to involve His people in this new work of creation.

Bezalel's story shows us what God's kingdom is like. As with others in the Old Testament, he was given God's Spirit in order to play a special role in God's big story of redemption. Moses once wished that every Israelite in his charge would be filled with the Holy Spirit (Numbers 11:29); now, because of Christ's perfect sacrifice, the Holy Spirit comes to live inside every believer, just as Moses had hoped. And God's Spirit wants to redeem every part of life stained by sin—including the creative work we do.

The original command God gave to Adam and Eve in Genesis 1:28 is still in full force for us today. We have been invited to "fill the earth and subdue it" with the work of our hands and hearts. For some, this is a call to create "traditional art" that reflects God's goodness. This is the work of painters, poets, musicians, and the like. But while art is needed in our world, God has also blessed people with skill in fields like mathematics, architecture, economics, baking, agriculture, and entrepreneurship, just to name a few.

You, as a believer in Jesus Christ, have unique talents, gifts, and abilities. Every time you put them to work, yielding your efforts to the Holy Spirit, you join God in His ongoing work of creation—and your story becomes entwined with His. With God as your creative partner, there's no limit to the good you can do.

YOUR LIFE IN THE STORY OF GOD

Having been made "in the image of God," humans are creative beings. The first man and woman, Adam and Eve, were given the responsibility to "fill the earth and subdue it," to join God in an ongoing act of creation—and we have the same privilege and responsibility today. As we do, whether in the fields of art or science or business, we can do much good, living out "the gospel here and now."

1. How do God's creation and acts of human creativity differ? How are they similar?

2. What creative activity is most enjoyable to you? Why?

3. How can acts of human creativity contribute to the spread of the gospel? When have you seen that occur?

God Presses Pause

JOSHUA 10:5–15

The armies of five kings joined forces and marched against the city of Gibeon. Normally, five against one would be an unfair fight, but Gibeon had a new ally, and that ally served the God of the universe.

Not long before this threat, some men from Gibeon had tricked Joshua and the elders of Israel into making a treaty with them. Rather than asking God for guidance, Joshua took the Gibeonites' word, believing they were from a far-off land rather than one of the nearby cities God had told the Israelites to conquer. He soon found himself bound by treaty to protect the people of Gibeon from attack—and in just a short while, the Gibeonites were calling on the men of Israel to help them fend off an invading horde of five armies. *What a mess!* Joshua must have thought.

Moses had died, and Joshua was now leading God's people. The days of wandering in the wilderness were over. The Israelites had entered the Promised Land and were fighting other nations. But more importantly, God was fighting for them. And it was a fight Joshua had wanted to see since his days as a much younger man. Some forty years earlier, Joshua and Caleb had been the only spies who returned from Canaan with faith to believe God would lead His people to victory over their enemies (see Numbers 13:30; 14:36–38). Now, he was finally seeing those battles take place.

In fact, Joshua had been there from the beginning, part of the generation that escaped slavery under Moses. Joshua had seen the rushing waters overwhelm the Egyptian chariots after God parted the Red Sea for His people. He remembered fighting the

Amalekites. On that day, he saw Aaron and Hur holding Moses' hands high to heaven, noticing that as long as those hands were up, his army also had the upper hand, so to speak. And when he became God's chosen leader of Israel, he had watched as the Lord turned the walls of Jericho to rubble without his army raising a single weapon against the city.

But on this day, as Joshua and his men marched from Gilgal to Gibeon to defend their regrettable allies, the Lord spoke to his servant: "Do not fear them, for I have given them into your hands" (Joshua 10:8). These were familiar words. When God first called Joshua, He had told him, "Be strong and courageous. Do not be frightened, and do not be dismayed, for the LORD your God is with you wherever you go" (Joshua 1:9). Even though Joshua had made an error in judgment, trusting the deceitful Gibeonites without consulting the Lord, God had not left him.

During the battle, Joshua prayed, but his prayer wasn't just for victory. With the enemy retreating and evening fast approaching, Joshua needed a way to keep the battle going. He knew that everything—absolutely everything in all of creation—belonged to the Lord, so Joshua prayed for nothing less than the sun to stop in its tracks.

And God answered.

We don't know how it was done. Perhaps the Lord tilted the earth for a time so that Israel, for those few hours, enjoyed the perpetual daylight normally reserved for the Arctic Circle. Maybe, for a time, He stopped the earth spinning in its orbit, while also holding back the calamity that would normally result. Or it could be that He redirected the sun's light to give the appearance that the sun was standing still in the sky. The Bible doesn't tell us how God stopped the sun, only that He did.

Between the Ordinary and Extraordinary

As the Creator of the universe, God holds everything together. Moment by moment, He sustains us. Contrary to the notion that God is a kind of watchmaker—He made the world, wound it up, and then walked away, leaving creation to run on its own natural processes—the Bible describes God as intimately involved with everything, from guiding the stars on their path in the sky to feeding the birds (Job 38:32, 41; Luke 12:6).

Here are just a few of the things God says about himself concerning His care of creation:

- He commands the mornings (Job 38:12).

- He keeps storehouses of snow and hail (Job 38:22).

- He decides the course of raindrops and thunderbolts, and orders them to fall from the clouds (Job 38:25, 34–35).

- He leads the constellations across the sky (Job 38:31–32).

- He makes sure young lions have enough to eat (Job 38:39).

- He watches over mountain goats as they give birth to their young (Job 39:1).

- He calls to the eagles, and they soar through the air in response (Job 39:27).

All of these examples come from two chapters in the book of Job, a passage in which God speaks to Job (from a whirlwind) about His authority and power. Using poetic language, God is not giving an exhaustive list of His daily chores as Lord of heaven and earth. Rather, it's to show Job—and us—that He rules over every square inch of the universe He has made, that His command extends to all of nature, and that He cares personally for the world He's created. Nothing is beyond His control or outside His provision. Joshua knew this, and that's how he had the confidence to ask God for something as extraordinary as reordering the heavens. He knew that if God commanded it, the sun would obey.

C. S. Lewis once wrote, "Miracle is, from the point of view of the scientist, a form of doctoring, tampering, (if you like) cheating. It introduces a new factor into the situation, namely supernatural force, which the scientist had not reckoned on."[2] God—the supernatural force to which Lewis referred—has not stepped away, leaving natural law to rule the cosmos. He is not an intruder in our world, and miracles are not an interruption. They are merely the choice of a sovereign God to do things in an unusual way once in a while.

■ ■ ■

In one sense, it's perfectly understandable to classify the sun pausing in the sky as a miracle. Such a phenomenon doesn't happen every day. It's exceptional, certainly out of the ordinary. The regularity with which our natural world acts is a gift—the rising and setting of the sun each day, the dependable change of seasons, allow us to plan and offer us a life of balance built on a rhythm ordained by the Lord. But because our God is a hands-on Creator, He reserves the right to suspend natural law as He sees fit, in much the same way that a sovereign earthly king might suspend the laws of his nation for a time if it served the good of his people. Natural laws are not really laws; they are only what we expect to find because of repeated experience. God is not bound by them.

God sustains His creation every second of every day, not just when there's a miracle happening. But miracles scream loudly of God's involvement in our world. When I have my three-year-old son, Jonah, in my arms, I am actively holding him up the entire time, though he may not realize the care I'm taking until he wriggles his way loose and I have to catch him to keep him from falling. It's that out-of-the-ordinary moment that shows him his dad won't let him down. The same is true of miracles. After that experience on the battlefield, Joshua never witnessed another afternoon when the sun paused in the sky, but I'm sure he was reminded of that special day and of God's power every time he saw a sunrise. (I imagine he even lingered now and then, just to be sure the sun was still advancing in its course.)

To be a Christian is to believe in miracles. Chiefly, it is to believe in history's greatest and most important miracle, the resurrection of Jesus Christ from the dead. But Scripture tells us that Christ's resurrection is only the first of many resurrections. To the church in Corinth, the apostle Paul wrote, "For as in Adam all die, so also in Christ shall all be made alive" (1 Corinthians 15:22). Death is what we would consider natural law. No one is immune. Everyone you or I have ever known has died or is in the process of dying. And, to my knowledge, no one I've ever met has climbed out of the grave. But as we've seen, God reserves the right to supersede that which we consider natural law. Paul called Christ "the firstfruits of those who have fallen asleep" (1 Corinthians 15:20). In the world of agriculture, the firstfruits indicate what an entire harvest will be like. Those of us who have put our faith in Christ will one day be raised to new life—just as He was—and we will never taste death again (see Revelation 20:4–6).

We are unlikely to see the sun stand still anytime soon, but ours is a world of miracles—the everyday ones to which we've grown accustomed and the out-of-the-ordinary ones that we sometimes doubt. Our God is a God of miracles, and there is one miracle that every follower of Christ is promised: to live with the Lord forever in a body free from corruption (1 Corinthians 15:42–49).

Until that day, we can ask God to intercede in our lives, to meet our needs as Joshua did. He trusted God for the seemingly impossible, and so can we. There are people in this world who go to church and believe all the right facts about Jesus. But the Christian life is more than that. It always has been. Trusting Jesus means following Him, talking to Him, sharing our lives with Him. It means making sure He is the first one to whom we go with our needs and our heart's longings. And it means resting in the fact that He upholds creation—and you and me—day in and day out.

YOUR LIFE IN THE STORY OF GOD

To be a Christian is to believe in miracles, trusting God for the seemingly impossible. The Creator and Sustainer of the universe is just as capable of meeting our everyday needs—and safeguarding our eternity—as He was of stopping the sun for Joshua and the ancient Israelites. God is always working in our world, but His miracles shout loudly of His involvement in our lives.

1. What is the most amazing thing you've seen or heard about? Would you call it a miracle?

2. Why do you think God sometimes answers prayers with obvious miracles and sometimes doesn't? How does that affect your faith?

3. How could you be more aware of God's work in your life, even in everyday occurrences?

Memories of a World to Come

1 KINGS 4:20–34; MICAH 4:1–5

In the heart of every person lives a desire that cannot be satisfied, at least not by anything in this world. This desire was planted in the soul of our first parents at the beginning of God's story—only then it wasn't so much a desire as it was something quite the opposite. It was a sense of belonging, of being known by their Creator, and of being at home in the universe. Living in intimacy with God, everything else fell into place. The world was made for Adam and Eve, and they for it.

With sin's invasion, this peace and wholeness was lost. Now, the void occupying its place reminds us that this world is not our home.

And yet it is home.

Though creation has been corrupted from end to end, the goodness of its Creator can still be experienced. Every time we sense this underlying goodness in the world around us, desire for our lost home is rekindled. We see that home in rare beauty, and we hear it in words of truth unmingled with compromise. These postcards from home trick our souls, for they come from a place we've never been. But the scenes portrayed on the glossy side are somehow more real than anything we've yet to experience in this life. And written on the back of each card is an invitation to hope.

David's Son and God's Son

After Joshua laid down his sword for the last time, a series of judges led the nation of Israel. For hundreds of years, the people contended with their enemies, who still occupied portions of the land God had promised. When Israel walked with the Lord,

43

He saved the nation from its oppressors by sending a judge to deliver them. But when the people forgot the goodness of God and went their own way, He allowed them to suffer the consequences. Good times or bad, though, God never abandoned Israel—He remained true to His people and His promises.

Even when the people of Israel cried out for a king to rule them, God obliged, though He understood what they were really saying. They were rejecting Him as their true King. They were choosing to be like the nations around them, nations that chased after false gods and perverted goodness and justice. But God never wanted that for His children—He desired Israel to be a land unlike any other, a special place that would be a light to the nations, an oasis of His love in a world soured and spoiled by sin. He wanted the people of Israel to play a special role in His story, to know Him and what it is to be truly alive.

The first king of Israel, Saul, was the man the people wanted, that king like the neighboring nations had. But he proved to be cowardly, prideful, and belligerent. For most of his reign, Saul did not follow the Lord, so God rejected Him as king and selected another man—David—for the job. Described as a man after God's own heart (1 Samuel 13:14; Acts 13:22), King David led the people of Israel faithfully, triumphing over her enemies and finally establishing peace in the land. By walking closely with God, David lived out the gospel story in his time, so much so that God promised to place His own Son on David's throne forever (Luke 1:32; compare with 2 Samuel 7:11–13).

Under David's son Solomon, the flower of prosperity blossomed in Israel. By necessity, David had been a man of war, but God blessed King Solomon with "peace on all sides" (1 Kings 4:24). The book of 1 Kings records that "Judah and Israel were as many as the sand by the sea" (4:20), a fulfillment of the promise God first made to Abraham, the father of the nation, a thousand years earlier (Genesis 22:17). The people not only multiplied; they also "ate and drank and were happy" (1 Kings 4:20). Further, "Judah and Israel lived in safety, from Dan even to Beersheba,[3] every man under his vine and under his fig tree, all the days of Solomon" (4:25). In modern terms, we might say that Israel enjoyed full employment and universal home ownership.

At the same time, Solomon's kingdom had become a light to the Gentiles, just as God wanted. "God gave Solomon wisdom and understanding beyond measure" (4:29), the Bible tells us, so that "people of all the nations came to hear the wisdom of Solomon" (4:34). Along with the gift of wisdom, God gave Solomon all the material blessings a king could ask for—and the people of Israel and Judah shared in those blessings.

But the good times didn't last, at least not with any consistency. At the close of Solomon's reign, the nation split in two, and both kingdoms—Israel in the north and Judah in the south—wandered from the Lord. Successive generations enjoyed brief periods of peace and prosperity as they walked more closely with God, interspersed with longer periods of hardship as they neglected Him and abandoned His ways. These chapters in God's story are a disappointing back-and-forth between faithfulness and unfaithfulness on the part of God's people.

Eventually, the northern kingdom was conquered by Assyria, and some years after that, the people of the southern kingdom were taken captive to Babylon. The good old days of Solomon's reign became nothing more than a distant memory.

Though 1 and 2 Kings appear in our Bibles before the small book of Micah, the latter was completed several decades prior to the former. So even though the reign of Solomon took place long before Micah the prophet came on the scene, the author of 1 and 2 Kings did not record the events of Solomon's life and rule until after Micah penned his oracles. Why does that matter? Because the author of Kings used a particular phrase that first appeared in Micah to describe life under King Solomon. And in Micah, we have a clue that tells us what God was showing Israel during Solomon's glorious time on the throne.

Micah 4:4 says, "They shall sit every man under his vine and under his fig tree, and no one shall make them afraid." Notice this is the same language used in 1 Kings 4:25 to recount life in Israel under Solomon. Here, though, Micah is not describing the nation of Israel during the reign of its third king—rather, he is speaking of "the latter days" (4:1). Micah is not looking back, but forward. And because these words from Micah were chosen for 1 Kings, it seems that God, in blessing Solomon's era the way He did, was also looking forward, giving His people a small preview of the new creation.

There are echoes of Solomon's reign in Micah's description of this new era, this new Promised Land. "For out of Zion shall go forth the law, and the word of the LORD from Jerusalem. He shall judge between many peoples, and shall decide disputes for strong nations far away" (Micah 4:2–3). Compare that description to what we read in 2 Chronicles about Solomon: "All the kings of the earth sought the presence of Solomon to hear his wisdom, which God had put into his mind" (9:23). In Micah, the Lord himself is on Jerusalem's throne, but it's as if a shadow from that glorious future reign stretches back into history to touch the kingdom of Israel under Solomon.

"They shall beat their swords into plowshares," Micah wrote, "and their spears into pruning hooks; nation shall not lift up sword against nation, neither shall they learn war anymore" (4:3; compare with Isaiah 2:4). Again, Micah's description of an age to come sounds a lot like the reign of Solomon, during which there was "peace on all sides" (1 Kings 4:24), only in Micah's prophecy, the peace has no end. Swords and spears are not just put away for a time; they're recycled.

■ ■ ■

Beyond the book of Micah, rumors of new heavens and a new earth, complete with a New Jerusalem, spilled from other prophets' pens. Often these passages describe a world in which the power and effects of sin are undone, and the Lord reigns as King. The end result is that creation itself is reborn. This should not surprise us—all of Scripture is one story, God's story, and He has already written the ending.

Isaiah, for example, wrote about changes coming to the animal kingdom. Wolves will nap with lambs, and leopards with goats (Isaiah 11:6). Cows and bears will eat grass side by side, and lions munch on straw (11:7). Toddlers will play with snakes without fear of being bitten (11:8). Whether literal or symbolic, the picture painted by Isaiah is of a secure and peaceful world. Fear and death have no place. It's as if the garden of Eden were opened to humanity once more, but now its boundaries encompass the whole of creation.

Prophecies of the new creation are meant to take us back, to remind us of bygone days of peace and prosperity. For the people of God in the Old Testament, life under Solomon had been a bright spot in history and the garden of Eden the ideal. But since "no eye has seen, nor ear heard, nor the heart of man imagined, what God has prepared for those who love him" (1 Corinthians 2:9; compare with Isaiah 64:4), nostalgia only serves as a dim preview of the world to come. In much the same way that memories of splashing in a backyard pool could never prepare us for the beaches of Maui, our experiences in this life can never fully prepare us for the new creation God has planned.

Still, God has given us seasons of blessing, along with the beauty that surrounds us every day, to pique our heart's longings—so that when pain and grief threaten to steal our hope, we might not forget we were made for eternal life with Him.

This promise of a new world is only possible because it was purchased for us. It was in the saddest moment of human history, at a time when evil appeared to have won the decisive battle, that Christ paid the entry fee on our behalf. And in so doing, the first rays of light from the new creation broke through the clouds of our world to signal the beginning of the end, the undoing of everything gone wrong, and the making of all things new.

While the rest of the world looks for happiness in everything from family to fun to finances, Christians can have joy in any circumstance. The eternal life God promised doesn't begin sometime in the future, after we die or Jesus returns. In a prayer for His followers, Jesus said, "And this is eternal life, that they know you, the only true God, and Jesus Christ whom you have sent" (John 17:3). Eternal life starts right here and right now! We have everything we need. All the peace, security, and prosperity that were there for the people of Israel under Solomon's reign are ours in Jesus, only without limit (see Ephesians 1:3).

This is why the apostle Paul, languishing in prison, could write: "I count everything as loss because of the surpassing worth of knowing Christ Jesus my Lord" (Philippians 3:8). He knew that his chains didn't provide a reliable picture of reality. As we live out God's story in our everyday lives, we too can have this kind of joy. Our surroundings may not reflect true reality any more than Paul's did, but they will catch up someday. God has promised as much. In the meantime, we already have Christ, who is far better than any circumstance imaginable.

YOUR LIFE IN THE STORY OF GOD

At some point in life, many people think, *There must be something more than this.* Our vague, unsatisfied desires—"memories of a world to come"—are actually God's way of drawing us into His work. This world, damaged as it is by sin, isn't really our home. But in another sense, this world *is* our home—the place we will ultimately live in perfect peace and safety, after God has made everything new.

1. When have you sensed the kind of dissatisfaction with the world described in this chapter? What did you do about it?

2. Where do you find the greatest beauty in this life? How might these pleasures point you to God?

3. Can you relate to the apostle Paul's statement, "I count everything as loss because of the surpassing worth of knowing Christ Jesus my Lord" (Philippians 3:8)?

The Most Beautiful Scars

JOHN 20:24–29

Every year on Good Friday, several pastors in and around my hometown in southern Connecticut come together to share a pulpit and preach the gospel throughout the afternoon. It's a wonderful tradition that's been taking place for many years. Attendees are free to stay as long as they like, but every hour, a different pastor preaches a new message. Often, a single theme ties all the sermons together.

One Good Friday some years ago, I was sitting in the back of the gym-turned-sanctuary of the Evangelical Free Church. My mind was taking in the fourth sermon of the day. That year's theme was the resurrection appearances of Jesus. I'd already heard about Mary Magdalene, the disciples on the road to Emmaus, and Peter. The current preacher—a Southern Baptist, if I recall—was beginning a message about Thomas.

In this sermon on faith and doubt—the necessity of one and God's grace for the other—a detail in the story of Thomas's encounter with the risen Jesus caught my ear: "Then [Jesus] said to Thomas, 'Put your finger here, and see my hands; and put out your hand, and place it in my side. Do not disbelieve, but believe'" (John 20:27). I thought it an odd thing that the Father had raised Jesus from the dead but hadn't patched up the holes in His hands or side.

Have you ever thought about how strange that is? When Jesus healed people, He healed them all the way, 100 percent. The lame could walk without a cane, the blind could see without glasses, and the ears of the deaf worked without a hearing aid. There was, of course, the blind man who required a second touch from Jesus, but he still left that day with twenty-twenty vision (Mark 8:22–25). So why did Jesus, who was God in the flesh, still have wounds left over from His crucifixion?

For Thomas, the holes in Jesus' hands and side were evidence that the man standing before him really *was* Jesus, the Rabbi he had followed for three years. Only someone who had been crucified and punctured with a spear could have had marks like that. But I think Jesus' scars served as more than mere proof of His identity for those who would doubt. They were—and are—an indication of the Father's heart in the new creation, of which Jesus' resurrection was the beginning.

Someday, every believer will be resurrected, though I hardly expect people who died from gunshot wounds to be raised to new life with holes in their chests, or those who died frail in their beds to appear just as sickly for all eternity. On the contrary, I believe what the apostle Paul wrote: "What is sown is perishable; what is raised is imperishable. It is sown in dishonor; it is raised in glory. It is sown in weakness; it is raised in power. It is sown a natural body; it is raised a spiritual body" (1 Corinthians 15:42–44). Jesus' nail and spear wounds, signs of dishonor in this world, were transformed into markings of glory for the next. They remain with Him because He is "the Lamb who was slain" and worthy to receive honor (Revelation 5:12).

But there's even more to Christ's piercings than that.

New from Old

When Laurin and I were planning our wedding, we asked Don, a carpenter friend, to build us an arbor for the reception. The wood he used came from an old barn that had been torn down in New Hampshire. As such, the arbor had unique character and texture. It was beautiful. Laurin and I sat under that wooden arch as we ate our first meal together as husband and wife, surrounded by our family and friends.

On the day we requested the arbor, we also asked Don to make us some bedroom furniture. Laurin showed him catalog pictures of a bedroom set she liked, and Don got to work. A few weeks after we returned from our honeymoon, Don arrived at our house with a headboard, a dresser, and two bedside tables, beautifully cut and stained. And he also delivered something of a surprise, telling us that he had repurposed much of the wood from the arbor we had used at our reception. So now we have a reminder of our wedding day every morning when we open our eyes to see that furniture Don made—a new creation built from an old one.

This is how it will be with the new creation God is planning. What happens in this life matters for the next. There is continuity between this world and the world to come. That is why Jesus could instruct His disciples to pray confidently, "Your kingdom come, your will be done, on earth as it is in heaven" (Matthew 6:10). Jesus didn't pray prayers that were merely wishful thinking—He prayed the will of His Father. And in this instance, He prayed for God's kingdom to come and make its home on *this* earth. Because that is the heart of the Father.

At the same time, we must reconcile Jesus' prayer with the fact that Scripture speaks of a judgment of fire for the heavens and the earth (2 Peter 3:7), and of the first heaven and first earth passing away (Revelation 21:1). Perhaps this fire will refine the earth as it judges, just like the flood of Noah's day—a judgment on mankind—reset the planet for a fresh start.

But what about the work *we* do, here and now? No one can quite say how our obedient, God-centered efforts will affect eternity. When we lead someone to Christ, of course, it's easy to see the ramifications for the next life. But what about those things we do for God that don't result in people coming to know Jesus? What happens when a community is revitalized or when peace is restored across racial lines? What about when great art is created for God's glory? Or a hungry person is fed in Jesus' name? All of these have value, but how exactly their good will translate into eternity is a bit of a mystery. And in this reality is a tension that every believer must live with: we must learn to long for the next world while loving this one. We can't grow too attached to this life while investing in it for the life to come.

As we learn to live in this in-between place, we can find rest because of Jesus' wounds. They are a tangible reminder of Romans 8:28, which says, "And we know that for those who love God all things work together for good, for those who are called according to his purpose." There is no limit to the "all things" mentioned. "All things" include every sin you have committed, and every sin that's been committed against you. Even something as grievous as the crucifixion of the Son of God was turned for good.

Because of Jesus' death at the hands of sinners, new creation has dawned. This, of course, is not meant to imply that sin birthed goodness. Rather, it's a loud proclamation of God's power to turn anything—even the vilest of actions—into something that brings Him glory and blesses His people.

The unfolding story of the new creation, though it is a new beginning, will not be the story of simply starting over. It will be the story of God's triumph over the power of sin and death in order to redeem His good world. It's one thing to defeat the enemy—it's another thing entirely for that enemy's work to be used against him in the service of God's good kingdom. But that is the beauty on display in Christ's hands and side.

Let's assume Thomas accepted Jesus' offer to inspect His crucifixion scars. When the doubting disciple pressed his fingers against Jesus' punctured flesh, he was touching the disturbed soil from which the firstfruits of the new creation had shot forth.

For those of us who only know of Jesus' scars from the pages of the Bible, the Lord says, "Blessed are those who have not seen and yet have believed" (John 20:29). His words still ring true today. We are blessed when we believe without seeing. The new creation has begun, God's story is still going forward, and you and I are invited to be part of it. Believing in Jesus and, in His name, recreating what is broken around us are ways we can bring the gospel to our communities.

"Now Jesus did many other signs in the presence of the disciples, which are not written in this book," John wrote, "but these are written so that you may believe that Jesus is the Christ, the Son of God, and that *by believing you may have life in his name*" (20:30–31, emphasis added). The life we are offered in Jesus' name is the life of the world to come. It is abundant life, lived here and now, in preparation for the day Jesus returns. It is nothing short of life in the new creation.

YOUR LIFE IN THE STORY OF GOD

Jesus' wounds, exhibited even *after* His resurrection, remind us that God can make "all things work together for good," as Romans 8:28 says. We need this encouragement as we live in a broken, sinful world still awaiting God's ultimate restoration. In the meantime, we contribute to the new creation by serving those around us, because what happens in this life matters for the next.

1. In your Christian experience, how have you viewed "eternal life"? What effect should the gospel have on us here and now?

2. In Matthew 6:10, Jesus prays for God's kingdom to come and God's will to be done. In our broken and sinful world, how are each of these things happening?

3. What can you do personally to participate in the coming of God's kingdom to earth?

The New You

2 CORINTHIANS 5:17

A few years ago, I got on a kick to reinvent myself physically. At the time, I had a beard, glasses, and an extra thirty pounds. I decided it was time for a change.

Losing the beard was easy, though it took several weeks to get back into the habit of shaving every morning. Taking off the glasses for good was a bit harder, but to my surprise, my ophthalmologist told me I was a good candidate for LASIK eye surgery, and I scheduled my appointment. Finally, there was the weight to be lost. I started by cutting out as much sugar as possible from my diet. I switched to stevia in my coffee, passed on desserts and snacks, and become a connoisseur of low-fat cheese and crackers. Then I committed to running at least three days a week. At first, it was more of a run/walk with lots of water breaks, but after a dozen or so sessions on the treadmill, I was able to jog five miles or farther at a time.

In just a few months, I felt healthier, looked younger, and had much more energy. In fact, my appearance was so different that one coworker, a guy who normally works remotely and hadn't seen me in a few months, didn't recognize me. He passed right by me in the hallway, offering only a polite nod of his head as he would to any stranger. When I spoke with him later, he did a double take and told me I looked completely different.

The Bible says that when we come to know Jesus, we become completely different too, though our transformation doesn't affect our outward appearance just yet. Second Corinthians 5:17 says, "If anyone is in Christ, he is a new creation. The old has passed away; behold, the new has come." In other words, because Jesus' resurrection sparked the dawn of the new creation, those of us who are connected to Him are also part of that new creation.

The Once and Future Kingdom

While the resurrection and transformation of our physical bodies is still a future event, the Holy Spirit living inside us brings our dead spirits to life. We become new. That's why, in one place, Paul could write, "Now if we have died with Christ, we believe that we will also live with him" (Romans 6:8; compare with 2 Timothy 2:11), referring to a future resurrection. But in another, he could say, "You were . . . buried with him in baptism, in which you were also raised with him through faith in the powerful working of God, who raised him from the dead" (Colossians 2:11–12), emphasizing that believers have already been "raised," a past event.

Jesus made this clear as well when He said Nicodemus needed to be born again: "Truly, truly, I say to you, unless one is born again he cannot see the kingdom of God" (John 3:3). Many people miss the significance of this truth because they equate the kingdom of God, also called the kingdom of heaven, with the afterlife. But this is not just another way of referring to heaven. The kingdom of God is the rule and reign of God, which, of course, is the way of things *in* heaven. But one day, all of creation will come under God's rule, just as it was in the beginning. God's kingdom will cover the whole universe.

As it stands now, though, our world is in rebellion. It's perfectly acceptable to talk about the kingdom in a future sense, as Jesus often did. But that's not the whole story. When people come to know Jesus, they enter into God's kingdom, right here and right now. And as individuals and families and communities and nations bow to Jesus, His kingdom takes new ground.

We saw in the last chapter that Jesus instructed His followers to pray for God's kingdom to come to earth (Matthew 6:10; Luke 11:2). That's the future aspect of the kingdom. But Jesus also referred to the kingdom as having "come near" (Luke 10:9,

11), having "come upon you" (Matthew 12:28; Luke 11:20), and being "in the midst of you" (Luke 17:21). That's the present aspect at work.

Nicodemus seemed to understand that Jesus was requiring a present change in order to enter God's kingdom here and now. The Pharisee's objection, while somewhat flippant, gets at the immediacy of Jesus' call to be born again: "How can a man be born when he is old? Can he enter a second time into his mother's womb and be born?" (John 3:4). As a highly educated religious leader, Nicodemus understood this "new birth" to be figurative language on Jesus' part. But his response, cloaked in literal language, demonstrates that he recognized the impossibility of Jesus' statement.

Had Nicodemus taken Jesus' demand of new birth as merely a requirement to enter the pearly gates of heaven upon death, he wouldn't have flinched. But he knew Jesus was telling him that God required a total change of life, right then and there, in order to be a part of the new thing God was doing. What Jesus asked was as impossible as a grown man getting back into his mother's womb to be born again. But, of course, "with God all things are possible" (Matthew 19:26).

No part of the old creation willed itself into being. In the same way, with the new creation God brings to each of Christ's followers, the miracle belongs to Him alone. None of us can take the slightest credit for what God has done. The apostle Paul goes so far as to say that the change in a believer is nothing short of the difference between death and life:

> But God, being rich in mercy, because of the great love with which he loved us, even when we were dead in our trespasses, made us alive together with Christ—by grace you have been saved—and raised us up with him and seated us with him in the heavenly places in Christ Jesus, so that in the coming ages he might show the immeasurable riches of his grace in kindness toward us in Christ Jesus (EPHESIANS 2:4–7).

Notice that Paul's description of the believer's experience is, once again, in the past tense. God has *already* "made us alive together with Christ" and *already* "raised us up with him and seated us with him in the heavenly places" (vv. 5–6). While we await a future bodily resurrection and the coming of new heavens and a new earth, we have already been awakened to the age to come. Our status as part of the new creation in Christ Jesus is already firm and secure.

God performs a miracle within every believer to make each one a new creation. This comes by nothing we have done—"by grace you have been saved" (v. 5). And the reason for this new birth? It is "so that in the coming ages [God] might show the immeasurable riches of his grace in kindness toward us" (v. 7). Just like the creation of the heavens and the earth—at the beginning of everything, way back in Genesis—this work of new creation in our hearts is from God and by God. Through and through, it is an overflow of His love.

■ ■ ■

Shortly after my eye surgery, I discovered that my mind did not immediately accept the new reality of twenty-twenty vision. Every morning for the first several days, I would wake up seeing clearly, but out of habit I would inevitably reach for my glasses next to the bed. And while driving, I would often find myself squinting unnecessarily to see things in the distance. The squinting didn't improve my eyesight one iota, but it somehow felt right to narrow my gaze, just as I had done before. In reality, I had new vision—but it took my brain a little time to accept the truth.

This is one of the ongoing challenges of the Christian life: learning to live in the truth of our new birth. We have been given a new nature, but we must choose to walk in it. While our status as a new creation is a gift from God, we must exercise the gift every day. That's why Paul encouraged the Christians at Ephesus "to put off your old self, which belongs to your former manner of life" (Ephesians 4:22), and also "to put on the new self, created after the likeness of God in true righteousness and holiness" (v. 24). God has given us a new spirit, which is now able to obey Him (Ezekiel 11:19; 36:26), and He has sent the Holy Spirit to live inside us (2 Corinthians 1:22; 1 John 4:13)—but it is up to us to obey His promptings.

As Christians, we have new life, but we must choose to walk in it. We must choose to wage an ongoing battle against sin. Too often, though, we give up before we even start. We are quick to say with the apostle Paul, "for all have sinned and fall short of the glory of God." That's Romans 3:23—a popular verse, one many people can recite from memory. But how many of us recall the next verse? Paul continues his thought: ". . . and are justified by his grace as a gift, through the redemption that is in Christ Jesus" (v. 24). We have been set free. We have been bought out of slavery. We have been made new. The new creation has broken into our lives, right here and right now. We are no longer at home in this world; we belong to another. And the sinful nature that we inherited from Adam, while it still attempts to pull us down every day, is just as alien within us.

The good news of the gospel extends to all of creation, but it starts with us. We have been made new, and we're no longer slaves to sin. One day, when we find ourselves living forever with our Maker in a restored and renewed earth that has been joined to a new heaven, we'll see the sin we'd struggled with for what it is: death. Sin is the very opposite of the goodness that was in our Father's heart at the very beginning—and has been His desire for us ever since.

Have you ever noticed that when a well-known Christian stumbles into sin, there are usually two responses? Some people celebrate, because those living in darkness hate light (John 3:20) and sin squelches an individual's light. Other people—even nonbelievers—mourn, because goodness lived out by a single person means there is hope for us all. In the Sermon on the Mount, Jesus told His disciples, "Let your light shine before others, so that they may see your good works and give glory to your Father who is in heaven" (Matthew 5:16). Many people are looking for the light of Christ. In God's story, we get to be the bearers of the flame.

Sin really is death. Yes, it may bring pleasure for a time, but deep down, most people know that choosing sin is eating poison, one rancid bite at a time. As we live out our role in the gospel story, choosing those things that bring life rather than death, we declare loudly that sin has been conquered—that there is hope in Jesus Christ.

YOUR LIFE IN THE STORY OF GOD

Jesus' resurrection was the beginning of the new creation. When we are "in Christ," we ourselves are "a new creation" (2 Corinthians 5:17), able to obey God's commands and enlarge the kingdom of God on earth, here and now. We can see sin for what it really is—death—and share the light of Jesus with a world in need of hope.

1. Is there anything you wish you could change about yourself physically? What would you like to change spiritually?

2. Why do we struggle, even as Christians, to leave sin behind us? How can we live in the freedom that Jesus brings?

3. How is the kingdom of God a future thing? How is it a present reality?

RELATION
God Draws Near

*"Some people think that God
does not like to be troubled
with our constant coming and asking.
The only way to trouble God
is not to come at all."*

—D. L. MOODY

The Peace beyond the Storm

GENESIS 3:1–13

My first child came into this world by caesarean section on a warm July evening in 2014. Just after nine o'clock, I saw Jonah's bright red face for the first time and heard his healthy lungs give voice to some apparent postnatal apprehension. After a momentary visit with his mother and me, Jonah was wheeled out of the operating room to be cleaned up, weighed, and measured. Once I was certain that Laurin was well cared for, I made my way to the next room to find my baby son.

I could hear Jonah's cries from the hallway. And when I entered the room, I saw the fear in his minutes-old face. The nurse counting his fingers and toes talked sweetly to him, but it made no difference. Jonah wasn't having it.

Then I came closer and spoke: "Hi, Jonah. I'm your dad." To my surprise, he stopped screaming. I put my finger in his hand, and he squeezed tightly. "I love you," I said, and Jonah responded with a peaceful coo and a firmer grip.

In a world of all new sights and sounds, I think my son recognized my voice. While Laurin was pregnant, I had talked to Jonah quite a bit—and played him a lot of Johnny Cash. He remembered my voice as a familiar, friendly tone he had known before everything changed for him minutes earlier. (In fairness, "Ring of Fire" might have had the same effect.)

Jonah won't remember the day he was born—or those beautiful moments in the neonatal recovery room—but I will. And when he's a teenager, I plan to remind him that my voice was once all it took to put everything right in his world.

Back in the garden of Eden, our heavenly Father had a special moment with His son, Adam. "The LORD God formed the man of dust from the ground and breathed into his nostrils the breath of life, and the man became a living creature" (Genesis 2:7). With the first man, God came closer to His creation than He had before. The sun, moon, and stars had been spoken into being; the same was true for the fish, birds, and animals. But with Adam, God got His hands dirty. The very breath expanding and contracting the man's lungs came from the Maker of heaven and earth. The message in this personal interaction is loud and clear: we human beings hold a special place in God's heart, and He wants to be intimately involved in our lives.

In fact, the Bible records that God would walk in the garden in the cool of the day (Genesis 3:8). Imagine Adam and Eve strolling through paradise with the Lord, talking together, laughing together, and enjoying one another. Think of the questions they asked God, and the answers He gave. Consider the joy our first parents must have felt walking in step with their Creator, seeing the smile on His face and hearing the delight in His voice as He shared His heart with them.

But note that this lone verse telling us how God walked in the garden in the cool of the day comes *after* Adam and Eve sinned. This means we don't actually know if the first humans, in their sinless state, enjoyed afternoon strolls with God. What's more, there is another way of translating this verse about God walking in the garden.

On the Wind of the Storm

Dr. Jeffrey Niehaus, an Old Testament scholar and a professor at Gordon-Conwell Theological Seminary, makes the compelling case that the scene described in Genesis 3:8 is one of judgment rather than casual walking. His argument centers largely on the Hebrew word translated "day" in our Bibles.

Just as many modern languages have similar words meaning similar things, ancient Hebrew also borrowed terms from other ancient tongues. With this in mind, note that the Hebrew word *yom* has an Akkadian cousin, *umu*. Both yom and umu commonly equate with our word "day," but umu can also be translated "storm." Dr. Niehaus suggests that there are a few places in the Old Testament where yom might be better rendered "storm" as well, based on the context. Genesis 3:8 is one of those places.

Though there is not space here to highlight the other translation issues at play,[1] it is possible to translate Genesis 3:8, "And they heard the sound [or voice] of the LORD God moving back and forth on the wind of the storm." This understanding makes sense of the second half of the verse: "and the man and his wife hid themselves from the presence of the LORD God among the trees of the garden" (compare with Exodus 20:18). Wouldn't you hide if you heard the thunderous sound of God coming on a windstorm in judgment?

But why get into the weeds here with a discussion of a seldom-heard alternate translation? Because it illustrates just how broken the relationship between God and His people became immediately after sin entered the world. Adam and Eve disobeyed God's command. By trusting the evil one, they pronounced God a liar and proclaimed His goodness to be wickedness. And just as their actions twisted and corrupted the truth, sin twisted and corrupted its way across creation—including the bond our first parents shared with their Maker.

While I prefer Dr. Niehaus's translation of Genesis 3:8 to the one found in most of our Bibles, I still find value in the thought of God walking with Adam and Eve in the cool of the day. I believe it happened. I can't see why it wouldn't have. It's hard for me to imagine God carefully forming the first man out of dirt and fashioning the first woman from the man's side, and then simply taking a leave of absence. I just can't picture God bringing the animals to Adam for naming, and then, after "zebu," barely speaking with him again. Before the fall, Adam and Eve enjoyed intimacy with the Father, so yes—I believe family walks would have been part of life in the garden.

And that makes this image of God so startling, His appearing in a windstorm with a voice that could shake the trees. It shows just how damaging sin is. God, in His holiness, can have no part with sin. By all measures, Adam and Eve's disobedience should have been enough for God to snuff out humanity. The Lord would have been justified in putting a stop to their lives right then and there. But—and thank God that, with Him, there's often a "but"—He chose to redeem the human race rather than end it.

On the day of their judgment, Adam and Eve hid when they heard the sound of the Lord—but Jesus did the opposite when He was judged for the sins of the world. He did not run in fear. He did ask God to "remove this cup," but then He willingly drank the cup the Father had for Him (Luke 22:42). Nails could never hold the Son of God to a Roman cross; Jesus remained there of His own accord.

With their innocence gone and their eyes opened, Adam and Eve were ashamed of their nakedness. Jesus, having been stripped naked by Pilate's soldiers, thought little of His shame in order to bear ours (Hebrews 12:2). In the garden, looking for the man and woman, God called out, "Where are you?" (Genesis 3:9). But at Calvary, it was Jesus who called out to God: "My God, my God, why have you forsaken me?" (Matthew 27:46).

In some way that we can't fully understand, Jesus experienced the judgment that Adam and Eve—and every one of their children down to the present—deserved. Though our minds cannot quite grasp the idea, in that moment the wrath of God fell on Jesus. As our representative, He experienced the God-forsakenness the Lord had warned Adam and Eve about.

Christ endured this unspeakable pain for us—for Adam and Eve, for you and me, and for anyone who professes sincere faith in Him. He did it so that when we hear the sound of the Lord, we will no longer feel the need to run and hide as our first parents did. Instead, we will recognize the Father's voice, and it will bring us peace. His familiar tone will be all it takes to put everything right in our world.

YOUR LIFE IN THE STORY OF GOD

A father's voice can strike fear into misbehaving children. But that same voice can bring comfort to sons and daughters who see their father as the source of protection, provision, and love. By their sin, Adam and Eve felt the fear of God; through Jesus Christ, who paid the price for our sins, we can come to God with confidence. His voice will put everything right in our world.

1. Can you describe a time when a parent's voice made you fearful? Can you describe a time when a parent's voice brought you peace?

2. What does God's grace to Adam and Eve teach us about Him? Why didn't He just destroy humanity as soon they sinned?

3. How do Jesus' interactions with God at the crucifixion contrast with Adam and Eve's after their sin in the garden?

Eyes to See

GENESIS 22:1–19

When I was a few years removed from college, I accepted a job as a youth pastor in California. But there were two problems: I was living and working in Connecticut at the time, and the church that offered me the position couldn't pay my relocation expenses. But I believed God was leading me across the country, so I took the job in faith, even though I had no way to get to it.

A few days later, my one-year Bible reading plan brought me to Exodus 12, and I read, "The LORD had made the Egyptians favorably disposed toward the people, and they gave them what they asked for; so they plundered the Egyptians" (v. 36 NIV). Something about that verse stuck in my brain, and I believed God was trying to get my attention.

The next morning when I still couldn't shake the idea, I began to pray about it. And I continued to pray. Before long, I was in my boss's office asking *him* to pay for my move across the country, hoping he would be "favorably disposed" toward me. Actually, I asked my boss if the company would be willing to offer me a severance package if I resigned my position.

It was a ridiculous proposition. What did the company have to gain by giving me an extra month's worth of paychecks when I had already decided to quit?

What I didn't know was that the organization was in a bit of financial trouble, and my boss needed to lay off a few employees. He'd actually been deciding on the layoffs when I interrupted him that afternoon. So when I volunteered to leave, he was more than happy to take me up on my offer. It meant someone else would get to keep their job.

God sees the whole story, but our vision is quite limited.

That's why it's never a good idea to trust our eyes alone. We have to trust the Author who knows the end of the story. I can't promise that God will use a particular Scripture in your life in the same way that He used Exodus 12:36 in mine. However, I can tell you that a relationship with the Lord always requires faith.

Just ask Eve. God had said that the tree of the knowledge of good and evil would bring death (Genesis 2:17). But rather than simply believing Him, Eve listened to the serpent. It was just Satan's word against God's, but she allowed her senses to be her heart's tiebreaker. "When the woman *saw* that the fruit of the tree was good for food and *pleasing to the eye*, and also desirable for gaining wisdom, she took some and ate it" (Genesis 3:6 NIV, emphasis added). When God's Word appears to contradict our experience, it can be tempting to place our trust in the "wisdom" we have conjured through our senses, but such trust is misplaced. Obedience to God never disappoints—not in the long run anyway.

■ ■ ■

Abraham discovered this when God called him to leave everything familiar and travel to a land he'd never seen. Though Abraham would later become the father of many nations, including the people of Israel, at the time of his calling his family served false gods (Joshua 24:2). As far as we know Abraham knew nothing of the true God until that incredible day when the Lord appeared to him in Mesopotamia (Acts 7:2). But Abraham proved to be a man of amazing faith; he took God at His word and dropped everything to sojourn in the land of Canaan—just because God told him to do so.

In the interest of full disclosure, it should be noted that God made Abraham some amazing promises: to give him descendants more numerous than the sand on the beach or the stars in the sky (Genesis 15:5; 22:17), to make his name great and make him into a great nation (12:2), to bless the entire world through him (12:3), and to give him the land of Canaan as an inheritance (17:8). Abraham was chosen to be a main character in God's story.

Still, Abraham believed God and acted on his faith before he received any of these gifts. In fact, Abraham lived out the definition of faith given to us in the book of Hebrews: "Faith is the assurance of things hoped for, the conviction of things not seen" (11:1). Though he stumbled and fell into sin along the way, Abraham walked through this world fully convinced that God is good and that He would fulfill the promises He made. But Abraham's greatest test of faith came when God began to deliver on those promises.

Believe It or Not

Twenty-five years after God promised to make Abraham into a great nation, Abraham heard the cries of a beautiful baby boy. Though Sarah had been barren and the couple was old enough to be great-grandparents, God gave them a son, Isaac—the first grain of sand to be deposited on the beach of descendants God had promised.

This promised miracle was beyond incredible—so incredible in fact that Abraham had a hard time understanding how God would accomplish it. Although he believed that God would make him into a nation (several nations actually; see Genesis 17:5), Abraham couldn't seem to imagine that he and Sarah would ever hold a child of their own. As a result, his story includes a few ugly chapters.

When God first spoke to Abraham, he and Sarah had no children. Initially, Abraham assumed that the promise would be fulfilled through his legal heir, a trusted member of his household, Eliezer of Damascus (Genesis 15:2). But Eliezer was not a blood relation to Abraham; he was most likely a slave. Any offspring through Eliezer would only be so legally. Abraham would be the end of his own bloodline.

When God insisted that Abraham's heir would not be Eliezer,

but "one who will come from your own body" (Genesis 15:4 NKJV), Abraham again tried to figure out how that could be. Since Sarah was barren, the solution seemed obvious to the couple: Abraham would have to father a child with another woman. And that's just what happened: Sarah gave her servant, Hagar, to Abraham as a wife, and through Hagar, Abraham fathered Ishmael.

But Ishmael was not to be the promised heir either. Instead, God himself visited the couple and promised that Sarah would become pregnant with a son in her old age (see Genesis 17:15–21; 18:1–15). And God was true to His word. At the ripe ages of one hundred and ninety-one respectively, Abraham and Sarah became the proud parents of Isaac.

You would think that with all that waiting and trying to bring God's plans to bear through his own efforts, Abraham would hold tightly to his miracle child, that he would never allow harm to come to him. Certainly, he cared for and protected Isaac, but Abraham's grip on his son was not adamantine. Abraham was willing to let go of Isaac and place him in the hands of One he trusted completely—even though that meant placing Isaac on an altar to be sacrificed.

When Isaac was a young man—perhaps a teenager or twenty-something—God told Abraham, "Take your son, your only son Isaac, whom you love, and go to the land of Moriah, and offer him there as a burnt offering on one of the mountains of which I shall tell you" (Genesis 22:2). No matter how many times I read this verse, I always expect it to be followed with "And Abraham took Isaac and hid him away," or "And Abraham responded with an airtight excuse."

But Abraham made no attempt to reason with God or to rationalize disobedience. He simply followed the Lord's command. Abraham took Isaac to Moriah and bound him atop an altar, the entire time trusting that God would somehow work everything out. In fact, when Isaac realized the most important part of the sacrifice—the lamb—was missing, Abraham told him, "God will provide for himself the lamb for a burnt offering, my son" (Genesis 22:8). At the last moment, when Abraham's knife was raised above Isaac, God intervened. Abraham had passed this test of faith, and God did indeed provide the sacrifice: a ram whose horns had become entangled in a nearby thicket.

The author of Hebrews tells us that Abraham was prepared to go through with the sacrifice of his son. He would have plunged his knife into Isaac and given his son's life to the Lord if need be, because "[h]e considered that God was able even to raise him from the dead, from which, figuratively speaking, he did receive him back" (11:19). That's the sort of faith God wants every one of His children to possess. It's the kind of trust in God that puts nothing out of the realm of possibility—because it puts no stock in circumstances but relies wholly on God, who is all-knowing, all-powerful, and good beyond measure.

Why should faith like Abraham's be the norm for every follower of Christ? Because the opposite is sin. It seems to me that every sin we commit, large or small, in secret or in public, is the final step in doubting at least one of these three things: that God is all-knowing, all-powerful, and good beyond measure.

We sin because we don't believe that God really knows best, so we deny the commands He's given us in His Word. Other times, we don't believe God is able to save us, so we do what we think we have to do to survive, whether that's lying, cheating, stealing, or worse. And sometimes we doubt God's good intentions toward us, so we take matters into our own hands to get the things we believe to be best for us. But Abraham didn't doubt God in any of these ways. "Abraham believed God, and it was counted to him as righteousness" (James 2:23; compare with Genesis 15:6).

Jesus said, "Abraham rejoiced that he would see my day. He saw it and was glad" (John 8:56). That's because God had promised Abraham, "In you all the families of the earth shall be blessed" (Genesis 12:3), and it was through Jesus, the many-times-over great-grandson of Abraham, that indeed every family in the world has been blessed.

The blood running through the veins of that ram caught in the thicket in Moriah had no power to remove sin or to bridge the chasm that exists between human beings and God. It was merely a road sign pointing to Christ, the substitute sacrifice we all need.

The scene in Genesis 22 foreshadows the climax of God's big story. God, in offering up His Son, in not staying His hand as He stayed Abraham's, was showing His love to the world. His perfect knowledge devised a way to bring sin to justice while offering mercy to His people. In His unlimited power, He rescued every follower of Christ from death and damnation. At Calvary (which is, incidentally, in the region of Moriah), God's infinite goodness was put on display for all to see.

There are moments in life when we allow our fears, our circumstances, and our sinful desires to drown out God's presence. Without realizing it, we can be tempted to write our own story, rather than play our part in God's. In these moments, when competing voices shout their loudest, we need to trust God simply because He is God.

In faith, Abraham had to imagine how God's salvation might come. But you and I do not—our faith can be centered on the completed work of Christ. Any time we begin to wonder about God's knowledge, power, or goodness, we need merely to look back to the cross. The gospel story tells us everything we need to know. Whatever you're facing this day, this week, or this year, God is able to carry you through it.

YOUR LIFE IN THE STORY OF GOD

Our view of life is limited, but God sees the whole story. So we trust in His knowledge, power, and goodness to bring us through those times that don't make sense. The faith of Abraham—a faith willing to sacrifice his beloved son at God's command—should be the norm for each follower of Christ. We need to trust God simply because He is God, playing our part in His story rather than trying to write our own.

1. Who or what would you identify as your own "Isaac"? What would you think if God told you to sacrifice that person or thing completely?

2. How might God's omniscience (complete knowledge) help us to trust Him? How would His omnipotence (complete power)?

3. Why do we sometimes struggle to believe that God is good? How can we move past that doubt?

God's Good Friend

EXODUS 33

After God freed the people of Israel from slavery in Egypt, He appointed Moses' brother, Aaron, as one of the men to lead them. But on one particular day—a very sad, dark day—Aaron let the people lead him instead. While Moses was atop Mount Sinai on a forty-day visit with God, here's what happened, in Aaron's own words:

> *"You know the people, that they are set on evil. For they said to me, 'Make us gods who shall go before us. As for this Moses, the man who brought us up out of the land of Egypt, we do not know what has become of him.' So I said to them, 'Let any who have gold take it off.' So they gave it to me, and I threw it into the fire, and out came this calf"* (EXODUS 32:22–24).

Before this incident with the golden calf, I think Aaron must have been an unusually honest man, because he certainly wasn't good at lying.

"Out came this calf," Aaron told Moses. Just like that, it sprang from the fire, wholly formed and ready to be worshipped. I wonder if Moses just shook his head and cringed. On top of all the sin Aaron had allowed to happen on his watch, he was now trying to lie his way out of trouble. Moses had witnessed some pretty unbelievable things in his time—his staff becoming a serpent, the Nile river turning to blood, the Red Sea parting—but even he couldn't entertain Aaron's spontaneous-calf story.

As ridiculous as Aaron's alibi was, the reality of the situation was nothing to laugh at. You may know the story. From all the earth God had rescued Israel to be His special people, and He was to be their God. As the people waited at the base of Mount Sinai for Moses to return from his extended meeting with the Lord, they grew restless. They fashioned a calf out of gold to stand in for the God who had brought them out of slavery—and they worshipped it. Creating a graven image, even as a representation of the true God, was strictly forbidden by the second commandment: "You shall not make for yourself a carved image, or any likeness of anything that is in heaven above, or that is in the earth beneath, or that is in the water under the earth. You shall not bow down to them or serve them, for I the LORD your God am a jealous God" (Exodus 20:4–5).

By committing this sinful act, the people of Israel broke their covenant with the Lord, and very soon after promising to keep it (see Exodus 24:3). With the covenant shattered, God would be perfectly justified in rejecting Israel as His chosen people. Their relationship was, in effect, severed. That's why God could tell Moses, "I have seen this people, and behold, it is a stiff-necked people. Now therefore let me alone, that my wrath may burn hot against them and I may consume them, in order that I may make a great nation of you" (Exodus 32:9–10).[2]

The truth is that every sin is treason against the Creator of the universe. As such, sin always carries a sentence of death (Romans 6:23). There is nothing extreme in God's response here. Nothing unjust. Nothing cruel. This is, rather, a rare look at justice unfiltered by the cross.[3] Or it would have been if God had not relented (Exodus 32:14). He did send judgment that day, and many people died because of their sin. But many did not.

In fact, God was so gracious that He told Moses, "Go up to a land flowing with milk and honey; but I will not go up among you, lest I consume you on the way, for you are a stiff-necked people" (Exodus 33:3). The Lord still planned to give His people the Promised Land, only now He would keep His distance so that His holy presence would not destroy them. Instead of leading the people himself, He would send an angel to go before them (v. 2). In effect, God was saying, "You broke your end of the covenant, but I'll still bless you with the land I promised, even though I don't have to."

Moses, however, knew the greatest blessing the Lord could give a person was not land or wealth or peace; it was God himself. So Moses said to the Lord, "If your presence will not go with me, do not bring us up from here" (v. 15).

More God, Please

We hear a lot today about Christian leadership. We read books that tell us how to have influence over the people God has put on our paths. We learn strategies for growing churches and ministries. And we listen to messages designed to help us find personal success in every sphere of life.

But in Exodus 33, Moses displayed the true secret to godly leadership. God had all but guaranteed him success in his mission to lead the nation of Israel to the Promised Land, but it wasn't good enough. Moses wanted more. He wanted to know the Lord, and he wouldn't settle for anything less.

Can you imagine what the church would be like if every believer made the same choice, if every Christian forsook success in life and ministry for the only thing that really matters? What if we all understood that the greatest blessing in this world is having more of God himself?

God's response shows that Moses hit the nail on the head: "This very thing that you have spoken I will do, for you have found favor in my sight, and I know you by name" (v. 17). Of course God knows everyone's name, but to say that He knew Moses by name was another way of saying that the pair had an uncommon closeness. In fact, we read that in the tent of meeting, "the LORD used to speak to Moses face to face, as a man speaks to his friend" (v. 11).

And Moses didn't stop there. In this moment, when God's wrath was still kindled against His people, Moses took another step closer to the Lord. He said, "Please show me your ways, that I may know you" (v. 13), and "show me your glory" (v. 18).

Once again, God obliged: "I will make all my goodness pass before you and will proclaim before you my name 'The LORD.' And I will be gracious to whom I will be gracious, and will show mercy on whom I will show mercy" (v. 19). God's ways are good. God's glory is infinite. Both are part of His identity and wrapped up in His name. They go before Him as a person's reputation precedes that individual.

As if to drive the point home to Moses, a short time later, the Lord again passed before him and said,

> "The LKN', the LKN', a God merciful and gracious, slow to anger, and abounding in steadfast love and faithfulness, keeping steadfast love for thousands, forgiving iniquity and transgression and sin, but who will by no means clear the guilty, visiting the iniquity of the fathers on the children and the children's children, to the third and the fourth generation" (EXODUS 34:6–7).

This is the heart of the God we are invited to know. This is the gospel here and now. In our sin, we hear that He will "by no means clear the guilty" and we look to hide from Him when we hear Him coming—just like Adam and Eve before us. But because of Christ, a way has been made so that He will forgive "iniquity and transgression and sin."

How can this be true? How can God both punish sin *and* forgive it? The answer is found at the cross. Jesus carried our sins with Him that day, and because of them God's judgment was poured out on the Son. Christ took the punishment we deserved. Because the Son of God came to earth as a man and lived a completely obedient and upright life, He was the perfect sacrifice on our behalf. Once we come to know Christ, we are joined with Him in His life, death, and resurrection. Our sin is cleansed, and the right relationship Jesus enjoys with the Father is ours for the taking. We just need to step up and receive it.

Too often, like Aaron before us, when we're found guilty we double down on our sin. We try to cover it up, to make excuses, to shift the blame. We think the best we can hope for is to keep our sin secret. But because of Jesus' death and resurrection—because of the gospel—we are now free to double down on God's goodness, as Moses did. So the best thing that can happen is for our sin to be exposed and forgiven.

At Calvary, Jesus paid for our sins. They no longer block our relationship with the Father. We now have this promise: "If we confess our sins, he is faithful and just to forgive us our sins and to cleanse us from all unrighteousness" (1 John 1:9). Every believer can speak to God "as a man speaks to his friend" (Exodus 33:11). We can know Him and be known by Him. This is how we were created to live in the first place.

YOUR LIFE IN THE STORY OF GOD

Moses wasn't perfect, but he was wise enough to know what he really needed in life: more of God. And God was happy to honor that request, interacting with Moses "face to face, as a man speaks to his friend" (Exodus 33:11). Such intimacy with God is available to each of us today through the work of Jesus Christ, who sacrificed himself for our sins. With the penalty paid, our sins need no longer to block our relationship to God.

1. How could the ancient Israelites fall into idolatry so soon after God miraculously led them out of their slavery in Egypt? How can we avoid that trap?

2. What do you think of the statement, "every sin is treason against the Creator of the universe"? How does God show grace to all people, Christians and those who don't follow Jesus?

3. How did Moses pursue more of God? How might you?

Moving Closer

2 SAMUEL 6:1–19

Pastor and author John Piper once wrote, "Missions exists because worship doesn't. Worship is ultimate, not missions, because God is ultimate, not man. When this age is over, and the countless millions of the redeemed fall on their faces before the throne of God, missions will be no more."[4]

After His resurrection, Jesus gave His disciples a directive that many call the Great Commission. In Matthew 28:18–20, He said:

> "All authority in heaven and on earth has been given to me. Go therefore and make disciples of all nations, baptizing them in the name of the Father and of the Son and of the Holy Spirit, teaching them to observe all that I have commanded you. And behold, I am with you always, to the end of the age."

This is a temporary directive from our Commander. One day, when history as we know it has spent its last moments, Christ will rescind that order. But the invitation to worship God will never run its course; it is the perpetual duty of every believer.

Worship is in our blood and in our bones. It's written on our DNA. We were designed to worship, and we can't *not* worship—no matter how hard we try. Since this desire is so ingrained in who we are as human beings, it's important that we know what worship is. It's more than singing. It's more than bowing our heads or bending our knees. It's more than taking part in religious activities. Each of these can be worship, but worship is so much more.

The truth is, whatever we give ourselves to, we worship. The problem is, we are prone to worship the wrong things: money, sex, power, comfort, the opinions of other people, and even ourselves. But anything that captures our devotion, save God himself, is an idol that has usurped the place in our hearts reserved for Jesus alone.

Because his life reflected godliness, David—Israel's second king—was called a man after God's own heart (1 Samuel 13:14; Acts 13:22). He was faithful and obedient, and he loved goodness. That's not to say he never sinned, of course. David was both an adulterer and a murderer. But even in these low points, his repentance was genuine and his love for God overarching. David was a man after God's own heart not only because of his personal character, but because he pursued God's heart. He was a man who worshipped with his whole being.

David is credited with writing more than half of the psalms recorded in the Bible. "Even though I walk through the valley of the shadow of death, I will fear no evil, for you are with me; your rod and your staff, they comfort me" (Psalm 23:4). That's David. "The LORD is my light and my salvation; whom shall I fear?" (Psalm 27:1). That's also David. "Create in me a clean heart, O God, and renew a right spirit within me" (Psalm 51:10). Yup. David. Many of the most familiar lines from the Bible's best-loved psalms came from the pen—and heart—of David.

And when David became king of Israel, he had the ark of the covenant brought to Jerusalem so that the presence of the Lord, which resided with the ark, would be nearby. In fact, during this unique period in Israel's history, there were actually two tabernacles—the one built under Moses' leadership, which was stationed in Gibeon, and a new tent pitched by David in Jerusalem. The difference between them? David's tabernacle housed the ark of the covenant, and with it, the power and presence of God (see Exodus 25:22).

The ark was a wooden box overlaid with gold ornamentation. When the Israelites were still in the wilderness, God commanded them to build it; once complete, the ark became home to God's manifest presence. Obviously, there is no place in creation where God is not present, but with the ark, He resided with His people in a special way. The ark was placed in the tabernacle when the people made camp, and it occupied a central location, visibly illustrating the prominence of God's presence in the life of the nation.

Under his leadership, David wanted God's presence once again to be central to the life of the nation, so he had the ark moved to Jerusalem, the capital that he had established for Israel. But beyond that, David wanted more of God in his own life. As I said, David was a man who chased after God's heart. You can't get to know someone very well if you're rarely together, so David made sure he could spend regular time in God's presence. That's one of the reasons he wanted the ark so close by.

King David also knew that God wants every person to pursue Him wholeheartedly, to trust Him and follow His ways. Having a relationship with the Lord is more than just friendship—God wants to be Lord of our lives. Actually, that's not quite right; by virtue of His being our Creator, He's already Lord. But we need to recognize His lordship and act accordingly. That means trusting Him and obeying His every word, even when we don't understand why. This is one of the ways we can live the gospel in our daily lives. David learned this lesson the hard way.

God had told Moses that the ark was to be carried using poles; no one was to touch it directly. And only members of the tribe of Levi were permitted to transport the ark from place to place. But when David first tried to bring the ark into Jerusalem, he had it placed on a cart and superintended by non-Levites. Then the unthinkable happened: the ark slipped, and a poor soul named Uzzah was struck dead when he reached out to steady it.

The incident made David angry with the Lord, and also very afraid. So three months passed before David tried again. But when he did, he got it right: he appointed Levites to carry the ark properly, saying, "Because you did not carry it the first time, the LORD our God broke out against us, because we did not seek him according to the rule" (1 Chronicles 15:13).

But David did more than just follow rules. He delighted in God and His Word. That's why, when the ark finally arrived in Jerusalem, it was met with musical instruments, singing, and dancing. The king wanted the moment to reflect how good God really is—and he wanted the people to sense the blessing of God's presence there in Jerusalem, the center of the nation's life and culture. David himself got in on the joy, dancing with abandon before the Lord (2 Samuel 6:14; 1 Chronicles 15:29).

Finally, David worshipped God with sacrifice and praise. The Bible tells us that "when those who bore the ark of the LORD had gone six steps, he sacrificed an ox and a fattened animal" (2 Samuel 6:13). While this may mean that David directed sacrifice one time at the beginning of the journey (after six steps), it's not unthinkable that he had offerings made *every* six steps. After all, some years later when David's son Solomon dedicated the temple in Jerusalem, he offered up quite a bit of sacrifice: "22,000 oxen and 120,000 sheep" (2 Chronicles 7:5). Either way, David was making a statement with these burnt offerings. He was proclaiming his thankfulness to the Lord while acknowledging his own sinfulness and that of the nation. David was honoring his Maker with "a pleasing aroma" (Leviticus 1:9).

Along with that aroma, David wanted to bring a pleasing sound to the Lord, so he instructed the Levites to sing and make music with "harps, lyres, and cymbals, to raise sounds of joy. . . . So all Israel brought up the ark of the covenant of the LORD with shouting, to the sound of the horn, trumpets, and cymbals, and made loud music on harps and lyres" (1 Chronicles 15:16, 28). David himself offered a song of gratitude and praise to God that day. It began, "Oh give thanks to the LORD; call upon his name; make known his deeds among the peoples!" (1 Chronicles 16:8).

Those opening lyrics capture David's hope for his people: he wanted Israel to delight in their God, to remember His faithfulness, to seek Him above all else, and to make Him famous in all the earth. All these are elements of worship, and David wanted to instill them in his subjects as he had in his own heart.

Camping with Jesus

The New Testament tells us that when Jesus came to earth, "the Word became flesh and dwelt among us" (John 1:14). Rendered more literally, the Greek word translated *dwelt* means "to fix one's tabernacle." The idea is that Jesus came to earth to camp with us, but His tent was not just any tent, for John added, "we have seen his glory, glory as of the only Son from the Father, full of grace and truth."

Jesus' tent, His earthly body (see John 2:18–22), was full of the glory of God, just as the tabernacle in the Old Testament was. But no one on earth had to make plans to set up this tabernacle, as David did with his; God, out of His love for us, did all the work by sending His son.

It is amazing to consider that the second member of the Trinity put on flesh and walked among us. But what's even more incredible is that because Jesus died for our sins, was raised to life on the third day, and ascended to the right hand of His heavenly Father's throne, we have even greater access to the tabernacle of glory. Paul wrote to the believers in Corinth, "Do you not know that your body is a temple of the Holy Spirit within you, whom you have from God?" (1 Corinthians 6:19). The tabernacle was a portable temple, and it was replaced by the glorious building Solomon constructed in Jerusalem. But God wanted to be closer to His people than that—Christ's Spirit now resides within every believer. His presence and power are alive inside us!

God did this to restore our relationship. We can now live lives of worship, just as David did. When we seek more of the Lord, we can know His presence and power is at work in everything we do. The Holy Spirit will instruct us, convict us, and bring to our minds the Word of God so that we can obey God's commands. He will produce the fruit of "love, joy, peace, patience, kindness, goodness, faithfulness, gentleness, [and] self-control" in our lives as we yield to Him (Galatians 5:22–23).

And, in thankfulness, we will have offerings and praises to give. But rather than bringing animals to be slaughtered, we ourselves are to be living sacrifices (Romans 12:1–2). Instead of the smell of meat being consumed by fire, our very lives should be a pleasing aroma wafting its way up to God, a holy fragrance that never dies out (2 Corinthians 2:14).

I am convinced that a lot of well-meaning Christians miss out on God's best for their lives because, day in and day out, they are worshipping something other than the Lord. If you'd like to perform a worship check on your heart, take a look at where your money and time go. Jesus said, "Where your treasure is, there your heart will be also" (Matthew 6:21). In other words, we give our resources to the things we cherish.

Of course, this doesn't mean that God calls every Christian, everywhere, to give every last dime to the local church and spend every moment of every day praying and singing praise songs. It does mean that decisions we make about our dollars and minutes should flow out of our love for Jesus. Having more of Him is far better than anything we'll give up in this life.

YOUR LIFE IN THE STORY OF GOD

Worship is part of humanity's DNA. We were designed to worship God, but sin causes us to idolize other things— whether money, sex, power, or the approval of others. These false gods must be recognized and removed from our lives, replaced by a pure pursuit of God's heart. To enjoy the Lord's presence, the biblical David brought the ark nearby; we as Christians, actually housing the Spirit, can be "living sacrifices" to our God.

1. What interferes most with your worship of God? Why?

2. What does the story of Uzzah (1 Chronicles 13) teach us about worshipping God? What can we learn from the fact that the Bible is so honest about people's failure—even of "heroes" like David?

3. What does the Holy Spirit's presence in our lives contribute to our worship of God? How is it still possible for us to miss out on God's best for our lives?

Jesus Invites Himself Over

LUKE 19:1–10

After three months of looking, I finally found a house I could afford. It had been vacant for more than two years, and the previous occupants had not treated the place very kindly. The floors and walls were stained and splattered (with what, I don't want to imagine). Many of the light fixtures had been ripped from the ceiling, and several of the faucets had been pulled out as well. The yard looked like a jungle in the front and the aftermath of a dust storm in the back. Insects of all kinds roamed freely in and out of the house through a broken window in the sunroom. As I toured the place with my real estate agent, I spied a large spider scurrying over a pile of trash—it paused for a moment as if sizing me up for a fight. The place was a mess, but I could see its potential. I submitted an offer, and several weeks later was the proud owner of the worst house in town.

I knew that everything wrong with the house could be fixed. Little by little, the walls were painted, the carpets and hardwoods replaced, and new fixtures brought in. I killed more spiders and scorpions than I care to remember. I even fought the good fight with the lawn, and won.

In a few months, the house looked great, inside and out. It was hard to believe that this was the same dismal property I had purchased. The best part was, because I had bought the place in such disrepair, I'd gotten a great deal on it.

As I met my new neighbors, several of them thanked me for taking care of the yard. I suppose they were tired of looking at all the tall weeds waving in the wind in defiance of basic suburban sensitivities. But my neighbors weren't the only ones who noticed the improvements. A short time later in the mail, I received a letter marked "Official Tax Matter." The county had decided that since my home was no longer such a mess, it was worth 50 percent more than I had paid for it—and my property taxes were raised accordingly.

There was a certain injustice to that tax bill. I had either done the work myself or paid someone else to do it, improving a dilapidated property that was an eyesore in the community. In doing so, I raised the resale value of every home on my street. What was the reward for my efforts? A fat bill from a local government bureaucrat.

I thought to myself, *Where was the tax commissioner when I was learning how to fix a shower from a YouTube video? Where was he when I almost fell through the ceiling adding insulation to the attic?* It seemed so very unfair. And that wasn't the only time I received such a letter. Every year I lived in that home, my taxes increased significantly.

When Lunch Changes Everything

No one likes paying taxes, but in the Roman Empire, most people despised tax collectors. And for good reason—their corruption seemed to know no bounds. Local tax gatherers bid for the privilege of levying taxes. Once awarded the office, they were free to charge above and beyond what Rome required— and keep the extra revenue for themselves. This made tax collectors very rich, but it also earned them few friends. In the Jewish corner of the Roman world, these men were viewed as traitors who colluded with the Romans to keep God's people in slavery. Therefore, tax collectors in Jesus' day were almost universally hated. I say "almost" because there was at least one person who loved them.

One time, after Jesus and His disciples arrived in Jericho, crowds of curious people surrounded them, hoping to see a miracle or hear a bit of the teaching that had all of Judea buzzing. Everyone wondered, *Could this be the Messiah?* So the people watched Jesus' every move.

But unlike politicians who take steps to shore up their own popularity, Jesus was concerned only with the Father's favor— and He knew His Father's heart was bent toward the broken and the outcast. That's why, when He saw the tax collector Zacchaeus up in a sycamore tree, clinging to a branch to get a better view, Jesus stopped for a moment to have a word with him (Luke 19:2–5).

The Jewish people within earshot no doubt expected Jesus to chastise the man. Even Zacchaeus may have braced himself for a tongue-lashing. After all, he was a *chief* tax collector. That meant he not only worked for the Romans and levied unfair taxes, he also took a cut from all the local collectors who reported to him, putting him at the top of a crooked pyramid scheme that hurt everyone in town.

But Jesus said nothing harsh. On the contrary, He said something quite unexpected: "Zacchaeus, hurry and come down, for I must stay at your house today" (Luke 19:5). The Son of God invited himself over for lunch.

■ ■ ■

This true story is a picture of Christ's mission in miniature. We, like Zacchaeus, had nothing to recommend ourselves to the Lord, yet He chose to draw near to us, unlovely though we were. He came without words of condemnation (John 3:17), and He dined at our table.

This is the way it had to be if our relationship with God was ever to be restored:

> *For while we were still weak, at the right time Christ died for the ungodly. For one will scarcely die for a righteous person—though perhaps for a good person one would dare even to die—but God shows his love for us in that while we were still sinners, Christ died for us* (ROMANS 5:6–8).

The gospel is a declaration that God has done the hard thing. He has bridged the chasm caused by our sin, and He has made a way, once and for all, to close the abyss that stands between us. On our own, we would never choose God. Sin has broken and tangled our heartstrings so that we could never find our way back to the Lord, even if we tried. Not in a billion years. So God, in the person of Jesus Christ, came to us. He died in our place, not because we were worthy, but because He loved us—because He is *that* good.

Zacchaeus was so overwhelmed by Jesus' love that day that he repented of his sins, right then and there: "Look, Lord! Here and now I give half of my possessions to the poor, and if I have cheated anybody out of anything, I will pay back four times the amount" (Luke 19:8 NIV; compare with Exodus 22:1). This is how it is with God: He loves us first, and we respond. It is never the other way around.

By this point in His public ministry, Jesus had earned a reputation as "a friend of tax collectors and sinners" (Luke 7:34). His opponents meant that label as a slur, but Jesus wore it proudly. He was indeed a friend to tax collectors and other notorious sinners. That's because, in His own words, "the Son of Man came to seek and to save the lost" (Luke 19:10).

The root of the Greek word translated *lost* means "to destroy." Jesus wasn't saying that He came to seek and save those who are merely in need of direction. The condition of those He came for is far worse. He came to rescue people who are destroyed—as good as dead, and without any reasonable hope of survival.

With his long list of offenses, Zacchaeus knew he fit squarely into this category. But the same could not be said of the people waiting outside for Jesus. They complained, "He has gone in to be the guest of a man who is a sinner" (Luke 19:7). These people didn't recognize that they too were just as lost, just as destroyed.

No amount of good deeds can save a person. Notice that Zacchaeus's good deeds—his decision to give half of his possessions to the poor and to repay his victims fourfold—came as a response to Jesus' love, not as a condition for it. His actions revealed the new state of his heart, but they did not budge God's heart one bit. Good deeds *are* important—they are the norm in God's kingdom, since they show the world the goodness of the Creator. But they are not an entrance requirement.

This is one of the things that makes Christianity different from every other religion, philosophy, and worldview on the planet. There is no ladder to climb to reach Jesus. There is no twelve-step program to achieve salvation. If you ever find yourself struggling to pull yourself one notch higher or to check a self-imposed task off your religious to-do list, remember that Jesus loved you before you ever did one good thing. When you were lost and broken, beyond all hope of rescue, Jesus showed up, just to be with you. And that's what He still wants more than anything—simply to be with you.

Having a relationship with Jesus Christ is the core of what it means to be a Christian. It's not what you do but who you know that makes all the difference. The good news is this: Jesus says, "Behold, I stand at the door and knock. If anyone hears my voice and opens the door, I will come in to him and eat with him, and he with me" (Revelation 3:20).

It seems the Savior is still in the business of inviting himself over. He's even willing to come to the worst house in town.

YOUR LIFE IN THE STORY OF GOD

We do nothing to earn our salvation. The story of Jesus and Zacchaeus proves that, showing how Jesus came "to seek and to save the lost" (Luke 19:10). Good deeds should be the outcome of our relationship with Christ, but they are never the thing that brings us to God in the first place. When Jesus "invites himself" into our lives, the only question is this: Will we, like Zacchaeus, welcome Him in?

1. Can you describe a difficult experience you had with an authority figure—tax collector or otherwise? How sympathetic were you to your "Zacchaeus"?

2. What does Jesus' compassion for Zacchaeus say about His interest in every person, from "the least of these" to those who take advantage of others? What does it say about you?

3. What do you think of the statement that good deeds "are not an entrance requirement" to God's kingdom?

A Gift to One Another

JOHN 13:34–35

"Comfort one another" (2 Corinthians 13:11). "Stir up one another to love and good works" (Hebrews 10:24). "Confess yours sins to one another and pray for one another" (James 5:16). I count forty-seven instances of these "one another" commands in the New Testament. It seems it is not enough to find peace with God; in doing so, we must also find peace with each other. As God brings a new creation, He is also healing every broken relationship and making peace where there was once no hope.

Jesus told His disciples, "A new commandment I give to you, that you love one another: just as I have loved you, you also are to love one another. By this all people will know that you are my disciples" (John 13:34–35). At first glance, this seems like an odd thing for Jesus to say. How is a command to love a "new commandment"? The Old Testament already included such a command: Leviticus 19:18 says, "You shall love your neighbor as yourself." And Jesus himself quoted this verse when asked about the greatest commandment in the Law. He said it came in second place (see Matthew 22:36–40; Mark 12:28–34). So what makes Jesus' commandment "new"?

Jesus said the world would know we are His disciples not just because we love each other, but also by the way we love: "*Just as I have loved you*, you also are to love one another," He said (John 13:34, emphasis added). And how did Jesus love us? All the way. No holding back. Nothing off limits. He loved us through His arrest, through false accusations, through an illegal conviction, through unspeakable torture, through a monstrous crucifixion, and into a cold, lonely grave.

That command to love had never been given before. It was indeed brand-new, just as Jesus said. And the rest of the New Testament's "one another" commands are given as reminders that we are to live as people set apart for love in a way the world had never seen.

In the garden, the close relationship that Adam and Eve enjoyed with their Maker wasn't the only intimacy that sin broke. When Eve was being tempted by the serpent, Adam was right there with her (Genesis 3:6)—but he didn't open his mouth to contradict any of the lies coming from the evil one's forked tongue. In essence, he shirked his responsibility as Eve's husband and protector, besides his duty as one of God's representatives on earth. Before Adam ever took a bite of the forbidden fruit, he yielded the holy ground the Lord had given him to an invader— and in doing so, he betrayed his wife. Eve yielded her authority too, allowing the serpent to question God's good intentions, then betraying her husband the moment she handed him the poisonous fruit.

Such betrayal has marked the human race ever since. Brokenness extends to every type of human relationship, not just marriage. Both the Bible and secular history contain a long, sordid record of relational dysfunction: murder, theft, adultery, cruel indifference—even, on a national level, war. Had Adam and Eve ever wondered if God had overstated the effects of sin, their son Cain's murder of his brother, Abel, was a grim affirmation that He had not (see Genesis 4:1–16). Every generation since has experienced the pain that comes from sin-infected relationships. None of us escapes.

We are all both victims and perpetrators of crimes. Each of us could have our own image displayed on the wall of the post office as a fugitive from justice. But our pictures should also appear on milk cartons, as the innocent victims of other people's crimes. We have all been hurt by someone, and we have ourselves hurt others. But the good news of Jesus Christ holds the remedy.

Scandalous Forgiveness

In October 2006, Charles Carl Roberts IV stepped inside a one-room Amish schoolhouse in Lancaster County, Pennsylvania, brandished a handgun, and opened fire, killing five young girls and wounding another five before turning the gun on himself. As shocking as the shooting was, more shocking was what happened immediately after: the Amish forgave the killer of their children.

Within hours of the murders, Amish neighbors arrived at the home of the Charles Roberts's widow to offer condolences and comfort in *her* moment of loss. More than half of the seventy-five people in attendance at Roberts's funeral were Amish, several having buried their own daughters the day before. The small Amish community even set up a fund to care for Roberts's widow and three children.

To those following media coverage of these events, this response was almost unbelievable. But the secret of the Amish was no secret at all. They understood rightly that because God has forgiven us, we can forgive others, no matter how terrible the pain (see Ephesians 4:32).

Jesus said, "If you forgive others their trespasses, your heavenly Father will also forgive you, but if you do not forgive others their trespasses, neither will your Father forgive your trespasses" (Matthew 6:14–15). Our forgiveness, or lack of it, reveals what's in our hearts. In other words, when we hold a grudge, what we're really saying is, "I don't trust God to take care of this." Forgiveness, then, is an issue of faith.

That's why Jesus can say that our choice to forgive or not forgive will surely affect our relationship with the Father. If we believe Christ has indeed paid for our sins on the cross, we must believe that He will also act justly in dealing with the sins of those who have harmed us. In forgiveness, we are agreeing with God when He said, "Vengeance is mine" (Deuteronomy 32:35; Romans 12:19).

Forgiveness stops the cycle of retribution, but it also provides healing to the one who forgives. By giving the matter over to God, we are set free from the bitterness that threatens to over-take us. The Amish of the Nickel Mines community knew this, so for them, there was never a question as to whether or not they would forgive. They trusted God and did their best to act as Jesus would, even if it didn't make sense to a watching world.

In our sinful state, forgiveness is not our natural response. That's why, when we come to Christ, God also gives us a new nature and the Holy Spirit. Though on this side of heaven we will never do things perfectly, we now have the power to live a life that honors God—and that means obeying all the "one another" commands. God's Spirit resides within us, enabling us to live like Jesus.

The apostle Paul told the believers in Galatia, "Those who belong to Christ Jesus have nailed the passions and desires of their sinful nature to his cross and crucified them there. Since we are living by the Spirit, let us follow the Spirit's leading in every part of our lives" (Galatians 5:24–25 NLT). We often live as if this is not possible, as if our sinful actions are a foregone conclusion—but that's a sure sign we've neglected the Holy Spir-it's presence in our lives.

Contrary to popular self-help methods, this kind of "one another" life is not the result of simply trying harder or invoking a special behavior-modification trick. Rather, it comes by walk-ing with the Spirit. Broken relationships, it seems, are healed by returning to life as it was in the garden, where we walked with God (Genesis 3:8).[5] Because God's Spirit dwells inside each of Christ's followers, we *can* walk with Him once again. And our relationship with Him affects our relationships with everyone else.

In Christ, we stand as people who have been scandalously forgiven. Not one of us deserves it. That puts us in a position of freedom, but also in a place to extend forgiveness to those who have wounded us, no matter how severely. There is incredible power in that. Being able to forgive is a sign of strength, not weakness.

This sort of forgiveness, of course, does not come easily. It flows from the heart of God, so we need to tap into His heart to be a conduit of radical forgiveness. In the heart of God, we'll also find love—enough to share with everyone we'll ever meet.

Anyone can hold a grudge. Anyone can act out of selfish ambition. But in God's story, we are warriors of goodness and love. That's the way He's written our parts. Now each of us must decide whether we'll take our rightful place in God's story or fade back into the crowd.

YOUR LIFE IN THE STORY OF GOD

Forgiveness is God's gift to us, one that we are then expected to share with others. For sinful human beings, there's nothing "natural" about it, so we must walk closely with God and tap into His heart for the ability to forgive. Only through Jesus Christ, by living in His Spirit, will we be able to fulfill the many "one another" commands of Scripture, to live the gospel here and now in our human relationships.

1. How many of the New Testament's "one another" commands can you recall? Why do you think God put so many of them—nearly four dozen—in the New Testament?

2. When have you seen forgiveness like that of the Nickel Mines Amish on the news or in movies and television shows? How common is forgiveness even of small offenses?

3. How does Jesus' example help us to forgive others? How can we tap into God's heart for the ability to forgive those who offend us?

SALVATION
God Rescues His People

*"You're born. You suffer. You die.
Fortunately, there's a loophole."*
—BILLY GRAHAM

Unquenchable Fire
and Unrivaled Love

GENESIS 3:8–24

Frane Selak, a retired music teacher from Croatia, knows a thing or two about surviving against the odds. It all started more than fifty years ago when he boarded a train in Sarajevo bound for Dubrovnik. Along the way, the train jumped the tracks and plunged into an icy river. While seventeen of his fellow passengers drowned, he escaped with only minor injuries.

The following year, after deciding trains were not for him, Selak took his first plane trip. But while the plane was in mid-air, one of the doors burst open, and he was sucked out of the fuselage, falling to earth without a parachute. The missing door caused the plane to crash, and everyone on board was killed. But not Selak. He was found unconscious atop a large haystack in the countryside.

Three years later, he was riding a bus that went off the road and into another icy river. Four people drowned, but—you guessed it—not Selak. Maybe it was muscle memory that helped him escape with only a few bruises and scratches.

But there's more. On two separate occasions, the car he was driving caught fire. Each time, he narrowly escaped before being engulfed in flames. Another time, to avoid a head-on collision with a truck on a winding mountain road, he veered his car through a guardrail and off a cliff. Selak was thrown from the car but somehow managed to grab a tree branch, and watched from his precarious perch as the vehicle plummeted three hundred feet into the valley below.

As if travel by train, plane, bus, and car wasn't dangerous

enough, another time Selak was simply walking down the street when he was hit by a bus. But don't worry—he walked away.

Seven times Frane Selak cheated death. That's enough to make most people consider him a very blessed man. But after all of those near misses, Selak told a reporter, "I never thought I was lucky to survive all my brushes with death. I thought I was unlucky to be in them in the first place."[1] But I don't believe Frane Selak's story has much to do with being lucky or unlucky—those are just terms we use when a thing seems improbable. Our lives are not left to chance. Not yours. Not mine. Not Frane Selak's.

He's not the only person who's skated on the edge of certain death. We're actually all right there.

Held Above the Flame

During the first Great Awakening, Jonathan Edwards preached the famous sermon "Sinners in the Hands of an Angry God," one of the messages God used to spark revival in New England. In that eighteenth-century sermon, Edwards wrote:

> The God that holds you over the Pit of Hell, much as one holds a Spider, or some loathsome Insect, over the Fire, abhors you, and is dreadfully provoked; his Wrath towards you burns like Fire; he looks upon you as worthy of nothing else, but to be cast into the Fire; he is of purer Eyes than to bear to have you in his Sight; you are ten thousand Times so abominable in his Eyes as the most hateful venomous Serpent is in ours.[2]

God holding sinners over hell like one might hold a spider over a campfire: it's not the most comforting image ever conjured. Does it accurately describe God's attitude toward human beings apart from Christ? Does God really "abhor" sinners? Does his wrath burn like fire toward the unrepentant? I mean, after all, "God is love" (1 John 4:8), right?

In the book of Romans, Paul teaches that, unless we are

reconciled to God through Jesus, we are God's enemies (5:10), deserving of nothing less than eternal torment. Every moment an unbeliever finds himself absent from hell is a moment of grace given to him by his Maker.

God takes sin very seriously. He will not tolerate it. So, yes—I believe Edwards painted a reliable picture of God's wrath. But I don't think the short passage quoted above contains the whole picture. God's fury toward sin is not the end of the story; it is overcome by His even fiercer love.

In fact, because sin is so serious, God's love is all the more extraordinary. If sin were no big deal to God, then delaying its punishment would also be no big deal. But sin is a *very* big deal. God's patience toward sinners is an extreme and ongoing gift of incredible love, though it's a gift that will not last forever.

Most unbelievers have become so accustomed to their day-to-day lives, upheld by God's gracious hand, that they don't truly believe they are a mere heartbeat away from eternal darkness. But God knows that's our situation. That's why He spared no expense—He gave His only Son—to save people from hell.

You see, God's delay in punishing sin is not merely a stay of execution. Wrapped up in that delay is also a daily offer of pardon. In every moment, sinners are welcome to come to Christ and be forgiven. As Jesus himself said, "For God so loved the world, that he gave his only Son, that whoever believes in him should not perish but have eternal life" (John 3:16).

Without exception, every sin that has ever been or ever will be committed must be paid for—either in the everlasting fire of hell or on the cross of Christ. Jesus died so that we might "not perish," that we might escape the punishment we deserve. He came to save us.

■ ■ ■

Shortly after Adam and Eve welcomed sin into our world, their hands stained with forbidden fruit and guilt, God pronounced judgment. While He cast them out of the garden, He did not send them all the way to hell. He could show grace to His children because He was already preparing the means of their salvation.

To the serpent, God said, "I will put enmity between you and the woman, and between your offspring and her offspring; he shall bruise your head, and you shall bruise his heel" (Genesis 3:15). This was the first gospel proclamation, a promise for Adam and Eve to grab hold of and repeat to their children and their children's children.

The serpent, we discover later in God's story, is the enemy of God and His people, a being known as Lucifer, or Satan (see Revelation 20:2). In the garden, God promised the birth one day of Someone who would put an end to Satan and his works, once and for all.

Then, as if to demonstrate how this Savior's heel would be bruised, "the LORD God made for Adam and for his wife garments of skins and clothed them" (Genesis 3:21). History's first sacrifice was performed by God himself. The first humans had never seen a physical life taken before; now they would begin to understand the cost of their sin. Just as Christ's blood would later be shed to wipe clean the sins of Adam and Eve and all their faithful descendants, on this day an animal's blood was shed to provide covering for the couple. Their new outfits were a striking picture and a continual reminder of the price that would need to be paid for their cosmic treason.

But the gospel is not simply about escaping God's wrath. Adam and Eve weren't saved from their just punishment only to be abandoned in the wilderness. All along, God's plan has been to welcome His children back into a right relationship with Him. On that day so long ago, the garden's entrance was cut off by cherubim and a flaming sword (Genesis 3:24), but the narrow way to eternal life was opened up by the promise of Jesus Christ.

Understanding our true situation before we're saved makes all the difference after we're saved. Those who don't know the seriousness of their sin can never be truly thankful for the gift of eternal life. And gratitude is fuel for walking in obedience to

God. Duty alone can never bring holiness. But once we understand what the Lord has done for us, it becomes our joy to follow Him and live out His story.

At the same time, understanding how God sees sin will give us a desire to see our neighbors and loved ones turn to Christ. Sharing our faith and praying for others to accept the gift of salvation is a serious responsibility, not an elective, for every follower of Christ. It seems like most people are introduced to Jesus by a friend—God uses broken men and women like you and me to offer the world His salvation, which is the greatest miracle of all. But it's a privilege we'll miss if we don't understand just how amazing salvation is.

In a fitting turn of events that mirrors the gospel itself, Frane Selak, the man who narrowly escaped death seven times, won the lottery two days after his seventy-third birthday. Of course, no amount of money can compare with the riches of heaven. But the story of Selak's life reflects God's story, which is playing out in the life of every believer. The Son of God died so that we might escape eternal death, yes—but also so we could be adopted as God's children, "so that in the coming ages he might show the immeasurable riches of his grace in kindness toward us in Christ Jesus" (Ephesians 2:7).

The fire of hell is no match for the love of God. When viewed side by side, one is a spark, and the other, an ocean.

YOUR LIFE IN THE STORY OF GOD

God takes sin very seriously. The eighteenth-century preacher Jonathan Edwards described Him as "of purer Eyes than to bear to have you [as a sinner] in his Sight." But because God is love (1 John 4:8), He spared no expense—He gave His only Son—not only to save people from hell but to bring us back into a right relationship with Him, here and now. Once we understand what the Lord has done for us, it becomes our joy to follow Him and live out His story every day.

1. What do you think of the title of Jonathan Edwards's famous sermon, "Sinners in the Hands of an Angry God"? Can God be both angry and loving?

2. In what ways does God show patience toward sinners? How long did it take you to respond to His call to salvation?

3. How might "living God's story" look in your life today? What can you do to help bring His redemption to your world?

How God Keeps Us Dry

GENESIS 6–9

The infection of sin is total. It is a dominant genetic trait that never skips a generation. With the exception of Jesus, no soul has been born free of the disease. And the strain does not weaken over time. Early in God's story, we read, "The LORD saw that the wickedness of man was great in the earth, and that every intention of the thoughts of his heart was only evil continually" (Genesis 6:5). Things were so bad that "the LORD regretted that he had made man on the earth, and it grieved him to his heart" (v. 6).

Ouch.

But there was one man who was different from the rest. The Bible says that Noah was a righteous man (v. 9), and as a result, He found favor in God's eyes (v. 8). Noah's righteousness did not mean he was sinless—like the rest of humanity, he too did wrong. What made Noah "righteous" was that he believed God and trusted Him. While the rest of mankind went their own way and indulged in evil, violence, and corruption, Noah bucked the trend and walked with the Lord, no doubt following in the tradition of godly men and women who had gone before him in the line from Adam and Eve's son, Seth (see Genesis 5).

So when God decided to destroy the earth, He also decided that He would save representatives of every kind of animal and just one human family: Noah's.[3] God hit the reset button on humanity, starting over with just eight people.

It's a story familiar to anyone who's ever attended Sunday school or flipped through a children's picture Bible. It's among the first of God's stories we tell our kids, and it's so ingrained in our collective cultural conscience that Noah, thousands of years after his time on earth, is one of the most famous people who ever lived.

God, in His mercy, called Noah to build an ark that would survive a flood, the likes of which the world had never seen. For forty days and forty nights, it rained (7:12), and everything except Noah's boat was destroyed. But "God remembered Noah" (8:1), and more than a year after he and his family entered the ark (see Genesis 7:11 and 8:14), God gave the command to begin again: "Go out from the ark, you and your wife, and your sons and your sons' wives with you. Bring out with you every living thing that is with you of all flesh—birds and animals and every creeping thing that creeps on the earth—that they may swarm on the earth, and be fruitful and multiply on the earth" (8:16–17; compare with 9:1, 7). Notice how God's word here echoes what He had said to Adam and Eve in the beginning: "Be fruitful and multiply" (Genesis 1:28). With Noah, the Lord inaugurated a new beginning to His creation and gave a fresh start to the world.

It's a picture of God's story in abbreviated form. The world had become sinful and corrupt, bringing judgment upon itself. But the Lord, not wanting everyone to perish, provided a way out, a way of salvation through the judgment. And when the price was paid for sin, creation was made new so that righteous men and women could once again walk with their Maker in a garden paradise.[4]

But the account of Noah and the flood, though true, is only a picture of the gospel story. In the end, after the waters subsided, the plight of humanity was unchanged. Without new hearts and a cure for the disease of sin, there could be no starting over. Not really anyway. God told Noah, "I will never again curse the ground because of man" (Genesis 8:21), but not because human beings had somehow changed their ways or proven themselves, and not because the flood itself carried any healing power. God's reason is just the opposite: "for the intention of man's heart is evil from his youth." Because sin had not yet been dealt with,

God decided to withhold His judgment. Until true salvation in Jesus Christ could come, He promised to stay His hand.

God put a sign in the sky—a rainbow—as a reminder of His promise to never again destroy the earth with a flood. But the reminder wasn't for us; it was for Him. God told Noah and his sons, "When I bring clouds over the earth and the bow is seen in the clouds, I will remember my covenant that is between me and you and every living creature of all flesh. And the waters shall never again become a flood to destroy all flesh" (Genesis 9:14–15).

The sign of the rainbow means many different things today, but in the ancient world, the image would have brought to mind one thing: war. The Hebrew word used in this passage has, as its most basic meaning, the kind of bow an archer uses in combat to fire deadly arrows at his enemies. By placing the bow in the sky, God may have been signifying that He was hanging up His bow, so to speak, since the time of judgment by flood had ended.

But in light of what we now know about the later chapters of God's story, it may be that the bow has another meaning. Perhaps, rather than being hung up, it is taut and aimed, at heaven rather than earth, ready to release its deadly arrow. Maybe God was announcing to mankind that judgment would indeed come again, and that He himself would take the fatal blow.

A Grave Reminder of Hope

Just six chapters into God's story, the Lord decided to judge the world with a devastating flood. While many generations came and went between Adam and Noah, in terms of God's story of redemption, only a few pages separate the two men. Have you ever wondered why?

The flood is background for every story that comes afterward. For example, When God brought plagues upon Egypt as punishment for its enslavement of God's people (Exodus 7:14–12:32), the flood story declares, "Even in this, there is grace."

Judgment wasn't total. Not every Egyptian was destroyed. God gave warnings throughout and provided a way of escape for those who would trust Him. Or when God's people rebelled, over and over again during the period of the judges, the flood story shouts, "God is keeping His promise. Your rebellion will not end in annihilation. God will send a Deliverer to take sin's punishment on your behalf." Even when the Babylonians breached the walls of Jerusalem and led the people of Judah into captivity because of their sin, the flood account was offering this assurance: "God's story doesn't end in defeat. A new day will come. All will be washed clean and made new."

The flood is a reminder of how life in a sin-plagued world *should* go. We should not receive second chances. There should not be grace for sinners. We ought to receive the punishment our sins deserve; justice requires that every generation be wiped out with some apocalyptic event or another. The flood occurred early in God's story to show succeeding generations that their days were given by God out of love—that they were not, for a single moment, deserved.

At the same time, the flood is a reminder of the way things *will* be. Evil will not go unpunished forever. There is a coming judgment, though not with water (see 2 Peter 3:10), in which rebellious and sinful humanity will face the wrath of God, both in this world and for eternity. And just as it was with Noah, those who put their trust in the Lord will be saved. Jesus Christ took the punishment our sins deserved so that you and I might be saved from the judgment to come.

God told Noah, "While the earth remains, seedtime and harvest, cold and heat, summer and winter, day and night, shall not cease" (Genesis 8:22). As long as the Lord is still writing His story of redemption, things will go on like this. But that doesn't mean every day will be sunny or that we won't experience the consequences of sin—our own or the sins of others. In this broken world, we will face "floods" from time to time. But the gospel reminds us that God saves His people through the flood. In the storm, Christ himself is our ark of safety.

The Gospels record an episode in which Jesus and His disciples were on the Sea of Galilee when a terrible storm erupted around them. While the disciples panicked, Jesus was asleep. They roused their Master, He stopped the storm with a rebuke, and everything turned calm once again. Then Jesus looked at His disciples, who, by this point in His ministry, had been traveling with Him for some time, and said, "Where is your faith?" (Luke 8:25). In other words, "Why weren't you asleep too?"

This is the confidence we can have in God when our own seas get rough. We can rest, knowing that He has power to calm the storm or to keep us afloat no matter how long it rains. Remember: it is always safer to be on a rough sea with the Lord than to be on the beach without Him.

YOUR LIFE IN THE STORY OF GOD

God's big story is depicted in miniature in the account of Noah and the ark. A sinful world had brought judgment upon itself, but God provided a way of salvation through the destruction. Though humanity was just as wicked after the flood, God showed His grace by withholding a universal judgment on evil. Thousands of years later, Jesus became another ark of sorts, ushering in a whole new chapter in God's story. Not only does He save us from judgment, but in His resurrection He began the redemption of all that God made.

1. What set Noah apart from all the other people of his day? How does his story foreshadow the work of Jesus?

2. What do you think of the idea that the rainbow signifies a weapon aimed at heaven itself? How can God hold people accountable for sin and yet show mercy to them?

3. What "floods"—the consequences of sin and evil—affect the world today? How does Jesus protect you through them?

The Prostitute
Who Became a Princess

JOSHUA 2

When I was seventeen, I went with my senior class on a life-changing mission trip. We traveled to the interior of Jamaica, far from the resorts and the pristine beaches, to work among the poor—building houses, putting on a vacation Bible school program for the community's children, and visiting the sick.

I left Jamaica feeling God's call on my life. Though I wasn't quite sure what that calling would look like in coming years, I had an intense desire to study the Bible and teach it to others.

One of the biggest influences on my life that week was a pastor named Paul, who had come from California to lead our high school ministry team. Paul had a way about him. It was obvious that he loved people, and he seemed to have a Bible verse in his heart for every action he took. Until that time, I'd never met anyone like him.

When I got back home to Connecticut, I wanted to stay in touch with Pastor Paul, but I hadn't gotten his address—I just knew his name and that he was from a small town in northern California. Over the years, I tried to look him up but never had much luck, so after a while, I let it go. I didn't forget Paul, but I assumed our paths were not meant to cross again.

Then, just a couple of years ago, I stumbled across Paul's Facebook profile. He was no longer living in California but had moved across the country to Atlanta, Georgia. This was incredible because I was also living in Georgia at the time. In fact, I discovered that he lived just a few miles away. Before long, we were enjoying lunch together and catching up, both amazed at how God had brought us together after twenty years and across thousands of miles.

Proverbs 16:9 says, "The heart of man plans his way, but the LORD establishes his steps." While this verse contains a warning against absolute self-reliance, it's also a reminder that God cares about the paths we take in life. Our neighbors, friends, and acquaintances are often in our lives for a reason. Reuniting with Paul was a blessing and a surprise to both of us, but it wasn't a surprise to God. He had it in mind long ago.

What Happens in Jericho

It wasn't by chance that when Israelite spies entered Jericho, they found lodging in the home of Rahab the prostitute. Though these two men didn't know it, they were not just there to spy out the city's defenses; they would also be used by God to save Rahab's life. Their mission of reconnaissance was also a rescue operation.

When word got out that there were spies in town, the king of Jericho sent a messenger to Rahab. Most likely, her home served as an inn for travelers on their way, so it makes sense that she would be one of the first to be questioned about any strangers in the area. Though Rahab could have turned the spies in—and been lauded for the act—she refused to give them up. Instead, she lied, saying the men had come to her but that she didn't know where they were from. Then she told the messenger it was no use anyway—the men had already left. In reality, she had them hidden away on her roof (Joshua 2:2–6).

In the book of Hebrews, we read, "By faith Rahab the prostitute did not perish with those who were disobedient, because she had given a friendly welcome to the spies" (11:31). Bible readers sometimes stumble over the fact that Rahab is celebrated, even though she lied to protect the spies. But at this point in her life, Rahab had never been confronted with God's law. Her lying, though sinful, came by way of faith. The only "gospel" that Rahab had heard were the stories of God leading His people out of Egypt and through the desert. In her own words, here is her confession of faith:

> "I know that the LᴋN' has given you the land, and that the fear of you has fallen upon us, and that all the inhabitants of the land melt away before you. For we have heard how the LᴋN' dried up the water of the Red Sea before you when you came out of Egypt, and what you did to the two kings of the Amorites who were beyond the Jordan, to Sihon and Og, whom you devoted to destruction. And as soon as we heard it, our hearts melted, and there was no spirit left in any man because of you, for the LᴋN' your God, he is God in the heavens above and on the earth beneath" (JOSHUA 2:9–11).

Rahab had faith to believe the stories she had heard. And she put feet to her faith. Right then and there, she transferred loyalty from her gods and her king to the true God, who is King over all.

For saving their lives, the spies made a promise: when they returned to conquer Jericho, they would spare Rahab and her family. The men instructed her to hang a scarlet cord out of her window—they needed a way to identify Rahab's home in the city wall, especially during the chaos of battle.

But I wonder if there was something more to that scarlet cord.

Years earlier, on the night the Israelites had escaped Egypt, God told His people to slaughter an unblemished lamb and to mark their doorposts with its blood. When the Lord's destroying angel passed through Egypt, he killed every firstborn male he found, but he did not enter the homes marked with blood. The Israelites were saved from death that day by scarlet, and every year following, they would commemorate that salvation at Passover.

Death was now coming to Jericho, and Rahab and her family would also be saved by scarlet. By hanging the scarlet cord out of her window, Rahab was identifying herself with the people of Israel—God's people. Whether she realized it or not, she was celebrating her own Passover of sorts as she joined with her new brothers and sisters.

■ ■ ■

Eating lunch with my friend Paul, I found out that he had started an inner-city ministry with the goal of helping people often forgotten: the homeless, gang members, and sex workers. In particular, Paul and his team reach out to at-risk women from the world of prostitution—Rahab's modern counterparts—and share God's story. They invite these women to change their allegiances and to trust Jesus for a new life.

Though Paul's ministry in Atlanta has a high success rate, each changed life comes down to a personal decision. Each of these women must believe something almost too good to be true: that God loves them and wants to make them a princess, a daughter of the King of the universe. This is part of what it means to trust in Jesus for salvation.

If we believe that Jesus died to pay for our sins, but we can't accept that our heavenly Father loves us enough to adopt us into His family, then we haven't really trusted Jesus. In the long run, we will still believe the lie that we must prove ourselves worthy of God's love.

Maybe you don't struggle with accepting God's love. If that's the case, wonderful. I've found that many people, though, whether they realize it or not, believe that while grace got them saved, they must perform in order to stay on God's good side. But the gospel isn't like that. There are no second-class citizens in God's family. There is no way we can be saved from the penalty our sins deserve while keeping God at a distance.

When Rahab was rescued from Jericho, she became one of God's people: "She has lived in Israel to this day, because she hid the messengers whom Joshua sent to spy out Jericho" (Joshua 6:25). Rahab gave up prostitution, marrying a man from the tribe of Judah named Salmon (Matthew 1:5), who some Bible readers speculate was one of the spies who visited her house in Jericho. Though the Bible never names the two spies, it wouldn't surprise me if God wrote Rahab's story this way.

Rahab wasn't just a stranger living among God's people. While she was "outside the camp" temporarily (Joshua 6:23), she was soon accepted and made a full citizen as if she had been traveling with the Israelites all along. The men of Israel were forbidden from marrying foreign women (Deuteronomy 7:1–4), so Salmon's marriage to Rahab was evidence of her status as a citizen of Israel. When she tied that scarlet cord from her window, she gave up her Canaanite citizenship in favor of something far better.

At the time, Rahab didn't know just how much better things would be. She didn't know she would become the great-great-grandmother of Israel's most revered Old Testament king, David (Ruth 4:18–22), nor did she ever imagine she would be included in the ancestral line of God's own Son (Matthew 1:2–16).

But this is the way it goes when we are written into God's story. It's always better than we can dare to dream.

YOUR LIFE IN THE STORY OF GOD

In protecting the Israelite spies who'd come into her house, Rahab—a prostitute in Jericho—was really acknowledging their God. In time, she became a full citizen of Israel herself and played an important role in God's story; she was an ancestor of Jesus Christ. Today, we have the same privilege: when God offers salvation, inviting us into the story He's telling, we can accept both forgiveness of sins and a position as a beloved member of His family.

1. How did Rahab come to believe in the one true God? What are some of the ways you've seen people come to Christ?

2. Why would God insert a foreign-born, former prostitute into Jesus' family tree? What does Rahab's story say to you today?

3. Why would someone struggle to accept God's love? What would you say to that person?

Even If Salvation Doesn't Come

DANIEL 3

After centuries of rebellion, sprinkled with but a few bright spots of faithfulness, God's people were conquered by the most powerful nation on earth. And God didn't deliver them.

Not that day anyway. When the Babylonians stormed Jerusalem's gates, the Lord didn't send His angelic armies to stop them. No plague. No miracle. No holding back the consequences of Judah's actions. God had promised long before that if His people broke their end of the covenant, He would allow them to be invaded, defeated, and humiliated before the eyes of the world (Deuteronomy 28:49, 64; 29:28).

Across the generations, there had been close calls, many times that God stepped in with a rescuer when it seemed time had run out. I wonder if the residents of Jerusalem, as they heard the rumble of the Babylonian cavalry outside their walls, looked heavenward to see if God would defend them one more time. But no rescue came on that summer day. God allowed the strong to defeat the weak and His people to be taken from the land He had given them.

But God did not abandon His people. He was there with them.

Daniel was one of the young men transported from Judah to Babylon, and in the book that bears his name, we have a record of God's enduring faithfulness. King Nebuchadnezzar had ordered the best of the best to be brought to serve in his empire. This meant that Daniel and other chosen Israelites, including Hananiah, Mishael, and Azariah (better known as Shadrach, Meshach, and Abednego), were given the finest education and training in the world, in addition to food from the king's table. With pictures of Jerusalem's destruction fresh in his mind, Daniel was given a place in the halls of Babylonian power. It was a blessing not without challenges.

Daniel and his friends found the very food they were given problematic, so they requested a different diet: nothing but vegetables and water. Why didn't they want the gourmet meals of the royal table? Some have suggested that Daniel, Shadrach, Meshach, and Abednego rejected the king's food because it was not kosher. But they also rejected the wine, and there is no commandment in the book of Leviticus that would prohibit these young men from consuming wine. Others believe they were trying to avoid eating food that had been sacrificed to idols, but it is likely that the vegetables they were given had been included in the ritual offerings, same as the meat.

The Bible doesn't tell us what made these young men become vegetarians, but Daniel's words to the king's steward may offer some explanation: "Test your servants for ten days; let us be given vegetables to eat and water to drink. Then let our appearance and the appearance of the youths who eat the king's food be observed by you, and deal with your servants according to what you see" (Daniel 1:12–13).

It was a test: Babylon's king versus Israel's God. Daniel, Shadrach, Meshach, and Abednego wanted to stand out. They wanted to show that they served God above the king of Babylon.

One would expect that men fed nothing but vegetables and water for ten days would lose weight—and muscle—but "at the end of ten days it was seen that they were better in appearance and fatter in flesh than all the youths who ate the king's food" (Daniel 1:15). God had performed a digestive miracle in the lives of his servants.

Seeing the results of this dietary experiment, the king's steward served only vegetables and water to everyone from then on. (And I'm sure everyone was thrilled at this development.) For Daniel and his friends, though, the choice to abstain from the king's portion had little to do with food. It had everything to do with their trust in God.

When to Kneel and When to Stand

Many of the other narratives in the book of Daniel follow this trend. Over and over again, Daniel, Shadrach, Meshach, and Abednego obeyed God above men. On one occasion, King Darius (a successor of Nebuchadnezzar) passed a decree that prohibited prayer to anyone but himself. Whoever broke this law was to be thrown into a den of lions. So what did Daniel do? "He went to his house where he had windows in his upper chamber open toward Jerusalem. He got down on his knees three times a day and prayed and gave thanks before his God, as he had done previously." The Bible tells us Daniel did this even when he "knew that the document had been signed" (Daniel 6:10).

I'm afraid that many of us today, if faced with the same threat, would make prayer an exclusively private matter. But Daniel prayed in front of an open window, for all to see, with full knowledge that he was breaking the king's law. He was bold and unafraid for God, and no consequence was too severe. A short time later, in the lions' den, God rescued Daniel, shutting the mouths of the hungry beasts and reversing their every predatory instinct.

Another time, Shadrach, Meshach, and Abednego took a stand of their own—literally. King Nebuchadnezzar had made a ninety-foot-tall golden statue, commanding everyone in the provinces to bow down and worship it. But Daniel's friends refused to bend low. They would not offer their worship, which belonged to God alone, no matter what the cost. And there was a cost. The king ordered them thrown into a furnace.

Nebuchadnezzar, though, was not without a soft side. He gave the young men one last chance to change their minds: "If you are ready . . . to fall down and worship the image that I have made, well and good. But if you do not worship, you shall immediately be cast into a burning fiery furnace." And then he said, as if to taunt Shadrach, Meshach, and Abednego, "And who is the god who will deliver you out of my hands?" (Daniel 3:15).

The three men did not budge. Their reply to the king was simple and straightforward, but I think it captures something about salvation that we often overlook:

> "O Nebuchadnezzar, we have no need to answer you in this matter. If this be so, our God whom we serve is able to deliver us from the burning fiery furnace, and he will deliver us out of your hand, O king. But if not, be it known to you, O king, that we will not serve your gods or worship the golden image that you have set up" (DANIEL 3:16–18).

"But if not." That's the beating heart of someone who trusts God completely. Shadrach, Meshach, and Abednego leaned wholly on God for their safety, and they knew that total trust meant recognizing that God is in control. While their murder at the hands of a maniacal dictator would be a great evil, they were not willing to disobey God by worshipping someone else. These three men were willing to lay down their lives in service to the God they loved, in one of the most horrific ways imaginable, if that's what He permitted. Even today, many Christians are unwilling to "play it safe" if that means disobeying God. But that's because safety is never the point of salvation. God is.

■ ■ ■

Shadrach, Meshach, and Abednego did not view their own well-being as paramount. Neither did Daniel. None of these men were willing to compromise, to slip into disobedience to save their own skin. Each one knew that he was not the central figure in the story he was living. As followers of God, these men were written into *His* story, and in God's story, God himself is the main character. It's about Him, and He gets all the glory.

When the apostle Paul was chained in prison, believing he was not long for this world, he wrote to the believers at Philippi, "To me to live is Christ, and to die is gain" (Philippians 1:21). Paul was not afraid of death, but instead looked forward to it: "My desire is to depart and be with Christ" (v. 23).

Don't misunderstand. Paul was not suicidal. He still valued the gift of life. But he also knew that Christ had settled his account with God. If Paul continued to live, that would mean Christ living through him and being glorified by him. If Paul died, he would enter Christ's presence and the Lord would be glorified in his death. Either way, God would get the glory.

When we are content to live out God's story rather than our own, we have nothing to lose, no matter what happens to us. *Because it's not about us.*

This is one of the secrets of the Christian life. It's how men and women who have endured unthinkable tragedy can continue on, not just surviving but thriving. It's how soon-to-be martyrs can boldly proclaim Christ before their killers. It's how fathers and mothers can speak of their confidence in God at the funeral of a child. It's the secret to finding peace in the midst of life's worst storms.

When we know that the story we're living belongs to God, we have confidence that He can turn even the deepest of sorrows for good. It seems impossible, but I've discovered in my own life and through the testimonies of others that walking with Christ brings with it a supernatural peace, "which surpasses all understanding" (Philippians 4:7).

Shadrach, Meshach, and Abednego could stand in front of Nebuchadnezzar in great freedom. Knowing that they belonged to God, the Babylonian king had no real power over them.

You and I have that same freedom in Christ. Nothing can separate us from God's love—"neither death nor life, nor angels nor rulers, nor things present nor things to come, nor powers, nor height nor depth, nor anything else in all creation" (Romans 8:38–39)—because that's what God's story is all about: His love.

So the parts God has written for us are bold and uncompromising. Not one of His children is to be bound by fear. He loves us too much for that.

YOUR LIFE IN THE STORY OF GOD

Following Christ is no guarantee of ease and safety in this life. God can and sometimes will save us from trouble, as He did with the ancient Israelites. But at other times He will allow trouble to overtake us—and then go with us *through* the difficulty. As players in His overarching story, God can write our parts as He chooses. Our job is to stay faithful, knowing that absolutely nothing can separate us from His love (Romans 8:38–39).

1. What is the closest thing you've had to a "Shadrach, Meshach, and Abednego experience"? How did you see God working in and through it?

2. What is the significance of the three words "but if not" in the story of Shadrach, Meshach, and Abednego?

3. How does a willingness to live out God's story give us freedom? Why would that give peace in the midst of trouble?

God's Dress Code

MATTHEW 22:1–14

Several years ago, I worked for one of the most influential Christian ministries in the world. It was a tremendous opportunity, especially since I was just starting my career. But, as with any workplace, there were things I enjoyed and others I did not. For example, I loved the campus. The office was tucked into the woods, and there were lots of trails to explore on my lunch break. On the other hand, I didn't like the dress code. Any day I have to wear a tie is one day too many.

One part of the job I enjoyed tremendously was the mandatory chapel hour each morning. I know what you're probably thinking: *if employees are forced to attend, how good can it be?* That's what I thought at first too. But after a few weeks, I began to look forward to starting my day with worship and teaching. Because of the ministry's prominence, we had a rotation of well-known musicians and speakers that was occasionally supplemented by local pastors and employees of the ministry.

My favorite chapel speaker was one of the employees, whom I'll call Jacob. He was a senior officer with the organization, and I had gotten to know him a bit through sporadic interactions. If I had to use one word to describe Jacob, it would be *kind*. Every time I talked with him, I felt heard and appreciated, even though the job I did at the ministry shouldn't even have been on his radar.

Whenever Jacob brought a morning chapel message, I left wanting to go deeper—to know Jesus more. There was something in Jacob's walk with the Lord that was exciting and attractive. That's why I was shocked when I heard Jacob speak in chapel for the last time before I left the organization. In that particular chapel session, he shared his testimony.

Years earlier, I learned, Jacob had been in prison. To look at him now, it was hard to believe, but Jacob had once worn an orange jumpsuit every day, and he had shared cells with thieves, murderers, and rapists. Jacob had been a drug dealer—though considering the volume of cocaine he moved, he was more like a drug distributor. When he was caught, he received a heavy sentence in the state penitentiary.

But Jacob told us how he had met Jesus in prison because someone cared enough to visit him and share the gospel. He described being eligible for parole and how God had orchestrated his early release—much earlier than Jacob expected.

As Jacob continued his story, it was clear that God's hand had been on his life. Jacob had been transformed in prison—the proof was the kindness by which he was now known. There was a look of shock on every face in chapel that morning as we all learned about his past.

I imagine that Jacob, after his release from the penitentiary, felt a bit out of place in church, especially at first. But I think he would have fit in just fine with Jesus' early followers. They were a bit rough around the edges too. The disciples were from a variety of backgrounds, but here's a sample:

- There were fishermen like Peter, Andrew, James, and John. Back then, as is true today, professional fishermen had to be tough. The work was both hard and dangerous. No one would have accused these guys of being sissies.

- Matthew, also known as Levi, was a tax collector. We saw in an earlier chapter that tax collectors in ancient Israel were despised by their neighbors. To do the job, Matthew had to have thick skin. He was used to being on the outside.

- Simon (not Peter) was a zealot, a political revolutionary who wanted to overthrow the heavy thumb of Roman oppression. Zealots earned their label by being zealous for God. These men would take extreme measures to destabilize the social order in their effort to bring justice, as they saw it. They were sometimes violent, and always ready for a fight.

- And then there was Judas Iscariot. No one knows for sure, but many scholars believe that "Iscariot" is related to the term *Sicarii*. The Sicarii were a first-century terrorist group known for carrying small daggers—*sicae*—and they weren't afraid to use them against the Romans and their supporters. It may have been that Judas was a part of this group before meeting Jesus.

These were the men with whom Jesus chose to share the most important three years of His earthly life. With the exception of Judas, of course, these were the guys whom Jesus commissioned to spread the gospel around the world.

It seems to me that the Lord has a soft spot for people who don't quite fit into polite society.

A Fashion Choice That Will Save Your Life

Jesus once told a parable about a wedding feast. In the story, found in Matthew 22:1–14, a king gave an elaborate banquet for his son and his new daughter-in-law in honor of their marriage. It's one thing when the rich host a party, but it's another thing entirely when royalty does. This would be an affair to remember, the social event of a lifetime. The best food. Top-notch entertainment. The finest of everything. No expense was spared. Who wouldn't want to attend such a banquet?

But when the king sent his servants out to call the invited guests, they ignored him. Again, he sent his servants out, "but they paid no attention and went off, one to his farm, another to his business" (22:5). And then it got worse: "The rest seized his servants, treated them shamefully, and killed them" (22:6).

Anyone living under a monarchy knows it's not wise to reject the king's invitation. It's not only rude, it's dangerous. But Jesus was describing a situation that goes far beyond social faux pas. The king's subjects were engaged in out-and-out treason. An attack on the king's servants was an attack on the king himself.

Jesus' listeners—a group of Pharisees and chief priests—would have been shocked by this turn in the story. And those religious leaders began to fume, because they knew Jesus was talking about them (see Matthew 21:45). In the parable, God was the king, the servants were His prophets, and the murderous wedding invitees were the Pharisees.

So what Jesus said next sounded even worse in their ears: "The king was angry, and he sent his troops and destroyed those murderers and burned their city" (Matthew 22:7). In the worldview of the Pharisees, they were the ones who followed God's laws—every last jot and tittle. They were the ones who remembered the traditions of their fathers. If any people were going to be honored guests at God's great banquet, it would be them. And most of their neighbors agreed. But Jesus, the Son of the King, was right there in their midst, inviting them to His Father's table—and they didn't recognize Him. They were ignoring God's invitation. They were living out the parable as Jesus was telling it!

Jesus continued His story. The king instructed his remaining servants to invite others to the party. "As many as you find," he told them (22:9). So the servants filled the king's hall with guests, "both bad and good" (22:10).

God's invitation is to sinners of all kinds. No one is too far gone to be welcomed into the King's home. These new guests were brought in because those who had been invited earlier, by their response, proved themselves unworthy (Matthew 22:8). The implication here is that "good and bad" are not measures of worthiness when it comes to God's great banquet.

These new guests had two qualifications that the original guests did not. First, they came! It's as simple as that. They responded to God's invitation. The gospel is a call for people from every walk of life—from every culture, from every place, and from every generation—to come and share in God's redemption of the world. But we must accept this offer in faith. Just as those guests had to believe that the sounds-too-good-to-be-true invitation they were receiving was indeed true, so do people today.

This second group of guests also wore the right clothes. It seems the king had provided fine clothes for the occasion, and every guest was to wear a special outfit as part of the celebration. On this point, Jesus' parable ends somewhat strangely.

The king came to see his guests but discovered one man, who had apparently decided he liked his own clothes better, wasn't wearing the wedding garment. The king's response? "Bind him hand and foot and cast him into the outer darkness. In that place there will be weeping and gnashing of teeth" (22:13).

Such an extreme punishment for showing up in the wrong clothes is a clue that Jesus isn't really talking about fashion or even an earthly wedding reception. The "wedding garment," it seems, refers to Christ's own righteousness.

No matter how good we may be, none of us can come to God on our own merit. None of us is worthy. As close as the Pharisees may have thought they came, they missed God's heart in His commandments. Only Jesus lived a perfectly sinless life.

That's why we need to "put on" Christ before we can set foot in God's presence. No matter how bad we've been, putting on Christ cleanses us from every dark stain. The Pharisees attempted to come to God in their own clothes. The ending of Jesus' parable was a warning for them—and for anyone else who might have the same idea.

■ ■ ■

In the church (and I don't mean a building, I mean the people of God in Christ Jesus around the world), every last one of us is wearing the same thing: Christ's righteousness. It doesn't matter if you grew up a pastor's kid, a senator's son, or the illegitimate child of a drug addict. It doesn't matter if you're a doctor, a missionary, or a gang member. When we come to God, we must take off our own clothes—that is, any striving to earn our own salvation—and put on the glorious wedding garment He gives us.

In God's story, the outcasts are brought near, and the elite are brought low. But everyone is invited to the wedding feast. *Everyone*—even if you've spent time in prison.

YOUR LIFE IN THE STORY OF GOD

The Pharisees of Jesus' day had the mistaken notion that their own efforts would commend them to God. But that idea has tempted people of all times and places. We are only acceptable to God as we receive by faith Jesus' work on our behalf—when we "put on Christ" like the wedding garment of the parable in Matthew 22. There are no preconditions, since Jesus said the king invited everyone, "both bad and good" (v. 10).

1. Can you think of a fellow believer who was saved out of a very difficult background? What makes that kind of testimony so compelling?

2. Why do human beings often want to clean up their act before coming to God? What does Jesus' parable of the wedding banquet (Matthew 22:1–14) say to that idea?

3. How do we "put on" Christ? How will that affect your behavior in the home, at work, or in your neighborhood?

Blood

HEBREWS 10:1–25

"We strictly charged you not to teach in this name, yet here you have filled Jerusalem with your teaching, and you intend to bring this man's blood upon us" (Acts 5:28). These were the words the high priest spoke to Peter and the other apostles after he found them mysteriously free of their prison cell.

There were a few things this high priest did not understand. First, he did not know that an angel had opened the prison doors and commanded Jesus' followers to carry on preaching in the temple courts (5:19–20). Second, the high priest would not believe that Jesus, in whose name these men were teaching, was no longer dead but instead more alive than anyone he had ever known. Finally, he did not realize that the greatest thing he could ever hope for would be to have "this man's blood" upon him.

Annas had once been the Jewish high priest, but now that job belonged to his son-in-law, Caiaphas. Together the two men wielded a great deal of power in Judea. Along with the other Jewish leaders in Jerusalem, they arrested Jesus and brought him before Pilate, the Roman governor, requesting a death sentence on false charges. They *were* guilty of His blood.

It was Pilate who officially ordered Jesus crucified, and it was Roman soldiers who put the nails in the Lord's hands and feet. But more than that, it was the sins of people around the world and across the centuries that necessitated Jesus' sacrifice. There was enough guilt to go around, so it's far too simple to say that the Romans or the religious leaders in Jerusalem killed Jesus. Besides, His life was not taken from Him—He laid it down willingly (John 10:18).

When Annas spoke the words of Acts 5:28, they had an unintended double meaning. Jesus' blood must be "upon" anyone who wants to be saved. I wonder if Peter or the other disciples caught the play on words. Perhaps one of them uttered a silent prayer for the wicked man's soul, even as he chastised them for their obedience to the Lord.

Written in Blood

If the Bible were a film series, it would be rated R for violence—and I'm not just thinking of the epic battle scenes. There is a river of blood that runs from Genesis to Revelation.

In fact, God's story cannot really be told without blood. For the people of Israel in the Old Testament, blood was a constant reminder of their sin and its cost. And for the followers of Jesus in the New Testament, blood became the reason for their hope.

As we've seen, blood was shed to provide skins to cover Adam and Eve after they sinned (Genesis 3:21). Blood welled up at every circumcision wound from Abraham on down the line as males were marked with the sign of their covenant with God (Genesis 17:10). Blood stained the doorposts of the Hebrews' homes in Egypt the night that death came for the firstborn (Exodus 12:1–13). And with the sacrificial system in place, blood became a part of life's rhythm for the people of Israel. Blood, blood, and more blood—all of it, in one way or another, pointing to Christ, whose blood has the power to cleanse us from every stain of sin.

During His final meal with the disciples before His crucifixion, Jesus instituted a new tradition. He told His friends to remember Him as they ate and drank together:

The Lord Jesus on the night when he was betrayed took bread, and when he had given thanks, he broke it, and said, "This is my body, which is for you. Do this in remembrance of me." In the same way also he took the cup, after supper, saying, "This cup is the new covenant in my blood. Do this,

as often as you drink it, in remembrance of me" (1 CORIN-
THIANS 11:23–25, compare with MATTHEW 26:26–28; MARK 14:22–24;
LUKE 22:19–20).

By no mere coincidence, this was a Passover meal that Jesus shared with His disciples. It was a commemoration of God's great rescue of Israel from slavery in Egypt.

After that first Passover, when the people had crossed the Red Sea and arrived safely at the base of Mount Sinai, God made a covenant with them. He promised that He would be their God and they would be His people. Israel, in return, had to obey the commandments He gave. But the people broke the covenant time and time again. They could not keep God's commands; they could not keep from sinning. And so, a new covenant was needed (Jeremiah 31:31–32; Hebrews 8:7). That new covenant, according to Jesus, could be found in His blood.

The blood of the old covenant was the blood of bulls and goats. Once a year, on the Day of Atonement, the high priest would enter the tabernacle (and later the temple), go into the Most Holy Place, and offer a sacrifice on behalf of the people (see Leviticus 16:1–34). This sacrifice would cover the Israelites' sins for the coming year. It was only a temporary remission of the punishment they deserved.

But Christ's blood—the blood of the new covenant—was not like the blood of animals. It did not merely cover sins; it washed them clean. And His sacrifice did not need to be repeated year after year. Once was enough for all time (Hebrews 10:12).

At every point, the new covenant surpasses the old one. The author of Hebrews goes to great lengths to show that each element of the Old Testament sacrificial system was a mere copy or shadow of a deeper and abiding heavenly reality (see Hebrews 8:1–10:18). For example, Israel's high priest was the only person permitted to go into God's presence in the Most Holy Place, and only on the Day of Atonement. But Jesus Christ, as both our great High Priest and our perfect Sacrifice, has made a way for anyone, covered by His blood, to draw near to God. This is why, at Jesus' death, the veil that separated the Most Holy Place from the rest of the temple was torn in two (Matthew 27:51). The tearing of that curtain was an invitation for everyone who is in Christ to come close to the Father.

The new covenant in Jesus' blood deals with the problem of sin in two ways. The first, as we've already seen, is that our sins are forgiven and washed clean. To be covered in Christ's blood is to be free from condemnation (Romans 5:18). The price has been paid, the score has been settled. God tells us, "I will remember their sins and their lawless deeds no more" (Hebrews 10:17; compare with Jeremiah 31:34). But the new covenant is more than just a get-out-of-jail-free card: the second way the blood deals with our sin is by changing our very hearts.

Under the old covenant, God wrote the Ten Commandments on stone tablets. But in the new covenant He says, "I will put my laws on their hearts, and write them on their minds" (Hebrews 10:16; compare with Jeremiah 31:33). The failure of the old covenant was this: sinful people, by their own efforts, cannot keep God's perfect law. The law itself is not to blame—its main job was to reflect God's perfect, holy standard, and in the process show us we needed a Savior, someone who could do on our behalf what we could not do ourselves. Under the new covenant, though, God gives us a secret weapon: himself.

Because we have been purified and made holy by Christ's blood, God's Spirit now comes to live inside each one of us. He speaks God's desires into our minds and hearts, giving us new life that wasn't there before we knew Christ. While we will continue to struggle with sin this side of heaven, the Spirit provides us with a new nature so that we actually *want* to obey God and walk closely with Him. Our old sinful nature now has an adversary, and a fight can be waged against sin's grip on our lives (see Ephesians 4:22–24; Colossians 3:9–10). In the precious drops of Christ's blood, the power and weight of sin are smashed. We are set free.

Being a part of God's story means living daily in His presence, the Holy Spirit speaking to our minds and hearts as we share life with Him. But our part in the story is not merely to sin less. That will happen if we're walking in step with God's Spirit, but it's only the beginning. As we listen to the Spirit's voice, we'll discover we've been drawn into something much bigger than ourselves.

God has unique plans for every one of His children. Life in His story will look different for you than it does for me. But that's the way relationships work; there is no one-size-fits-all option. We are saved by the same Savior, washed in the same blood, and renewed by the same Spirit, but we must each spend time walking and talking with Him daily to discover the particular adventure He has for us. And He is weaving our individual stories together to change the world.

In the meantime, I can tell you this: I've never met anyone who regretted walking closely with the Lord. As the psalmist said, "You make known to me the path of life; in your presence there is fullness of joy; at your right hand are pleasures forevermore" (Psalm 16:11). And that's only possible because of the blood.

YOUR LIFE IN THE STORY OF GOD

God's story cannot be told apart from blood. From the ongoing offering of animals in the Old Testament to the once-for-all sacrifice of Jesus at Calvary, blood is a constant reminder of sin and its cost. Jesus' blood washes our sins clean and makes us a proper home for the Holy Spirit. He changes our nature and gives us the desire to obey God and walk closely with Him. Being a part of God's story means living daily in His presence.

1. How does Jesus' blood—the blood of the new covenant— differ from the blood of bulls and goats in Old Testament times?

2. Where did God write His laws under the old covenant? Where does He write them under the new covenant?

3. How can we live in God's presence? What does it mean to "walk with the Lord"?

NATION
God Brings His Kingdom

"The whole of history since the ascension of Jesus into heaven is concerned with one work only: the building and perfecting of this 'City of God.'"
—THOMAS MERTON, on St. Augustine's *The City of God*

The War All Around Us

GENESIS 4

For our honeymoon, Laurin and I decided to take a Mediterranean cruise. We took a flight to Italy and spent a few days in Rome before boarding a ship in the port city of Civitavecchia. From there it was on to Sicily, Athens, Santorini, Ephesus, and Pompeii, with several other stops along the way. The trip awakened our inner history buffs, and we were fascinated as we walked through the ancient ruins of famous and not-so-famous sites.

In Rome, we found the Arch of Titus with its carving of Jewish slaves and temple treasures being brought to Rome in procession after Jerusalem was destroyed (in AD 70), just as Jesus predicted it would be (Matthew 24:1–2). In Athens, Laurin and I broke away from our tour group to find Mars Hill, where Paul preached one of the most famous sermons in the New Testament (see Acts 17). And in Ephesus, we walked onto the stage of the theatre where Paul's friends, Gaius and Aristarchus, were brought during the riot recorded in Acts 19.

The trip was a dream come true for a couple of Bible geeks like us. But one of my favorite memories is of something *not* connected to God's story—at least not in the way one might think. A few miles from the ancient city of Ephesus, we saw the remnants of the temple of Artemis, the one mentioned in Acts 19: "The city clerk quieted the crowd and said: 'Fellow Ephesians, doesn't all the world know that the city of Ephesus is the guardian of the temple of the great Artemis and of her image, which fell from heaven?'" (v. 35 NIV). There, in the middle of an empty field stood a couple of broken pillars and some rubble—all that's left of one of the seven wonders of the ancient world.

Across the way from the fallen temple stands a centuries-old mosque, its lone minaret piercing the Turkish sky, still calling Muslims to pray five times daily. As we took in the view, Laurin and I stood on the grounds of the sixth-century Basilica of St. John, a once grand church commemorating the tradition that the apostle John, one of Jesus' closest friends and the recognized author of five New Testament books, was buried in that very spot. Like the temple of Artemis, John's basilica had seen better days, but what remained of the pillars, floor, and walls formed a cross, a fitting tribute to the Lord John served so well.

In that picturesque setting, three worlds converged: pagan, Muslim, and Christian. It would seem, based on the fact that the only building left standing was the mosque, that Islam had won the day. But the Bible says that the knowledge and glory of the Lord will one day cover the earth (Habakkuk 2:14; compare with Isaiah 49:6; Acts 13:47), and that includes this small hillside on the Turkish coastline. It is fitting, therefore, that the mosque in that place is called *Isa Bey* in Arabic, which means "Jesus is Lord." The mosque was named for an Ottoman military commander called Isa, or Jesus, but the statement holds more truth than any who worship there realize.

■ ■ ■

God's story is a love story about a valiant Prince who lays down His life to rescue His bride. It's also a rags-to-riches tale of friendship and redemption, in which our heavenly Father invites broken people into His family to find healing, wholeness, and an unimaginable inheritance. But it's also a war story. Ever since Adam and Eve yielded their authority to the serpent back in the garden of Eden, our world has seen unceasing combat, a war between the kingdom of darkness and the kingdom of light.

There have been two wars in our history called "world wars," but the ongoing conflict between darkness and light is truly global. There is no place on earth free from the devil's attacks, no strata of society above his schemes. We are all in this war, whether we realize it or not.

I say it all started when Adam and Eve failed to confront the serpent in the garden—because, at that point in the story, the enemy had no territory to call his own. He was an unlawful invader in paradise with no right to slither along any branch or to speak to the mother of the human race. It was only when Adam and Eve were deceived by the devil that he gained authority in our world.

In fact, he became this world's ruler (see John 12:31; 14:30). That doesn't mean this world is no longer the rightful property of its Creator or that God has somehow given up His sovereignty. On the contrary, God temporarily allows Satan a position in our world because humanity willingly handed it to him.

When God first made Adam and Eve, He said to them, "Be fruitful and multiply and fill the earth and subdue it, and *have dominion* over the fish of the sea and over the birds of the heavens and over every living thing that moves on the earth" (Genesis 1:28, emphasis added). God, as the High King, appointed Adam and Eve to be His representatives and granted them royal authority to rule over the world He made. One duty of a king or queen is to protect their realm from foreign invaders, but Adam and Eve failed to recognize the serpent Satan as the invader he was. Believing his lies and eating the forbidden fruit were acts of submission, and in that exchange, our first parents handed their God-given authority to Satan. He eagerly snatched it up and never looked back.

That's how the war started.

Since then, every child descended from Adam and Eve has been born into the kingdom of darkness. Most don't realize it; they've never known anything else. Many don't even notice there is a war taking place all around them. But all the same, the battles rage, in every generation. In fact, in the generation that followed Adam and Eve, we have a vivid example of the struggle between good and evil played out in the lives of their sons—Cain and Abel.

Murder One

The two men brought offerings to the Lord. This was before God had given His people commandments concerning sacrifices, so these gifts were completely voluntary. Cain, being a farmer of sorts, brought God some of the produce he had grown. Abel, a shepherd, brought the firstborn of his flock.

There was nothing wrong with either offering, but there was something wrong with Cain's heart (1 John 3:12). Abel offered his sacrifice in faith (Hebrews 11:4), but Cain offered his with other motives. We don't know precisely what was going through Cain's mind when he presented some of the fruit of his harvest, but God knew—and "for Cain and his offering he had no regard" (Genesis 4:5).

Cain fumed, and the Lord said to him, "Why are you angry, and why has your face fallen? If you do well, will you not be accepted? And if you do not do well, sin is crouching at the door" (Genesis 4:6–7). Cain was caught up in a deadly battle between good and evil, and with every action he took, he chose a side.

Cain's anger showed that he didn't think he was being treated fairly. Clearly, he didn't believe God was right to reject his offering. It seems that Cain, like his parents before him, chose to believe that God was not good after all. When that happens, Satan springs into action, ready to suggest something that brings death rather than life.

The devil's handiwork is known by its marks—pain, suffering, confusion, loss, and death. He is a murderer and a liar (John 8:44), who "comes only to steal and kill and destroy" (John 10:10). God said that sin was "crouching" at Cain's door. The image is of a wild animal waiting to devour the man if he's not careful. But notice that God didn't say to run from this beast or to kill it. He said Cain "must rule over it" (Genesis 4:7).

It wasn't too late. Cain could still choose to do good rather than evil. There was still time for him to turn from the darkness to the light. God never rescinded His command for humans to have dominion over the earth (Genesis 1:28), but now that dominion must extend even to the sin that wanted to rip Cain to shreds. He had to rule over it.

Cain could still be a faithful servant. He could step into the role God's story laid out for him, but only by mastering the sin that threatened to overcome his heart. In the end, though, Cain failed. It was one of the saddest scenes in God's story. As Cain killed his brother, Abel (Genesis 4:8), Satan won the battle.

But it was only one battle. Jesus won the decisive victory in the war when He died and rose again. His blood was spilled so that Abel's blood would not be lost forever. He died so the kingdom of darkness could be dismantled and destroyed for good—so there would come a day when sin no longer crouches at anyone's door.

Though we live on the other side of Christ's victory, the war is not yet over. To be sure, God could end all the hostilities right now. He could put an end to Satan and his evil works in a single moment, but that would mean ceasing rescue operations—and God wants to give prisoners of war still trapped behind enemy lines the opportunity to be set free.

Why doesn't God stop the evil in our world? Crime, terrorism, racial tension, and unending wars riddle the evening news. Why is Jesus so slow in returning to set everything right? The Bible gives us an answer: "The Lord is not slow to fulfill his promise as some count slowness, but is patient toward you, not wishing that any should perish, but that all should reach repentance" (2 Peter 3:9).

So as we wait for Christ to return, we do so in a war zone. We must be on guard where Cain was not. We must resist the lies that Cain did not. We must cultivate life instead of death. We look forward to a day when "all the earth shall be filled with the glory of the LORD" (Numbers 14:21), but we do so as soldiers in the thick of the battle. Our job in God's story is to stay close to our Commanding Officer, listen to every word He says, and obey every order issued from His mouth.

Near Ephesus, Turkey, there is a mosque that declares "Jesus is Lord." Someday soon, everyone—absolutely everyone—will know how true that pronouncement is.

YOUR LIFE IN THE STORY OF GOD

Is God's story a tale of love or of war? Actually, it's both. It is the story of a valiant Prince who lays down His life to rescue His bride, as an ongoing worldwide conflict makes that rescue necessary. By convincing Adam and Eve to disobey God, Satan claimed the authority they'd been given over the earth. He does all he can to enslave people, but Jesus in His love died and rose again to set them free. The decisive battle has been won—but until Jesus returns, we live our lives in a war zone.

1. What evidence do you see of the ongoing conflict between Satan and God?

2. How did Satan usurp Adam and Eve's authority over the world God created? What was the decisive battle that sealed Satan's defeat?

3. Why does God keep us living in a war zone? How can we come through this war zone successfully?

Here Be Dragons

EXODUS 7:1–13

In the New York Public Library's rare books section, there is a copper globe about five inches in diameter. It's a little more than five hundred years old, but what makes the Hunt-Lenox Globe truly special is the small engraving along the coast of Southeast Asia that reads *Hic sunt dracones.* That's Latin for "here be dragons."

It's been said that many old maps contained such warnings. But the actual phrase was never found in print until the discovery of the Hunt-Lenox Globe. (It has since been found again on an early sixteenth-century globe, etched on an ostrich egg.)

I mention these globes because of the stark contrast between them and our modern navigational aids. You could scroll all the way around the planet in Google Maps and you wouldn't find a single warning about dragons. Likewise, no GPS system on the market will alert a driver that an area may be rich with monsters.

When we read that people were once concerned with creatures we consider the stuff of make-believe, it's easy to chalk their fear up to ignorance, superstition, or misunderstanding. And often, this is how people—even Christians—approach parts of God's story in the Bible.

We read about the various gods of the ancient Near East: the deities of the Canaanites, the Egyptians, or the Greeks. These are false gods, often associated with idols. Or sometimes they're puffed-up kings who have declared themselves divine. We consider them merely the imagined deities of men and women who have not yet come to know the true God, the one and only Creator of heaven and earth. We may also think about the religious hierarchy in those societies—the priests and kings who used the terror of the gods to keep uneducated peasants in line.

Some readers may even entertain the idea that God is no different, so they investigate the claims of Scripture carefully to see if there is any truth to His Story. For what it's worth, I believe God welcomes such inquiries. Through the prophet Jeremiah, He said, "You will seek me and find me, when you seek me with all your heart" (Jeremiah 29:13). The Lord wants to be discovered. He wants to be known.

Those other so-called gods, though—Baal, Marduk, Ra, and the rest—they're imaginary, right? While it's true that there is only one God, if you know where to look in the pages of the Bible, you'll find markers that have been preserved for thousands of years. In an ancient tongue they warn, "Here be dragons."

■ ■ ■

Moses knew well the gods of Egypt. He had grown up in Pharaoh's household, most likely educated and trained among the elite. From an early age, he would have been exposed to the various beliefs and traditions of the Egyptian religion.

But Moses would have known of another God too. Contrary to many popular retellings of the exodus story, including the classic film *The Ten Commandments*, the Bible gives us no indication that Moses grew up unaware that he was a Hebrew.[1] While he enjoyed the status of having been adopted by Pharaoh's daughter, it seems he also knew his birth mother, Jochebed, and the rest of his family, including his sister, Miriam, and his brother, Aaron. It's likely that Moses heard the portions of God's story that now make up the book of Genesis (Exodus 2:1–10; Numbers 26:59).

No doubt Moses found those accounts markedly different than the tales that were part of the Egyptian religion. Instead of a pantheon, there was only one God. And He was neither capricious nor needy. The Hebrew God was a personal friend to Moses' ancestors, Abraham, Isaac, and Jacob, and He rescued

His people when they were in need. One day, on a mountainside in the wilderness, God introduced himself to Moses, telling him it was time, once again, for a rescue.

Moses had fled Egypt forty years earlier after murdering an Egyptian he'd seen mistreating an Israelite (Exodus 2:12). Since that time, he had settled in Midian, become a shepherd, gotten married, and started a family (2:15–22; 3:1). But now he would have to give up this new life in order to follow the Lord. He would have to return to the land of his birth to face Pharaoh, the most powerful man in the world. And not just Pharaoh—Moses would also be challenging the gods of Egypt.

God didn't send Moses into Pharaoh's court alone, though. Moses' brother, Aaron, would go along with him. Beforehand, God gave the men this instruction: "When Pharaoh says to you, 'Prove yourselves by working a miracle,' then you shall say to Aaron, 'Take your staff and cast it down before Pharaoh, that it may become a serpent'" (Exodus 7:9). When it was time, things happened just as the Lord had said. Aaron threw down his staff, and it turned into a snake. But then the magicians of Egypt threw down staffs of their own, and theirs, too, became snakes.

Many people would like to believe that nothing exists beyond our senses—nothing supernatural, nothing otherworldly, and nothing unrestrained by the laws of physics that govern our universe. Some of these people may make an exception for God, but that is where they draw the line. *There is no devil. There are no demons. God may employ angels—that's His business—but we won't see them poking around here.*

Whether or not they say these things out loud, many live as if this were the case. However, if we are to take the Bible at its word, that simply will not do. On that day long ago, the gods of Egypt showed up in Pharaoh's court with their dark power at the ready.

Here be dragons.

Of course, the gods of Egypt were nothing like the one true God—not in any real sense—but neither were they imaginary.

So what are we to make of them and the other colorful characters that fill up the mythologies of the ancient world? We can
trace the answer to a city in Asia Minor, more than a thousand
miles north of Egypt, to a tentmaker writing a letter more than
a millennium after the events of the exodus.

The apostle Paul, writing from Ephesus, sent a letter to
Corinth addressing several controversial issues affecting the
daily lives of believers there. Among these was how to live in a
society saturated with idols.

Paul wrote, "The things which the Gentiles sacrifice *they
sacrifice to demons* and not to God, and I do not want you
to have fellowship with demons" (1 Corinthians 10:20 NKJV,
emphasis added). The idols of wood and stone and bronze and
gold may be nothing in and of themselves, but the spirits behind
those idols are nothing short of demonic. False gods are, in many
cases, demons—evil spirits in rebellion against God, themselves
pretending to be gods. Their power is real, but it is darkness
through and through.

Bugging Pharaoh

Time and time again, Moses appeared before Pharaoh to deliver
God's message: "Let my people go!" But Pharaoh's heart was
hardened, and getting harder all the time. So with each stubborn
refusal and broken promise from Egypt's king, God brought a
different plague upon the Egyptians.

First, the Nile turned to blood (Exodus 7:14–25). Next, God
overwhelmed the people with frogs (8:1–15). Then came gnats
(8:16–19), and then flies (8:20–32). After the bugs, the livestock
in Egypt got sick and died, though the herds of the Israelites were
spared (9:1–7). Soon after, the people got sick too, breaking out
with painful boils (9:8–12). Hailstones rained down from the
sky, bringing destruction to everything in their path (9:13–35).
Locusts swarmed the once-lush Egyptian fields, devouring anything the hail had left intact (10:1–20). Then came a darkness

unlike anything the people of the ancient world had ever seen (10:21–29).

Finally, the tenth plague arrived, the worst of all. Death came for the oldest child of every family (11:1–12:32). "At midnight the LORD struck down all the firstborn in the land of Egypt, from the firstborn of Pharaoh who sat on his throne to the firstborn of the captive who was in the dungeon, and all the firstborn of the livestock" (12:29).

With each plague, as Numbers 33:4 indicates, the God of Israel was judging the gods of Egypt. Because the Egyptians worshipped hundreds of gods whose domains and areas of influence often overlapped, we can't identify just one god for each of the ten plagues. For example, Hapi was the god of the Nile. But Egypt's greatest river was also said to be the bloodstream of Osiris, the god of the underworld. The Nile turning to blood was an attack on both. Similarly, the plague of darkness challenged Ra, the sun god, but also Nut, the god of the sky. Each calamity had the same effect: to show the Egyptians that their gods were no match for the one true God. "The Egyptians shall know that I am the LORD, when I stretch out my hand against Egypt and bring out the people of Israel from among them" (Exodus 7:5).

When God turned the water in Egypt to blood, and later brought swarms of frogs over the land, Pharaoh's magicians were able to perform similar wonders (7:22; 8:7). Each time, the power of God seemed to be matched by the power of darkness. But it only seemed that way. The sorcerers of Pharaoh could do nothing to *stop* the plagues, and soon they couldn't even mimic them. After Aaron threw his staff down and it became a snake, Pharaoh's servants were able to do the same (7:10–11). But that wasn't the end of the battle between good and evil that day: "Aaron's staff swallowed up their staffs" (7:12).

In the same way, the plagues brought by God "swallowed up" whatever power the gods of Egypt wielded over their particular realms. This is especially true of the last plague—the death of the firstborn. This plague was an attack on all the gods of Egypt (Exodus 12:12); none of them was powerful enough to stop this supreme tragedy. More directly, the final plague was a judgment upon Pharaoh himself, the god-king of Egypt.[2] His firstborn son, taken by the plague, was next in line for the job.

In God's story, there are villains. While the kingdom of heaven is making its way across creation's grand landscape, taking territory with every heart that is made new, there is a kingdom of darkness that will not surrender quietly. As we live out the parts that God has written for us in His story, we will face this enemy.

Modern life may seem a world away from the ancient Near East, but false gods remain with us, if often in less obvious forms. Satan and his dark army still oppose God and His people. They will do whatever it takes to keep us believing they're not real, and their job is so much easier if we go on thinking the war is against other people. Paul reminded Christians in Ephesus, and God's Word reminds us today, that "our struggle is not against flesh and blood, but against the rulers, against the authorities, against the powers of this dark world and against the spiritual forces of evil in the heavenly realms" (Ephesians 6:12 NIV).

The gospel is, in part, a declaration that Satan and his kingdom of darkness have been overthrown for good. Their end is certain; their destruction, assured. But until that beautiful day when evil is no more, we would do well to remember: *Hic sunt dracones.* Here be dragons.

YOUR LIFE IN THE STORY OF GOD

Like an ancient map that warns of dragons ahead, the Bible points out dangers that followers of Christ will face. Behind the scenes, Satan and his demons stir up trouble, even posing as gods themselves. More often today, they try to convince us that our conflict is completely internal or with other people rather than spiritual forces. The gospel declares that Satan has been defeated, but until he is finally neutralized, we must be alert to the "dragons" among us.

1. How did the one true God prove His superiority over the various gods of Egypt? How might the ten plagues have affected the religious views of the Egyptian people?

2. Who is the enemy that Christians face daily (Ephesians 6:12)? Why do we often see our battle as being against other people?

3. What are some of the false gods of our modern world? How might Satan be using them against humanity?

Where God Is King

1 SAMUEL 8

My sister Kerry loves piecing together our family tree. She spends hours online researching dead relatives I never knew we had. She's even made trips to far-off cemeteries and records libraries to learn more.

A few years ago, to go back further than birth certificates and baptism records allow, Kerry had a genetic ancestry map created from a sample of her DNA. Because we're siblings, her genealogy map is my genealogy map. As I looked over our results, a few surprises caught my eye.

I always thought I was about one-eighth Irish. I'm actually only 1 or 2 percent. I also thought I was 75 percent Italian. As it turns out, that was a little high too. But the biggest surprise of all was that somewhere back through the centuries, I had ancestors who were Jewish.

As I read the Bible now, knowing that at least a small part of me was descended by blood from Abraham, I can't help but geek out a bit. Reading stories about men and women like David, Deborah, and Daniel is like turning up the most amazing family history.

But the truth is, as a follower of Jesus Christ, I have been adopted by God. I am already part of the "one new man" God has created from Jewish and Gentile believers (Ephesians 2:15). There are no second-class citizens in God's family; the world is no longer divided along Jewish and Gentile lines, circumcised and uncircumcised. Now the dividing line is Jesus—it's what we do with Him that makes all the difference in our standing before God.

When Abraham looked into the sky to number the stars

(Genesis 15:5), there was a sparkling light there for every person who would come to know Jesus Christ—Jewish and non-Jewish alike, from "all tribes and peoples and languages" (Revelation 7:9).

God's Plan for All Those Stars

Just like a star set against the backdrop of space, the tiniest spark of light glows all the more brightly when surrounded by acres of darkness. Its flame may be small, but the blackness cannot snuff it out. Darkness has no power to destroy light, but light—even the most insignificant of flashpoints—pierces whatever darkness it finds in its path.

There must be something in the heart of God that loves small beginnings. Think about it: God can do anything He wants. There is no scale too large for Him to display His works. But when it comes to His story—the story of redemption as written in the Bible—more often than not God chooses to start things small.

At the dawn of creation, He began the human race with just one man. Then, after the floodwaters subsided, He began again with just one family. When it was time to establish a nation on earth that would be like no other, He chose an old man and his barren wife to be the beginning of a new people—a people who would be set apart in a special way for their Creator.

When God called Abraham, in one sense He was preparing to do something unprecedented in the history of the world. Never before had God stepped into history to build a nation, and then live among that people and show them His ways. At the same time, however, nothing was entirely new about the Lord's plan for Israel. God had always intended to rule as King over a people who enjoyed a special relationship with Him.

That was His will for Adam and Eve. When God told them, "Be fruitful and multiply" (Genesis 1:28), He was calling them to be parents of a nation that would cover the whole earth. With Abraham, God was starting this project again—only this time, because of sin's hostile takeover of our world, there would be continual opposition, both from within and without.

For a long time, the nation of Israel had no earthly king of its own. In Egypt, the people had been slaves under Pharaoh. In the wilderness, they were led by Moses and Joshua. Once in the land, the Israelites were ruled by various judges, with Samuel the prophet being the last. He instructed the people and modeled how a life walked in step with God should look.

From slavery to Samuel, God was the people's king. But in Samuel's old age, they began asking for someone else: "Appoint a king to lead us, such as all the other nations have" (1 Samuel 8:5 NIV).

It was a sinful request. The people of Israel were envious of their neighbors. They wanted the security of a warrior-king who could lead them in battle. They also wanted the prestige and pomp of royalty at the center of their cultural life. But God had set the nation apart from her neighbors. He was her security. And His presence was to be at the heart of the nation's culture. The people weren't just requesting a king; they were rejecting God (1 Samuel 8:7).

Of course, the Lord was not surprised by this. He had known all along that His people would one day ask for a king. He had told Abraham, "I will make you exceedingly fruitful, and I will make you into nations, and *kings shall come from you*" (Genesis 17:6, emphasis added). And He had even given Moses laws to govern the kings of Israel, hundreds of years before Israel's first king would sit on his throne (Deuteronomy 17:14–20). As is often the case, God used the sinful actions of His people to bring about His good purposes.

At first, the two ideas might seem contradictory. On the one hand, God had established a nation over which He would rule directly as the people's king, setting them apart from every other people group on the planet. On the other, He had long planned on giving His people a human king, "such as all the other nations have." If it wasn't God who "breathed out" the

Scriptures (2 Timothy 3:16), we could chalk up such an apparent continuity error to bad writing.

But God did inspire the Scriptures and, as He established a line of kings in Israel, He slowly unveiled the greatest plot twist of all time. Israel would have her kings, and God would remain High King over the nation—but from the family tree of one of those kings, a Ruler would be born. He would be "God with us" (Matthew 1:23; compare with Isaiah 7:14), His reign would have no end (Daniel 2:44; Luke 1:33), and His kingdom would extend to the ends of the earth (Zechariah 14:9).

Jesus would bring everything together: in Christ, God himself would rule over His people. And King Jesus would be the hope not just of Israel, but of every nation on earth (Isaiah 42:1–4; Matthew 12:21). Someday His kingdom will encompass every corner of creation.

In the previous two chapters, we saw how Satan gained a foothold in our world and how his demonic agents deceive people, turning their hearts and minds away from their Maker. But there is good news: God is undoing all of that. Though His plan to bring a kingdom was initiated with Abraham and the Jewish people, the nation of Israel was never really the kingdom of God. However special they were, the Israelites knew that the Lord would need to deliver the sort of kingdom that could live up to all His promises—they couldn't build it on their own.

So they waited for a prophet like Moses and a king like David (Deuteronomy 18:15–19; Isaiah 11:10). They looked for the signs of the coming Messiah to be fulfilled. They watched as king after king failed to lead them along the path of righteousness. They endured as empire after empire took turns ruling over the Promised Land and oppressing its people. Centuries passed, and it began to seem like God had forgotten His promises.

But remember how I said God likes to start small?

On a dark night in Judea, some four hundred years after the last writing prophet put down his pen and the Old Testament (as it came to be known) found its completion, a small spark of light from God's kingdom burst into our world. The first bit of territory retaken from Satan's dominion was a single cell in a virgin's womb. But nine months later, a newborn King was placed in a manger. Israel's wait was over, though most didn't realize it. With Jesus came the kingdom of God—and it has been spreading across the globe ever since.

The kingdom has not yet come in its fullness. We merely need look around to know that. But the kingdom's gradual progress is not due to any weakness in its King. On the contrary, God is patient, wanting to save as many as possible before He comes to judge sin finally (2 Peter 3:9).

Today, we find ourselves in the latter chapters of God's story. The decisive battle has already been fought. The cross and the empty tomb settled the matter once and for all. Our role in these final days is to proclaim God's kingdom to everyone who has not yet heard. We declare it by sharing Christ with those we meet, inviting friends, neighbors, and strangers alike to take their place in the kingdom. We also make the kingdom known by living as its citizens, soaking in its culture, and bringing its goodness, truth, and beauty to whatever we touch.

In God's name, we are to be agents of change, ambassadors of healing, and missionaries of hope. And we're all in this together. Broadcasting news of the kingdom in word and deed is our family business, no matter how much (or how little) of Abraham's blood may course through our veins. After all, it's Jesus' blood—not Abraham's—that has the power to remake the world.

YOUR LIFE IN THE STORY OF GOD

From its founding, the nation of Israel had God himself as its king. When the people foolishly demanded a human ruler, God granted their request—but with a plan to ultimately raise up a different kind of Ruler from the royal line. Jesus would be "God with us," the eternal king whose rule would one day cover the entire earth. By believing in Him, we join God's story—no longer divided as Jews and Gentiles, but part of the "one new man" God has created (Ephesians 2:15).

1. How do we know that Israel's demand for a human king had been anticipated by God? What does that tell us about Him?

2. What is the "plot twist" that God wrote into the story of His kingdom? How would Jesus differ from even the best earthly kings?

3. Why has God's kingdom not yet reached its full extent (see 2 Peter 3:9)? What is our role in God's story until the kingdom is fully revealed?

The All-Consuming Fire

1 KINGS 18:16–46

Elijah was a powerful prophet—a man used by God to change the nation of Israel. In response to Elijah's prayers, God shut up the sky, and it didn't rain for three and a half years. Through Elijah, the Lord multiplied flour and oil so that a poor widow and her son would have enough to eat for as long as necessary. God even used His prophet to bring the widow's son back to life after he fell ill and died.

There can be no doubt that Elijah was a man of God. But Elijah was also arrogant. He was a liar. And on at least one occasion, he doubted God so much that he wanted to die. (More on all that in a bit.) Elijah was far from perfect. He was broken and messy, just like the rest of us. Still, when it came time for a showdown between the forces of good and evil, God picked Elijah as His man to lead the charge.

Fire on the Mountain

On top of Mount Carmel, 450 prophets of Baal (plus an additional 400 prophets of Asherah) stood against Elijah as the people of Israel—men and women who had turned from God—looked on with curiosity. The wicked King Ahab and the wickeder Queen Jezebel championed idolatry and made it central to life in Israel. To be sure, the worship of false gods had begun long before Ahab and Jezebel were in charge, but this couple brought the sin in the nation to a whole new level.

All of Israel's neighbors were polytheistic, meaning they believed in a pantheon of gods. Some of these gods were thought to be active mainly in local communities, while others were viewed as regional or national. Many gods exhibited their power only over a particular sphere of nature or season of the year. So when the people of Israel began worshipping Baal, they didn't set the true God aside altogether—they simply placed Baal alongside Him. That's why Elijah could rightly say to the people, "How long will you go limping between two different opinions? If the LORD is God, follow him; but if Baal, then follow him" (1 Kings 18:21).

That was the question to be settled on this particular day: *Who is God—Baal or the Lord?* The contest was simple. Baal's prophets would place one bull, cut up in pieces and prepared as an offering, on their altar. But they could not light the fire; they would need to call on their god to do that. Then Elijah would do the same, and ask his God to set his bull aflame. Whoever answered the call was the one to be worshipped in Israel.

Baal's prophets went first. They danced around the altar, whooping and hollering, shouting for Baal to send fire and consume their burnt offering. When that didn't work, "they shouted louder and slashed themselves with swords and spears, as was their custom, until their blood flowed" (18:28 NIV). They started in the morning (18:26), and "they continued their frantic prophesying until the time for the evening sacrifice. But there was no response, no one answered, no one paid attention" (18:29 NIV).

Many people read this account and conclude, "Of course 'no one answered,' and 'no one paid attention.' These other gods aren't real." But I don't believe that's a fair assessment of the situation, for two reasons.

First, as we've already seen, false gods were often the twisted and deadly manifestations of demons. They weren't *gods* in any real sense, but they weren't imaginary either. Second, people in the ancient world weren't stupid. They may not have understood the science behind our world, but they learned from their experiences, just as we do. If these prophets of Baal danced around in a frenzy, eventually spilling their own blood, "as was their custom," then it's reasonable to assume that they'd seen such tactics work in the past. For a god to gain a following, he has to answer a summons every once in a while.

Why else would these prophets agree to such a contest with Elijah? These were true believers; they expected to see their bull catch fire on the altar. They expected Baal to show up.

But he didn't.

Next came Elijah's turn. And here's where God made the contest a true show for the ages. Elijah built an altar out of twelve stones, a number meant to remind the people that God loved them very much.[3] Once the stones were in place, Elijah dug a trench around his altar, and after the bull for his offering was prepared, he had twelve jarfuls of water dumped over everything. There was so much water that it ran down the sides of the altar and turned the trench into a moat. Then Elijah prayed:

> "O LKN', God of Abraham, Isaac, and Israel, let it be known this day that you are God in Israel, and that I am your servant, and that I have done all these things at your word. Answer me, O LKN', answer me, that this people may know that you, O LKN', are God, and that you have turned their hearts back" (1 KINGS 18:36–37).

That's what the contest was all about: winning back the hearts of God's people.

God's love is not restrained or polite. It's powerful and all-consuming. It does not hold back. If the intensity of God's love could be seen with human eyes, it would look something like this: "The fire of the LORD fell and consumed the burnt offering and the wood and the stones and the dust, and licked up the water that was in the trench" (18:38). The heat from heaven's fire burned with such passion that it incinerated not just the sopping wet bull and the wood, but also the twelve stones Elijah had used to construct the altar.

■ ■ ■

This same love of God is the force behind the kingdom that is now invading our world and toppling the powers of darkness. The cross, which in the moment must have seemed like a victory for evil, was actually Satan's defeat. For everyone who trusts in Him, Jesus took sin's punishment and wiped away its stains of guilt.

There is now no validity to any accusation the devil lays against a believer. We can stand firmly on Christ's work, knowing the indictments of the evil one have been answered at Calvary. Any doubts we might have about this good news are answered by the resurrection, which proves Jesus' sacrifice on our behalf was accepted by God the Father. All of this has revoked the foothold in our world that Adam gave Satan all those years ago. The kingdom of God is advancing, and the dominion of darkness, though it will unleash its worst on any who challenge it, ultimately has no choice but to retreat.

On that day at Mount Carmel, God's victory came not merely with fire from heaven; it came when God's people responded to the Lord. "When all the people saw it, they fell on their faces and said, 'The LORD, he is God; the LORD, he is God'" (1 Kings 18:39). It is the same way today. God could destroy Satan in an instant, but He is really after the hearts of men and women who have turned to other gods. He reveals His love in a million unique ways to us as individuals, but His affection can be seen most clearly at the cross.

I began this chapter by noting what a mess Elijah could be. Standing there on the mountain before the contest got under-way, he announced, "I, even I only, am left a prophet of the LORD" (1 Kings 18:22). But that was a lie told in arrogance, per-haps masking an insecurity. Elijah was not the only one of God's faithful servants left—and he knew it. Just a short while earlier, Elijah had run into Obadiah, who had told him about a hundred prophets of God he had hidden away (18:13). Then, after God's victory on Mount Carmel, after the Lord brought rain back to Israel (18:45), and after God temporarily allowed Elijah to run faster than the Flash (18:45–46), the prophet sat down under a broom tree and asked God to take his life (19:4)—because Jezebel had vowed revenge. In spite of all the things Elijah had seen, he couldn't muster the faith to trust that God would protect him from the queen's royal tantrum.

It's important for us to see the kind of struggles Elijah endured, because as God fights for the hearts and minds of people today, He wants to use people like you and me to share His love—no matter how imperfect we are. In much the same way that Elijah stood before the men and women of Israel, confident in what the Lord would do that day, we can stand before our communities and culture, confident in Jesus' death and resurrection.

History is drawing ever nearer to the day when Jesus will set all things right. On that day, Satan will no longer be free to seduce people away from goodness. There will be no need for a showdown like the one on Mount Carmel. Everyone will see clearly enough to proclaim, "The Lord, he is God; the Lord, he is God!"

YOUR LIFE IN THE STORY OF GOD

Elijah's fiery victory over the prophets of Baal at Mount Carmel is a picture of God's love—powerful and all-consuming, not restrained or polite. Today, He still advances His kingdom, relentlessly, in spite of every attempt by Satan to defeat it. God uses imperfect people—like Elijah, like you and me—to carry out His story on earth, until that day when Jesus arrives to set everything right.

1. What two things did Elijah ask God to do for the Israelites as He defeated the prophets of Baal (1 Kings 18:37)? How did the spectators respond after God sent His fire (1 Kings 18:39)?

2. How do you see God winning people's hearts today? How does He capture yours?

3. Why should Jesus' death and resurrection give us confidence as we stand before our culture today?

A Colt, Crying Rocks, and the Crucified King

JOHN 12:12–19

It is only a short walk from the Mount of Olives to the city of Jerusalem. Under normal circumstances, no able-bodied person would need a ride to make the trip. So when Jesus asked two of His disciples to go ahead of the group and fetch a donkey for Him, it wasn't about relieving His tired feet.

The prophet Zechariah had written, "Rejoice greatly, O daughter of Zion! Shout aloud, O daughter of Jerusalem! Behold, your king is coming to you; righteous and having salvation is he, humble and mounted on a donkey, on a colt, the foal of a donkey" (Zechariah 9:9). Jesus knew the prophecy, as did most faithful Jews. And He decided to make it come true that day as He entered Jerusalem.

In the ancient world, it was common for military leaders and high-ranking officials to ride into town on a warhorse or in a finely appointed chariot, leading a procession of supporters and conquered enemies in their wake. Though the scene is not recorded in Scripture or Roman history, it is likely that such a procession took place sometime during the week prior to Jesus' donkey ride as Pontius Pilate came to Jerusalem for the Passover.

Pilate was the Roman governor of Judea, but the Roman capital of the province was the coastal city of Caesarea, not Jerusalem. So, for large national festivities, Pilate would take up temporary residence in Jerusalem in a palace built by Herod the Great a generation earlier. As the highest imperial official in the land, Pilate's entrance into the city would have been something to see.

But Jesus, the rightful King of Israel, did not choose a stallion for His entrance; He chose a humble donkey, a foal on which no one had ridden before (Mark 11:2). Matthew tells us the donkey was so young it had to stay next to its mother the entire time. The mother walked alongside Jesus as her colt brought Him into Jerusalem (Matthew 21:7).

Is there anything less intimidating than a baby barnyard animal with its mother? It's as if the Holy Spirit, who inspired Zechariah's words, was intent on painting a picture that would completely contradict politics and power as usual.

Those who knew the prophecy of Zechariah understood the statement Jesus was making with His slow but steady entrance through the city's Golden Gate. "So they took branches of palm trees and went out to meet him, crying out, 'Hosanna! Blessed is he who comes in the name of the Lord, even the King of Israel!'" (John 12:13). The Jewish people who surrounded Jesus that day connected the dots from Zechariah's prophecy to the colt following his mother to the Man who was the young animal's first-ever passenger. They knew Jesus, by His actions, was claiming His place as King of Israel.

Hosanna comes from a phrase that means "Lord, save (us)" in Hebrew and Aramaic. It comes from Psalm 118, as does the exclamation, "Blessed is he who comes in the name of the Lord" (vv. 25–26). The scene of praise in that psalm is one of victory and thanksgiving. And that was the mood on the day that Jesus came to Jerusalem for His final Passover. In Jesus, every hope the people had for the Messiah was about to come true—or so they thought.

You may have heard it said that the same crowds who shouted "Hosanna!" on Palm Sunday also shouted "Crucify Him!" on Good Friday, but that's not quite right. Luke tells us that on Palm Sunday, it was a "whole multitude of *his disciples*" who cheered Him on (19:37, emphasis added). John says that the crowds were made up of people who "had come to the feast," that is, out-of-towners, possibly Galilean pilgrims who already knew about Jesus (12:12; compare with Mark 15:40–41), plus men and women who were present when Jesus raised Lazarus from the dead (John 12:17).

The people calling for blood on Good Friday, on the other hand, had no apparent connection with Jesus. "Now the chief priests and the elders persuaded the crowd to ask for Barabbas and destroy Jesus" (Matthew 27:20). Mark records that they were "stirred up" (15:11). These were people over whom the religious establishment in Jerusalem held sway, not the sorts of people identified in the crowd on Palm Sunday.

The gospel writers describe a scene on Palm Sunday that was genuine. The people who laid down their coats on the road and greeted Jesus with palm branches offered sincere praise to God for their coming King. They knew, at least in part, who Jesus really was. Many of them had just seen Jesus call a dead man from his tomb, and they watched as that man—no longer dead—stumbled out, still wrapped in his grave clothes.

If we collapse Good Friday into Palm Sunday, we can only conclude that Jesus' triumphal entry into Jerusalem was a sham, or at best a misunderstanding. In that case, it would have been far better for Jesus' arrival to be lauded by rocks crying out, as Jesus suggested they could have (Luke 19:40), rather than phony shouts of "Hosanna!" from the fickle.

A Kingdom Just Like Its King

Some people imagine Jesus is a conservative. Some think he's a liberal, or a Communist, a hippie, a vegan, a member of the National Rifle Association, or even a vampire slayer. We have no shortage of creativity when it comes to remaking Jesus in our own image.

There is something inside us, placed there by God, that drives us to be more like Him. Sadly, sin has twisted that desire so that we find comfort in merely believing we are on His side—or rather, that He is on ours. But the kingdom of God isn't simply an idea that changes over time or shifts in the blowing winds of culture and popular opinion. Its values are found in its King, not in the competing imaginations of its citizens—or its fans.

I believe the people who praised God as Jesus arrived in Jerusalem were genuine followers—at least on some level. That's not to say that they knew the week would end with Jesus' death on a cross or that He would be resurrected the following Sunday. But such understanding was not yet among the standard beliefs of a genuine disciple.

Even the twelve, who had been with Jesus for three years, had not yet grasped His mission. The people who walked the road into the City of David hailed Him as the King of Israel because, based on what they'd seen and heard, they believed He fulfilled the Old Testament's vision of the Messiah. They believed Jesus was on their side.

Their side wanted the Romans destroyed—or at a minimum, sent packing back to Italy. Their side wanted the kingdom of God and the kingdom of Israel to be one and the same. Their side wanted the Messiah to take up His throne in Jerusalem and usher in a golden age of peace. This was the hope of the Jewish people in Jesus' day. It's why, even after Jesus died and rose again, the disciples asked, "Lord, will you at this time restore the kingdom to Israel?" (Acts 1:6).

Jesus didn't come to Jerusalem on Palm Sunday to topple the Romans. He had no interest in leading a revolt. On the contrary, He told His supporters to "render to Caesar the things that are Caesar's, and to God the things that are God's" (Luke 20:25). Jesus came to die, not only for faithful Jews with hopes of a coming kingdom, but for those who shouted, "Crucify him!" (Mark 15:13), and for the Romans who supplied the wood and the nails for the cross. Jesus' kingdom is not like the kingdoms of this world. He established it not by the blood of His enemies, but at the cost of His own.

The young donkey that Jesus rode was a key to this mystery. Jesus came to wage peace, not war. In the same passage in which he prophesied the colt, Zechariah wrote, "The battle bow shall be cut off, and he shall speak peace to the nations" (Zechariah 9:10). Jesus spoke peace to the nations on the cross, making friendship with God possible for anyone who believes. This is the upside-down nature of the kingdom: Victory comes through surrender. Enemies are conquered through love. Power is undone through meekness.

Jesus will enter Jerusalem once more at His second coming (Zechariah 14:4–5; Acts 1:9–12). When He does, people will again say, "Blessed is he who comes in the name of the Lord" (Matthew 23:37–39). But this time there will be no partial understanding of His identity, no mistaking the nature of His kingdom, and no need for Him to die in order to make peace. The rocks may cry out, but not because of a lack of praise. If they celebrate, it will be because they, too, have been eagerly waiting for creation's rightful King to come (Romans 8:19–22).

The Jewish people in Jesus' day were not wrong about God coming to judge the world or about the Messiah taking up residence in Jerusalem. The Old Testament speaks of both events. But that day is not yet here.

Right now, we live between the inauguration of the kingdom in peace, which came through Jesus' death and resurrection, and the consummation of the kingdom in justice, which will take place when Jesus returns to reign over the earth. Our privilege as citizens in God's kingdom is to live God's story by working to bring peace and justice to our communities. With both the gospel and our own tales of forgiveness at the ready, we invite all those who might be inclined to shout "Crucify! Crucify!" to instead join in the celebration, proclaiming "Hosanna! Hosanna!"

YOUR LIFE IN THE STORY OF GOD

In terms of God's story, we live in the in-between—after Jesus' death and resurrection inaugurated the kingdom in peace, but before His second coming to consummate the kingdom in justice. As citizens of His kingdom, we play an important role: working to bring peace and justice to our own communities, here and now. When Jesus comes again, all of creation—even the rocks—will acknowledge Him as the rightful King.

1. How did Jesus' "triumphal entry" into Jerusalem contrast with arrival of the political leaders of His day? What can we as His followers learn from this?

2. How did the people of Jesus' time—even His disciples—misunderstand His kingship? What mistakes do people make today in their view of Jesus?

3. Can you name two or three practical ways you could live out God's story by bringing peace and justice to your community?

The Death of Darkness

ACTS 9:1–22

God's story begins with a garden and ends with a garden city (Genesis 2:8–15; Revelation 22:1–5). The journey from Genesis to Revelation follows the vein of human history from Eden to New Jerusalem, and everything in between—the space in which we live—is the valley between two paradises. But this valley is unnatural, a deep rut in creation carved out by sin and broken relationships, keeping all who live in it trapped in the darkness of the basin's rocky floor.

If you know where to look, rays of God's goodness can be seen breaking over the horizon. Light from heaven streaks across the valley; these illuminated moments come whenever a page turns in God's story—whenever He moves or speaks, propelling redemption forward. Then, for a time, everything changes. Some people clamor for a taste of what life was like in the garden. Others, having grown accustomed to the perpetual twilight of the lowlands, hide from the unfamiliar brightness.

In truth, some measure of divine goodness is always flooding the valley. Life could not be sustained without it. God, in His mercy, has put certain limits on the power of darkness.

When the Son of God came to earth, He entered our "valley of the shadow of death," bringing with Him the light of heaven. People either embraced the light or hid from it, though Christ's light was so bright and convicting that some plotted to put it out altogether. These folks, jealous for their own authority and preferring the shadows, were incited by none other than the prince of darkness.

But the light of heaven cannot be snuffed out.

At first, the death of Jesus seemed to squelch the brightness.

But with the stone rolled away from the tomb, it was clear to all that its intensity had only grown. And when the Son of God left the valley floor and returned to the Father, He didn't simply take His light with Him—He sent that light to live inside every one of His followers. Then they could bear heaven's glory and be living reminders of the garden-city destination God has willed for all who trust in His Son.

The light Jesus sent is the Holy Spirit, and He does more than illuminate the dark valley—though He certainly does that. God's Spirit changes our home address. He marks Christ's followers as members of God's family and as citizens of heaven (John 1:12; Philippians 3:20). You see, God's desire is for heaven and earth to be intimately intertwined (see Revelation 21:9–11; 23–25).

In a previous chapter, we looked at Jesus' prayer for this: "Your kingdom come, your will be done, on earth as it is in heaven" (Matthew 6:10). Notice how that prayer connects the kingdom with heaven, because God's kingdom is wherever He reigns as King. Heaven is God's kingdom, and so is every outpost on earth where a believer in Jesus Christ bends her knee to the Lord.

The Making of a Kingdom Citizen

In a letter to the church at Colossae, Paul wrote, "[God] has delivered us from the domain of darkness and transferred us to the kingdom of his beloved Son, in whom we have redemption, the forgiveness of sins" (Colossians 1:13–14). That's the great exchange that happens when a sinner gives his life to Jesus. And Paul would know. He was once quite at home in the "domain of darkness."

In another letter, Paul wrote, "This is a faithful saying and worthy of all acceptance, that Christ Jesus came into the world to save sinners, of whom I am chief" (1 Timothy 1:15 NKJV). Paul considered himself the worst of sinners, and that wasn't an exaggeration. The statement did not grow out of some deep, self-deprecating humility. He truly believed there was no one worse than him, because he had once been a persecutor of Christians.

The book of Acts records that Paul—then known as Saul—approved of the murder of a man named Stephen (Acts 7:58; 22:20). Stephen was a deacon in the early church, a man through whom God had done signs and wonders to show that Jesus was the Messiah (Acts 6:8). Stephen's light was bright. But so intense was Saul's hatred for Christ and His followers that he stood by, guarding the garments of the Jewish leaders who took Stephen's life.

For Saul, that was just the beginning. Soon after, he "began to destroy the church. Going from house to house, he dragged off both men and women and put them in prison" (Acts 8:3 NIV).

But on the road to Damascus, on one of his missions to put more Christians in prison, Saul was confronted by heaven's light. In a moment, he was knocked to the ground and blinded, never to be the same again. Disoriented, he heard a voice saying, "Saul, Saul, why are you persecuting me?" (Acts 9:4).

"Who are you, Lord?" Saul asked (9:5). But in that instant, he already knew the answer.

Luke, the author of Acts, doesn't tell us explicitly. But there are good reasons to believe that all the rage swirling in Paul's heart, all the zeal for tradition, all the ambition for a façade of purity were drowned in a sea of glorious light when Jesus spoke. We can tell that by Paul's response: "Lord" was more than a polite greeting. For Jews in his day, the term was regularly used to refer to God.[4]

In his blindness, Saul saw clearly. He had been on the wrong side. He had been fighting against the God he thought he loved. It seems the light from heaven knocked him to the ground—and to his senses.[5] With his question, Saul was, in effect, asking Jesus to do more than simply identify himself. He was pleading, "Confirm this for me, Lord."

Saul was rescued "from the domain of darkness and

transferred . . . to the kingdom of [God's] beloved Son" (Colossians 1:13). His blindness was only temporary, but his new sight permanent.

The Son of God had freed Saul, calling him to use every gift and ability at his disposal (plus a few new ones) to build up what he had once tried to tear down. Rather than stifling the good news of Jesus Christ, Saul poured out his life to become the gospel's greatest champion. Calling himself Paul—a name more at home in the Gentile world, where he would do most of his work—he zealously traveled from city to city, not to lock people up, but to set them free.

In his former life, Paul was a Pharisee. You may remember them from the Gospels, where they were usually the bad guys. The Pharisees were a first-century Jewish sect focused on outward purity and strict compliance with the law of Moses—and the myriad traditions that flowed from that law. The reason for this was simple. The Pharisees studied the Old Testament and saw how the sin and idolatry of their forefathers brought trouble to Israel time and time again: when the people turned from God, He withdrew His blessings. Eventually, God allowed the nation to be conquered and its people enslaved.

For the Pharisees, the solution to the problem of holiness was clear: get rid of all the sinners, or at least push them to the margins of society and shame them into compliance with the law. That's why the Pharisees were outraged when Jesus made it His common practice to eat and drink with this crowd—tax collectors, prostitutes, and the like (Matthew 9:10–11; Luke 15:1–2).

But Jesus knew the problem of sin is not merely a behavior issue. Sinful acts are symptoms of a brokenness that goes far deeper than what can be seen on the surface. That's why He warned:

> *"Woe to you, scribes and Pharisees, hypocrites! For you are like whitewashed tombs, which outwardly appear beautiful, but within are full of dead people's bones and*

all uncleanness. So you also outwardly appear righteous to others, but within you are full of hypocrisy and lawlessness" (MATTHEW 23:27–28).

The Pharisees had figured out how to fake it—how to look good on the outside while concealing the sin in their hearts. Even worse, as the self-appointed spiritual leaders in their communities, they didn't do a thing to help others struggling with sin—those people who weren't as good at masking their heart problems. Instead, the Pharisees added the weight of condemnation to their burden. This is what it meant to be a Pharisee, and Paul was one of them.

Until the day he met Jesus.

Following Jesus has never been about following rules. It's about a relationship with God, which is possible because Jesus dealt with the guilt and stain of our sin once and for all on the cross. Apart from Jesus, the best we can hope to be is Pharisees—people who have their act cleaned up on the outside. But when we're connected to Jesus, His goodness actually flows out of us. Jesus said, "I am the vine; you are the branches. If you remain in me and I in you, you will bear much fruit; apart from me you can do nothing" (John 15:5 NIV). Branches have no power to produce a harvest on their own, but when they are connected to the vine, they can produce rich, delicious fruit.

Today, there may no longer be a group identifying itself as Pharisees, but there are people living like Pharisees in every corner of the world. You may know several. You may be one now—or you may have been one in the past, just as I have. But Jesus came to free us from this slavery, this need to pretend we have it all together when we really don't.

Even Christians—some might say *especially* Christians—can succumb to the temptation. The good news seems just too good. *You mean God loves me the way I am? I don't have to wear this mask? But all my insecurities and struggles will be laid bare.*

To any who have ever felt this way, don't worry! Jesus

promises not to leave us in our weakness. He came to heal us of everything that robs us of His joy. Jesus said, "The thief comes only to steal and kill and destroy. I came that they may have life and have it abundantly" (John 10:10). This is the difference between the kingdom of the evil one and the kingdom of God.

Paul discovered the joy of no longer having to fake it. God's Spirit changed him from the inside out, and he became an agent of healing for the kingdom. He spread the same joy to everyone who saw the King's light aglow within him—to all who did not shy away.

This is the story God is writing today. It is the undoing of the domain of darkness as person by person discovers the light and passes along the joy of living in step with God's Spirit. It's the way life was meant to be lived all along, before the world was plunged into darkness.

YOUR LIFE IN THE STORY OF GOD

The Christian life—our role in God's story—is much more than just looking good on the outside. Through Jesus, God has "delivered us from the domain of darkness and transferred us to the kingdom of his beloved Son" (Colossians 1:13). Jesus brings light to our lives, a light that shines out from within us to others. We don't have to pretend we're okay—through Christ, we are good in God's eyes, and His Holy Spirit empowers our daily lives.

1. What was Jesus' complaint with the Pharisees (Matthew 23:27–28)? How does the Pharisees' attitude live on today?

2. Why did the apostle Paul consider himself the "chief" of sinners? How can his story encourage us as Christians today?

3. What illustration does Jesus use to depict our relationship to Him (John 15:5)? What is required for His goodness to flow through us?

FORMATION
God Makes Us More like Jesus

*"As God nurtures, protects,
prepares, and initiates us,
he restores us to the truth of who we are
and the reality of the life
we are living and meant to live."*
— STASI ELDREDGE

Like God

GENESIS 3:1–8

There is something magical about being the first one up and outside the morning after a snowstorm. I should know—I grew up in New England. On a snow day, creation seems to rest, curled up under a blanket of white—a blanket that covers over imperfections. It forgives neglected yards, while also hiding cracks in the sidewalk and potholes in the road. Everything is so pristine. So perfect. New. The world is full of possibilities.

But there is also a sadness to such a moment. Any step taken will punch a hole in the perfection. As children play, driveways are shoveled, and cars begin to take back the streets, white gives way to gray and brown. Winter wonderland's spell is broken, and the breathtaking panorama is transformed back into cold, slippery inconvenience. Once the world is in motion, there is no way to unbreak the snow, to see it again as it was in those first moments of early morning. Any progress into the day mars the landscape. Every step taken is a step away from that initial state of peace.

This is how I used to think about the garden of Eden—as a state of perfection that was to be maintained, kept, and protected. When Adam and Eve sinned, they failed in that responsibility. They made footprints in the snow, allowing for the pollution of the world in grays and browns.

As an analogy, I think this is helpful—up to a point. Fresh snow does carry with it a sense of unspoiled newness. But I've come to believe that when we see perfection in the early chapters of Genesis, we're reading something into God's story that just isn't there.

Sinless? Yes. Joyful? Certainly. Good? Without a doubt. But perfect? I'm not so sure.

God's plan had always been for human beings to work the soil in order to grow crops for food (Genesis 2:5). And as we've already explored in an earlier chapter, the Lord invited our first parents to join in the ongoing work of creation, to "be fruitful and multiply and fill the earth and subdue it" (Genesis 1:28). There was, apparently, room for improvement.

God never intended for the world to remain static. We should expect this though. A world without change—without surprises or new adventures—would be boring. God's goodness is better than that.

But what about Adam and Eve? Were they perfect before sin invaded the Garden? It can be tempting, from our vantage point, to answer yes. And it would be understandable. Adam and Eve enjoyed a level of holiness that none of us has yet experienced. They knew God and were known by Him without interruption. Their worship was pure, focused solely on their Maker. Their love was free of selfish motives. They had what we all now long for, even if we don't recognize the source of those longings.

Being sinless, however, is not the same as being perfect.[1] Just as the plants of the garden sprouted and flowered with water, sunshine, and cultivation, there was also room for growth in Adam and Eve. I realize the Bible doesn't explicitly tell us this, but I draw this conclusion from a reliable case study.

Luke 2:52 makes this shocking claim: "Jesus grew in wisdom and stature, and in favor with God and man" (NIV). Have you ever thought about that? Jesus grew in wisdom, and He grew in favor with God the Father. At least at this point in His earthly life, there was still wisdom and favor to be gained. If this was true of Jesus, God's one and only Son, it would certainly be true of Adam and Eve.

I bring up this issue of perfection because I've heard a horrible rumor about holiness. It's important, at the outset of these short chapters on becoming more like Jesus, that we set the record straight: *holiness is not the same thing as having every-thing figured out.* Even as I write those words, I feel a weight lifting from my shoulders.

Somewhere along the way, many of us got the idea that to be holy is to have arrived at the summit of a great mountain—there is nowhere left to travel and nowhere to look but down. Maybe that's because we've known people with an air of holiness about them, people who seem to have it all together. But they may also seem more sanctimonious than sanctified, and sometimes we fear they *are* looking down—on the rest of us who stumble along the rocky, steep mountain path.

But this is miles removed from the holiness God wants for His people.

Programmed for Holiness

By now, you can probably tell that I love to explore the places in God's story where we are pressed to ask questions. These are the verses that, at first glance, appear to reveal inconsistencies in Scripture, or seem out of place, or don't quite square with our personal experience in this world. These are often the passages where skeptics report "weak spots" in the Bible. But I've found that these are the places where God speaks deep truth, if only we will pause, reflect, pray, and listen. And, at times, we may need to dig for it.

One of these passages comes in the early chapters of Genesis, during Eve's temptation. Satan, disguised as a serpent, offers the forbidden fruit and tells the first woman, "God knows that when you eat of it your eyes will be opened, and *you will be like God*, knowing good and evil" (3:5). The devil promised Eve that in eating the fruit she would become like God. But this should not have been a great incentive to sin: remember, Eve was already like God, having been created in His image (Genesis 1:27).

Satan appears like a salesman trying to peddle air condition-ers in the arctic or flood insurance in the Atacama Desert. Still, he made the sale—so he must have been on to something.

Within each one of us, God has placed a desire for more of himself—to know Him better, to be with Him, and to be like Him. This is not like the unmet desires we have because of sin— our need for joy, for wholeness, for love, and so on. This desire is sacred, it predates the fall, and it remains even when it is met. C. S. Lewis put it this way:

> *God made us: invented us as a man invents an engine. A car is made to run on petrol, and it would not run properly on anything else. Now God designed the human machine to run on Himself. He Himself is the fuel our spirits were designed to burn, or the food our spirits were designed to feed on. There is no other.*[2]

For Adam and Eve, this hunger for God came from a place of fullness rather than lack. Satan knew that if he could tap into their good desire and twist it, he'd have a snare that could hook our first parents. But Satan did not create the desire; God did.

Too often we think of holiness as a chore, a task that must be done (and is never done) but is nonetheless ours. "Becoming like Jesus" means a sort of living purgatory, in which we are purified through discomfort and self-denial. But this episode in the garden shows that this is not the case. Growth toward God and with God—growing to be like God—is part of what it means to be human, deep down at the core. The path of holiness is, in fact, a gift.

Do you know that first cup of coffee in the morning? How in that initial sip everything in the world seems right, if only for as long as it takes the coffee to slide past your back teeth? Imagine if every sip was like that, and the experience never got old. Or what about that first bite of a mouthwatering cheeseburger when you haven't eaten all day? Think how good and inviting that moment is, especially knowing there is more burger to be enjoyed. Now imagine if every bite were more delicious than the last, satisfying in itself but bringing with it a craving for the next. These are my less-than-perfect analogies to describe the ongoing pleasure of walking with God. But the Bible has its own illustration.

In Psalm 36, David wrote, "For with you [God] is the fountain of life" (v. 9). In Jeremiah, God referred to himself as "the fountain of living waters" (2:13; compare with 17:13). In the New Testament, Jesus picked up this language and described the Holy Spirit as "a spring of water welling up to eternal life" (John 4:14). The water from a fountain or a spring is constantly on the move. There is no chance for stagnation. A person can drink, drink again, and drink some more without the water running low, and be refreshed.

Just as there's never a point in life when water becomes unnecessary for survival, there will never be a moment when we've had our fill of God. As we grow closer to God, we find new levels of joy in Him. He fills our hearts even as our desire for Him grows stronger. Walking in holiness—walking in close step with God—is the furthest thing from a life of punishment.

Jesus came not only to save us *from* our sin; He also came to save us *to* a life of holiness. It's in our DNA, since we were made to be like our Creator. The gospel frees us to get back to this life of holiness, to continue where Adam and Eve dropped the ball back in the garden.

Because Jesus paid the penalty for our sins on the cross, we can have peace with God. We can walk closely with Him once again. We can become like Him, more and more so with each passing day—not to prove our worth, not to earn our way, and not as a condition of our salvation. It's just who we are meant to be in the story God is writing.

YOUR LIFE IN THE STORY OF GOD

Within each person, God has placed a desire for more of himself. And unlike our other human desires, this one can be fulfilled perfectly—the more we get of God, the more we want, and the more we want, the more we get. This is called holiness. In a sense it takes us back to the garden of Eden, walking and talking with God like Adam and Eve did before their sin. We actually become like God, more and more with each passing day.

1. What things or activities do you find most fulfilling? How completely do they satisfy?

2. How does a desire for God differ from our desire for other things?

3. Think of the common biblical picture of God mentioned in this chapter—flowing water (Psalm 36:9, Jeremiah 2:13, John 4:14). How does that image relate to our quest for holiness?

The Secret to Holiness

JOB 1:1–2:10

After his great aunt Ruby passed away, Michael Rorrer had the unenviable job of putting her worldly possessions in order—cleaning her home and figuring out what to toss and what to keep. In the basement, Rorrer found a treasure, though he didn't realize it at the time.

This treasure consisted of a neatly stacked collection of old comic books that had once belonged to Ruby's late husband, Billy, Michael's great uncle. The nostalgia of the decades-old comics certainly qualified them as *cool*, but that was all Michael Rorrer thought of the stack—that is, until sometime later when he thumbed through the pile at home and noticed a copy of *Action Comics* No. 1, which contains the first-ever appearance of Superman. In the mix there was also a *Batman* No. 1, as well as *Captain America* No. 2 from 1941, in which the superhero confronts Adolf Hitler.

Rorrer had in his hands the kind of comic collection that die-hard fans can only dream of. In early 2012, he sold most of the collection for $3.5 million. What was once a stack of Uncle Billy's old comics, just taking up space in a basement closet, was actually a family fortune.[3]

I like this story, and not only because I had childhood fantasies of coming across such a find. I also like the story because it illustrates the importance of proper labels.

When this was just a pile of old comic books in a basement in the suburbs, it was considered worthless. But as one of the rarest collections of golden-age comic books in existence, its true value comes through. And so it is with people: when we come to understand that all human beings were created in the image of God, we see their real worth in God's eyes. When we come to know Jesus Christ personally and are adopted as sons and daughters into God's family, we can comprehend divine love in a way that simply wasn't possible before. Labels matter.

And because they matter, labels offer Satan a favorite line of accusation.

With Friends like These

In what is likely the earliest-written book of the Bible, Satan challenged Job's reputation as a man who was "blameless and upright, one who feared God and turned away from evil" (Job 1:1). The devil's complaint was that the label God gave Job hadn't been tested; anyone, he argued, can be good and love God if all God ever does is bless that person.

So Satan pressed the Lord: "Stretch out your hand and touch all that he has, and he will curse you to your face" (1:11). Satan was willing to bet that if Job were put to the test, his label would peel right off.

God knew his faithful servant's devotion was the real thing, so He allowed the devil access to Job—and Satan took Job's wealth, his family, and even his health. Righteous Job was left to suffer, sitting in a pile of ashes, scraping his head-to-toe sores with a piece of broken pottery in a futile attempt to find relief from the itching.

But he never cursed God. Job refused to do that, despite the counsel of his wife and the incessant pecking of his so-called friends, who pushed him to admit that God was punishing him for some secret sin.

These friends of Job's were the religious type. They believed that God was perfectly holy and perfectly just, and in that regard they were spot on—as orthodox as they come. But the friends took those truths to the next step. And then they tripped over that step.

Job's friends believed that if someone was suffering, he must deserve it. God wouldn't allow otherwise. There was no room in their theology for the brokenness of this world or the reality of dark spiritual powers working behind the scenes. And there certainly wasn't room for the thought that God, in His wisdom, might allow something tragic in order to bring about greater good.

This type of thinking gives Satan much of his strength. Job didn't have to curse God and remove the label of righteousness himself; his friends were happy to do that for him. What should have been an opportunity for love and compassion became an occasion of judgment and shame.

Job wasn't sinless, and he never claimed to be (see Job 6:3; 7:21; 9:2, 28; 19:20), but he could be called righteous because he trusted in God and lived out that trust every day of his life. You and I aren't sinless either, though we can be declared righteous because of the price Jesus paid on the cross.

But that's where Satan comes in. His barbs of condemnation are a common feature in the Christian life, and often we don't need friends to accuse us; we do it to ourselves with a little help from the enemy. When we've messed up, or we're faced with a temptation that's hard to resist, we might hear a thought that says, *God doesn't really love you. How could He?* or *Are you even a Christian? How could someone who trusts Jesus do something like that?*

That's not God speaking; that's the enemy. He is the accuser of God's people (Revelation 12:10). And that's why God tells us to put on our spiritual armor, including "the shield of faith, with which you can extinguish all the flaming darts of the evil one" (Ephesians 6:16).

The shield of faith is the right tool for the task because it takes faith to believe God's good promises. If we were to rely on what we can see with our eyes, we would have no choice but to agree with Satan. Based on the physical evidence, he's right: We do sin, no matter how mature we are in our faith. We are not perfectly holy, as God declares we are in Christ. We make sinful choices and bow down before the false gods of money, success, comfort, security, or a million other things. And we routinely choose the good thing in front of us rather than the best thing that comes from the hand of our Father. Faith is required to rest in God's love, and it is by abiding in that love, through faith, that we resist the evil one.

The gospel is a declaration that God loved us "while we were still sinners" (Romans 5:8). But the good news doesn't stop there. God doesn't want to leave us that way: "For those whom he foreknew he also predestined *to be conformed to the image of his Son*, in order that he might be the firstborn among many brothers" (Romans 8:29; emphasis added). In short, God wants to make us more like Jesus.

Many people, when they hear this, feign excitement. The prospect of a holy life sounds about as pleasing as a prolonged tax audit. There may even be some who are honest enough to ask what difference holiness makes. After all, if a person is saved and going to heaven when they die, why does it matter how little or how much that person sins here on earth?

That cynical idea misses the point of holiness.

Salvation without sanctification (the process through which God makes us holy) would be like a judge overturning a conviction on paper but doing nothing to free the prisoner—at least not while he's alive. Or like a generous benefactor paying a sick person's hospital bill while that person nears death but not offering him the cure for his disease. At the moment of salvation, God declares us to be saints ("holy ones"), and just as it was when God spoke creation into being, His words birth the reality of this declaration in our lives. Through the process of sanctification, He forms us into what He already says we are.

Some people's eyes glaze over at the mention of holiness because they've come to think of holy living as merely a set of rules, as certain things they must do and others they should never do. Commandments and statutes are helpful in restraining evil, up to a point, but they will never produce true godliness. Laws are a measuring rod, and (spoiler alert) we never measure up.

But walking in step with God is another thing entirely. This type of holiness—real, genuine, deep-down-in-your-soul holiness—frees us from the condemnation of ourselves and others, because it looks outward to God and to other people. It's not about measuring up at all; it's about becoming more like Jesus, and the closer we get to Him, the more beautiful and fulfilling life becomes.

Rules ask the question, "What am I doing wrong?" You can almost hear the enemy's accusations coming. But falling in love with God's heart brings wholeness and makes obedience a joy. And that joy spurs on more obedience, and more joy.

■ ■ ■

Clues from the book of Job tell us its title character was a Gentile and that he didn't have access to the Old Testament law.[4] This has always amazed me about Job's story: he pleased God without having a set of written rules to follow.

Job knew what good to do because he knew God. His holiness flowed from years spent close to God's heart. Take it from Job himself: "My foot has held fast to his steps; I have kept his way and have not turned aside. I have not departed from the commandment of his lips; I have treasured the words of his mouth more than my portion of food" (Job 23:11–12). Keep in mind that when Job said these things, there was no Bible—not a single page. "The commandments of his lips" and "the words of his mouth" were not the Scriptures; they were part of the intimate relationship Job enjoyed with God, talking with and listening to his Creator.

I believe one of the greatest tragedies in the church today is that millions of people believe embarking on a holy life is a burden, just the cost of being saved that was somehow hidden in the fine print. If following Jesus were the same as following a bunch of rules, this attitude would be justified. But God's story isn't written that way.

We weren't saved from the condemnation of our sins only

to be condemned to a long list of impersonal commandments. Becoming like Jesus isn't supposed to be drudgery. If your journey toward holiness feels more like slavery than freedom, you can be sure it's not the path God wants you on. That's not how He does things.

Jesus said, "My yoke is easy, and my burden is light" (Matthew 11:30). Difficulties in this life are a certainty, but Jesus does not put rocks in our backpacks to weigh us down.

Remember Uncle Billy's comic book collection? It had tremendous value because of the exorbitant price someone was willing to pay for it. Now think of the price God paid for you. He loves you that much, and He wants to spend time with you. In those moments and hours of togetherness, more of God is the goal; holiness is the byproduct.

Job lived long before Christ, and long before God's story was recorded in the Bible. But he trusted that God loved him, that God would not let sin overtake him or allow the accusations of his friends to stand. In the midst of tremendous pain—physical, emotional, and spiritual—Job still had the strength of spirit to declare, "I know that my Redeemer lives, and at the last he will stand upon the earth" (Job 19:25).

Somehow, Job knew that God would take it upon himself to redeem him from the curse of sin and its punishment—and that God would silence his critics in the end. Amazingly, Job had foresight to understand that God would "stand upon the earth," as Jesus did.

No matter what befell Job, he kept talking to God, waiting on God, and trusting God. It's what separated him from the crowd. It's the secret to developing godly character.

YOUR LIFE IN THE STORY OF GOD

Becoming like Jesus isn't supposed to be drudgery. Holiness isn't living up to a set of rules; it's falling in love with God, finding a wholeness that makes obedience a joy. That was the experience of Job, who was "righteous" not by his knowledge and following of Scripture (it didn't yet exist) but by his close relationship with God. As we talk to God, wait on Him, and trust Him, we live out the story He has written for His children.

1. How did Job and his friends differ in their view of God? Why was Job called "blameless and upright" (Job 1:1)?

2. What is God's goal for those who follow Jesus (Romans 8:29)? What role do rules play in this pursuit?

3. How did God prove His love for people (Romans 5:8)? What does that say about the value you have to God?

DAY 29

Set Apart for Good(ness)

RUTH 2

Have you heard that it is illegal for citizens of Milan, Italy, to frown in public? Exceptions are made for hospital visits and funerals, but smiles are required everywhere else. Or what about this one? In Canada, the law requires one out of every five songs broadcast on the radio to be sung by a Canadian. Or this one? In the state of Victoria, Australia, light bulbs must be changed by a certified electrician under penalty of fine. And in Switzerland, it is illegal to flush a toilet in an apartment complex after ten o'clock p.m.

There is good reason to doubt the validity of some of these "laws." For example, I'm not sure how the Canadian radio law is enforced. Is it someone's job to listen to the radio all day and make sure Justin Bieber gets his airtime? Still, they get repeated as true and valid, and many people believe them to be so. But whether these strange laws are real or a hoax, most would agree that when lived out in the real world, they make little sense.

Now what if I told you of a place where it was illegal to eat lobster—and if you did, you'd need to wash your clothes and other people would have to stay away from you all day? It's true. In this same place, it would be against the law to wear anything made of 50 percent cotton and 50 percent polyester. And if you were a wheat farmer, you couldn't drive your combine in a straight line to the edges of your property—you had to leave the corners of your field shaggy with wheat.

These laws are real, and they're from Leviticus, the third book of the Old Testament—or as some people have come to think of it, the book that single-handedly destroys New Year's resolutions to read through the Bible in a year.

Leviticus is full of strange, seemingly arbitrary laws that governed the people of ancient Israel. Alongside well-known and more universally accepted laws against crimes like theft and murder (Leviticus 19:11; 24:17), there are prohibitions against eating shellfish (11:9–12), using two different fabrics to make a single item of clothing (19:19), and harvesting the corners of your fields (19:9). These laws might seem haphazard to us, but that is only because we are separated from them by thousands of years.

Though God doesn't always spell out the rationale behind each law in the pages of Scripture, every one was given for a reason. For many, we are left to speculate. Take, for example, the law against blended fabrics (Leviticus 19:19). It's hard to figure out what this one is all about. What moral issue was God trying to address? No one is hurt by wearing a garment made of two materials, and apart from knowing that doing so would be a violation of the law itself, it doesn't trigger the conscience.

But if you were to read through all the Old Testament laws carefully, you'd notice that the only time mixed fabrics are mentioned is in reference to the tabernacle and the priesthood (see Exodus 26:1, 31; 28:6, 15; 39:29). It appears that with this law, God was illustrating to the people of Israel that there should be a distinction between the holy and the common. As part of the legal code meant specifically for God's people, Israel, laws like this don't apply to believers today. But the principle behind it—the importance of living a life set apart for God—remains.

Many Bible scholars see three types of laws in the Old Testament: moral, ceremonial, and civil. Moral laws are those that transcend culture and remain in force for people today, such as the commandments against murder and adultery. Ceremonial laws have to do with the festivals, the priesthood, and the sacrificial system of ancient Israel. And civil laws are those that governed the nation of Israel as a theocratic monarchy.

While these categories are helpful, the laws in the Old Testament are not presented in neat divisions. There's no one section of moral laws, another of ceremonial, and a third of civil laws. They're often mixed together. There is also some overlap, and always an underlying principle that supersedes the letter of the law. We can't simply ignore the commands that seem odd to us.

The Law at Work

Some laws were designed to help the people of ancient Israel avoid the idolatry of their neighbors. Others were meant to be a reflection of heaven, showing the world and the Israelites themselves the goodness of the Lord.

This is the case with the commandment to leave the corners of a field alone at harvest time (Leviticus 19:9). God didn't want landowners to take every last bit of their crop. Instead, He wanted them to leave some of the field's produce for the poor. Anyone who was in need could take from these leftovers and provide for herself and her family.

■ ■ ■

We see the goodness of this commandment on display in the lives of Ruth and Boaz. Their story takes place during the time of the judges—after the people of God had entered the land of Israel but before they had asked God to place a king over them. "In those days there was no king in Israel. Everyone did what was right in his own eyes" (Judges 17:6). This meant that many people were not following the commandments of God. Some acted justly, and others selfishly. Some men sought peace, while others looked to gain strength through violence. It was a scary time to be vulnerable—and that's just what Ruth was.

Ruth was a widow and a Gentile. Her connection to the land of Israel came through her late husband and through her mother-in-law, Naomi, whom she followed home after they were both widowed in Moab. She didn't have to do this; Ruth could have returned to her own family and remarried, since she was still young (Ruth 1:11–13). But she loved Naomi and told her, "Your people shall be my people, and your God my God" (1:16). The two women arrived in Bethlehem together, though without men in the family to protect and provide for them, life was not easy. But Ruth found relief in Boaz's field.

Boaz was a righteous man, one who followed the laws of God. He instructed his workers not to harvest every last bit of the barley crop, but to leave some for men and women in need. So, as Ruth gleaned grain behind Boaz's servants, she discovered firsthand the kindness of the Lord. In His commandments, He had thought of people just like her. In Boaz's field, Ruth was able to collect enough food to sustain herself and Naomi each day.

But it was a different commandment from the book of Leviticus that provided lasting help for Ruth and her mother-in-law: "If your brother becomes poor and sells part of his property, then his nearest redeemer shall come and redeem what his brother has sold" (Leviticus 25:25). God knew that without any restriction on buying and selling land, in just a few short generations a handful of successful families would own most of the territory in the Promised Land. To stop this from happening, God set up a system in which all land had to be returned to its original owner every fiftieth, or Jubilee, year (Leviticus 25:8–17). In addition, God created a provision for a close relative, or a "kinsman-redeemer," to buy back land sold during a time of great need. Boaz, as it turned out, was a relative of Naomi's husband—and he was eligible to be her redeemer. More importantly, he was a godly man. He married Ruth and saved the family.

■ ■ ■

The laws of the Old Testament reveal God's character. He is just, so His laws are just. He cares for the poor—the orphan, the widow, and the sojourner—so His law code has special rules designed to help ease their suffering. He hates sin, so acts of rebellion carry a heavy weight. And He is holy, so God's laws set His people apart from the rest of the world so that they, too, might be holy. These rules and commandments are the corrective words of a loving Father speaking to a world of chaos and revolt.

I don't know about you, but when I read through portions of the Old Testament law, I'm thankful I wasn't born an Israelite in the years BC. There were a lot of rules, a lot of places where one could slip and fall. Just the thought of it feels like a weight on my shoulders.

But that seems to have been largely the point. The apostle Paul wrote, "I would not have known what sin was had it not been for the law" (Romans 7:7 NIV). The commandments make us aware of our sin—and our desperate need of a Savior. And that is a very good thing.

It's this purpose of the law that has led many Christians to dismiss it, as if now that we have Christ, the law is no longer God's Word. But Jesus himself said:

> *"Do not think that I have come to abolish the Law or the Prophets; I have not come to abolish them but to fulfill them. For truly, I say to you, until heaven and earth pass away, not an iota, not a dot, will pass from the Law until all is accomplished"* (MATTHEW 5:17–18).

God is not done with the Law. It has been fulfilled in Christ, which means that its requirements have been met and its purpose of pointing people to Him has been accomplished. But it has another purpose, one that will remain "until heaven and earth pass away": to be a faithful revelation of God's character.

On this side of the cross, we who live God's story tend to have a complicated relationship with the Old Testament Law. It seems foreign and strict, strange and, at times, bloody. But it is for our good. While we don't have to worry about the edges of our fields, we are still called to provide for those in need. A snack of crab cakes will not make us unclean, but an unchecked heart, out of step with God's Spirit, will.

The commandments of the Old Testament—even those

meant specifically for ancient Israel—give us an opportunity to look back on Christ's sacrifice, breathe a sigh of relief, and respond with gratitude. Jesus completed it all; Jesus paid it all.

The law, therefore, need not be a source of condemnation. Rather, it can be a means of stepping toward holiness. It can be an encouragement, an occasion to see God's goodness on display. That's what it became in the life of Ruth when she discovered that God had provided for her in the written code of her late husband's ancestors. Little did she know that Jesus, a greater Kinsman-Redeemer, would come from her family line (Matthew 1:5). He would obey the law perfectly in order to save her—and us—from a death sentence.

YOUR LIFE IN THE STORY OF GOD

The Old Testament law contains both moral rules that apply to all people at all times and civil and ceremonial codes that were specific to the ancient Israelites. But all of the law reveals God's character, and is therefore helpful to us as Christians in understanding the roles we play in His story. God's law for us is not a source of condemnation, but a means of advancing in holiness.

1. What are some examples of moral rules in the Old Testament law? What are some examples of civil or ceremonial rules?

2. How does the Old Testament law reveal God's character? How can it help us to grow in holiness?

3. What did Jesus say He came to do with the law (Matthew 5:17–18)? What does that mean to us, who live "on this side of the cross"?

The Return to Faith

PSALM 51

Across the Valley of Elah, David saw Goliath's nine-foot, six-inch frame planted firmly in place, sword in hand, waiting for him to come near. But David did not. He chose to fight from a distance, and not with a sword as Goliath expected, but with his sling.

David could probably get one clean shot before Goliath realized what was happening. If the stone wasn't a direct hit, Goliath would be on the move, barreling toward him, ready to slice him open and end the fight. If David had time to fire off a second stone, he would have the more difficult task of hitting a moving target. He had to get it right the first time.

It wasn't the odds that led David to meet Goliath that day; they certainly weren't in his favor. Nor was it his skill with a sling, impressive as that was. And he wasn't there in hopes of looking good to King Saul; God had already promised David the throne one day. David was in that valley, staring down a giant of a man, for one simple reason: he had faith in God.

For forty days, Goliath had taunted Israel. "I defy the armies of Israel!" he would shout (1 Samuel 17:10 NIV). But when David listened to Goliath's trash talk, he heard something different, so he asked, "Who is this uncircumcised Philistine, that he should defy the armies *of the living God*?" (v. 26, emphasis added). A challenge to the people of God was no different than a challenge to God himself, so David had faith to believe that God would see him through the battle to victory. The win would be God's: "The LORD," David told Saul, "will deliver me from the hand of this Philistine" (v. 37).

It's one of the most famous stories ever told, and you already know how it ends. God does deliver David, whose stone lands a direct hit in the center of Goliath's forehead. The giant falls to the ground, face first. David runs to him, but without a sword to kill Goliath, he uses the Philistine's own heavy blade to remove his head from his body.

I imagine an experience like this would stick with a person, that a win of this magnitude would make an indelible impression on your life's journey. Whatever future struggles you faced, whatever challenges or tests, having this moment of unthinkable victory burned into your memory would be fuel for more faith. Remembering the surging adrenaline and the sound of cheering crowds, you could stand—no matter how large your enemy—knowing that God would come through again and deliver you.

For much of David's life, this appeared to be the case. The years that followed were difficult, as shortly after the fight with Goliath, Saul grew jealous, became somewhat unhinged, and sought to kill David. The giant-slayer found himself on the run. He hid out in caves (1 Samuel 22:1) and even pretended to be crazy in order to find temporary refuge in the land of the Philistines (1 Samuel 21:10–15).[5] But David survived and demonstrated enough reliance on God to spare Saul's life on two occasions (1 Samuel 24:1–22; 26:1–25).

Then, once David became king, there were all the challenges that came with establishing his realm and expanding the borders of Israel. But David proved himself to be a man of incredible faith and resilience, battle after battle. That is, until one day when he found himself staring across another valley of sorts—the kind between houses in the city of Jerusalem.

David was walking along the roof of his palace when he saw that he wasn't alone above the city. Not far away, Bathsheba, the wife of Uriah, one of David's "mighty men" (2 Samuel 23:8, 39), was taking a bath on her roof. While that might sound strange to us today, bathing on one's rooftop was common in the cities of David's day.[6]

What was not common, however, was for a king to be at home while his troops were fighting to expand his kingdom. It was springtime, so David was supposed to be at the front, alongside his men in battle—but he had decided to take a break from war. Nevertheless, whether he realized it or not, he *was* in a battle, and it turned out to be one of the most difficult of his life.

King David, the man who was said to have killed tens of thousands in combat (1 Samuel 18:7; 21:11), was taken out by the sinful desires of his own heart. In the crucial moment, at the sight of a beautiful woman, he put down the shield of faith and was picked off by "the flaming darts" of the enemy (Ephesians 6:16). Looking at Bathsheba became lust. Lust gave way to an abuse of his power as king. Then lies and murder followed—all because David, at every point along the way, abandoned his trust in God.[7]

The passage that follows this episode makes it clear that David was responsible for his actions. God, speaking through Nathan the prophet, said to the king, "Why have you despised the word of the LORD, to do what is evil in his sight? You have struck down Uriah the Hittite with the sword and have taken his wife to be your wife and have killed him with the sword of the Ammonites" (2 Samuel 12:9).

In a short time, David committed a list of atrocities. He had Bathsheba brought to his palace. He slept with her. When she revealed she was pregnant, David ordered Uriah home from battle so he could sleep with his wife and be tricked into believing the child on the way was his. But Uriah refused even to cross the threshold of his home while his brothers in arms endured the hardships of war, so David sent him back, ordered him to the front lines, and made the other troops pull back. Uriah was a sitting duck. And David had blood on his hands.

All this is true. But there was much more going on in those hours, days, and weeks.

The Sin before the Sin

The apostle Paul, writing to Christians in ancient Rome, said, "Whatever does not proceed from faith is sin" (Romans 14:23).

Paul was addressing issues related to food sold in the market-places of Rome and the celebration of certain holy days, neither of which are particularly relevant to our understanding of David's sin with Bathsheba. However, Paul unearths a universal principle in this passage that speaks directly to David's sin, as well as yours and mine.

"Whatever does not proceed from faith is sin." At first, this sounds crazy, as if your choice of breakfast cereal might offend God if it comes from a place of hunger rather than devotion. But Paul is hitting on something fundamental to all of life, an idea that goes beyond breakfast cereals, food sacrificed to idols, and even lust and murder. That idea is this: we were designed to live with a permanent connection to God. That's why Jesus said we are to live as branches connected to a vine (John 15:1–11). Jesus is the vine. Good fruit will grow if we remain in Him, but sin will take over if our connection to the vine is broken. Jesus was describing active faith.

Think of any sin recorded in Scripture. Think of any sin you've committed today, this week, or at some point in your life. What do they all have in common? They were all birthed in moments when faith was lacking, when the branch lost its connection to the vine. Trust in God would have kept David from allowing a look to become lust. If he had invited a heart check from God in that moment, he would have seen that the momentary pleasure he was contemplating could not compare with the good things that come from God's hand. Faith would not only have brought God's commandments to mind, but also all the times in David's life when God saw him through. He would have seen the sin he was contemplating the way that God sees it: as ugly, twisted, and heartbreaking. In a word, as *death*. True faith would have choked the sin growing in David's heart before it produced its poisonous fruit.

David learned all of this the hard way, when it was too late. But one of the blessings we enjoy, finding ourselves in such a late chapter in God's story, is that we can benefit from all those who have gone before us. Thankfully, we have David's prayer of repentance recorded in the Psalms:

> *Have mercy on me, O God, according to your steadfast love; according to your abundant mercy blot out my transgressions. Wash me thoroughly from my iniquity, and cleanse me from my sin! . . . Create in me a clean heart, O God, and renew a right spirit within me. Cast me not away from your presence, and take not your Holy Spirit from me. Restore to me the joy of your salvation, and uphold me with a willing spirit* (PSALM 51:1–2, 10–12).

Repentance is not a promise to try harder. It's not an excuse for sin. It's not a way of making a deal with God. To repent, biblically speaking, is to agree with God. About everything. It's agreeing that sin is sin. It's agreeing that His commandments are good and just. It's agreeing that our sins carry a hefty price tag. It's agreeing that He is the only source of true life. And it's agreeing that He is good and merciful to sinners.

There is no halfway repentance. For a believer, repentance is coming back to faith, reestablishing a lost connection with the Lord. That's what David gave voice to in Psalm 51.

He lived about a thousand years before Jesus, but it was Jesus' death on the cross that made David's prayer of repentance possible. In turning to God, David agreed with Him on everything. David came clean about his sin. He acknowledged the weight of his guilt. But he also came into agreement with God about His mercy. "Wash me, and I shall be whiter than snow," David prayed (v. 7), but this prayer would have been utterly meaningless if Jesus never came to lay down His life for David—and us—on the cross.

The life of holiness is a life of repentance. I know; that sounds horrible, as if there is nothing more for a Christian to do than wallow in the misery of his sin. We should mourn over our sin, as God does. But there is much more to repentance than that.

And if we get stuck in our sorrow, it may be that we have missed the good news.

Several years ago, when Laurin and I were engaged, we read a marriage book together. The author focused on the reality of marrying another sinner and the need to be prepared for such a potentially volatile union. At one point while we were reading, Laurin turned to me and asked somewhat facetiously, "This guy knows our sin has been paid for, right?" It has, and our constant, daily connection with Jesus makes it possible to put sin to death and bear good fruit in this life. The life of holiness is a life of repentance, because it's in repentance that we reestablish faith for the big things and the seemingly little things. It's where we check our connection with God and make any necessary repairs.

Remember that God's story is about God. He is at the center of Scripture, the center of history, the center of what we mistakenly refer to as our "own" lives. Sin tricks us into thinking we can recast the role we have been given, get the part we really want, and make the story all about us. But God is good—in His story, there is life and victory and joy. It's in repentance that we find our way home again.

YOUR LIFE IN THE STORY OF GOD

Though we each play our own roles, God's story is all about God. Like the ancient King David, when we try to make the story about ourselves, we sin. But also like David, we can turn to God in repentance. Agreeing with God that sin is sin, and that He is good and merciful, keeps us connected to the vine, as Jesus described himself.

1. What was the progression of David's behavior that brought him to the point of committing sin with Bathsheba and having her husband killed? What lessons does his story offer for us?

2. What exactly is "repentance"? What did David do to return to his good relationship to God (Psalm 51)?

3. How does repentance keep us connected to Jesus, like branches to a vine (John 15:1–11)? What happens when the branches have a healthy connection to the vine?

The Deeper Law

MATTHEW 5:17–48

As host Peter Tomarken greeted contestants for that day's fifth episode taping of *Press Your Luck*, there was the usual banter and congenial good wishes one expects in the opening minutes of a daytime television game show. Michael Larson, the first of two players challenging the current champion, said he wanted to win enough money that he could stop driving his ice cream truck during the summer months back in Ohio. Tomarken made a joke about eating too much ice cream, offered Larson his customary "Best of luck," and moved on to the next contestant.

Larson smiled. He had more than luck on his side. Before the day was over, he would cheat the show out of tens of thousands of dollars—and get away with it.

Press Your Luck worked like this: Contestants would compete to answer trivia questions. Correct answers earned them spins around an electronic game board. The "spin" part of the game was where contestants could earn their winnings, since most of the tiles contained cash, prizes, or extra spins. But there was one hazard to spinning: the board also contained Whammies, animated creatures that would appear on the screen to wreak havoc on a person's accumulated earnings. If a contestant landed on a Whammy, he or she would forfeit all winnings for the game. Players had to know when to stop, or they risked losing everything.

While watching taped episodes of the show with his home VCR, Larson had discovered a secret. The Whammies' appearances on the board were not random, as most people assumed—there was a pattern. Larson surmised that contestants who timed their "stops" correctly could avoid the rally-ending Whammies altogether. So for hours each day, over the course of six months, he set about learning the complicated pattern, committing it to memory. From his recliner, Larson practiced hitting the big money, using the pause button on his remote control.

Soon after, he got the opportunity to try his technique before a live studio audience, and in June 1984, CBS aired a two-part episode that featured Larson walking away with more than $110,000 in cash. His turn lasted so long that it could not be edited down to a single show.

Since no one had ever won that much cash on *Press Your Luck* before, CBS investigated the anomaly and discovered Larson's trick. But in the end, the network let Larson keep the money he had won. Technically speaking, they concluded, he hadn't cheated; the rules did not forbid a player from memorizing the pattern of the game board to avoid elimination.

A short time later, though, producers of *Press Your Luck* retooled the board so that its pattern was truly random. No one else would be able to use Michael Larson's strategy to beat the Whammies.

He may have followed the letter of the law, but he had obliterated its spirit. Larson focused on the rules, changing his strategy to fit what he saw. But that wasn't how the game was meant to be played, and I'm all but certain his fellow contestants weren't impressed by Larson's ability to "play by the rules." Once he got control of the board, they lost theirs for good.

The Christian life is not a game, yet many people think they can "win" by closely following the letter of the law. When we focus on mere outward morality, behavior modification *will* happen. But there is a cost to "playing the game well," following the rules while ignoring their spirit.

A person can look moral and upright on the outside, but if that's all she's concerned about, the seemingly more acceptable sins—the kind that are less easily spotted, like pride, gossip, and unchecked anger—may go untouched. Another person might hide his struggles from fellow believers in Christ for the sake of appearing to have it all together. That's how he perceives the game is won. Still another wants to be the critic who remains backstage while the action takes place, speaking up only to dispense judgment rather than grace when a brother or sister falls.

It's no wonder people fake it in church. And it's no wonder so many Christians prefer to come up with a personal sin management system for playing the game rather than fighting for true holiness.

But, thankfully, Jesus came to set us free from this whole mess.

Jesus, the Dishwasher

In the Sermon on the Mount (Matthew 5–7), Jesus did something extraordinary. Several times He cited some part of the Old Testament Law—"You have heard that it was said to the people long ago, 'You shall not murder' . . . 'You shall not commit adultery' . . . 'Love your neighbor and hate your enemy'"—before He said, "But *I* tell you . . ." (Matthew 5:21–22, 27–28, 43–44 NIV, emphasis added).

Rabbis often used a method like this in their teaching. It was a way of explaining God's commands, similar to a preacher today reading a Bible passage and then sharing a bit about the original context, giving insight into the verses' meaning and how to apply them today. Jesus was doing that, but He was also doing much more. The law is God's unchanging Word, and yet Jesus was saying, "I have something to add on that subject." Such statements must have dropped the jaws of Jesus' disciples and anyone else within earshot.

Take, for example, Jesus' teaching on murder:

"You have heard that it was said to those of old, 'You shall not murder; and whoever murders will be liable to judgment.' But I say to you that everyone who is angry with his brother will be liable to judgment; whoever insults his brother will be liable to the council; and whoever says, 'You fool!' will be liable to the hell of fire" (MATTHEW 5:21–22).

In the Old Testament, God made murder a capital crime, but Jesus' statement got behind the law to God's heart. In effect, Jesus was saying, "It's not enough simply to avoid bludgeoning someone to death. The seething, unrelenting anger in your heart—that's the root problem."

Jesus' "new" commands were all about true holiness, a purity that flows from the inside out. It's what God wanted all along for His people. The heart is what matters: our thoughts, attitudes, and actions will all flow in the right direction if our hearts are cleaned and maintained by God.

On the outside, the Pharisees were the most well-behaved, moral people of Jesus' day. They kept the letter of the law like no one else, gaining notice for tithing even their spice racks (Matthew 23:23; Luke 11:42). But Jesus reserved his harshest words for this group:

> *"Woe to you, scribes and Pharisees, hypocrites! For you clean the outside of the cup and the plate, but inside they are full of greed and self-indulgence. You blind Pharisee! First clean the inside of the cup and the plate, that the outside also may be clean. Woe to you, scribes and Pharisees, hypocrites! For you are like whitewashed tombs, which outwardly appear beautiful, but within are full of dead people's bones and all uncleanness. So you also outwardly appear righteous to others, but within you are full of hypocrisy and lawlessness"* (MATTHEW 23:25–28).

I'm a firm believer that Jesus loved at all times, even when He was throwing over tables or yelling at folks. Jesus' identity demands that we read these words through the lens of love.

So this is the sound of a car horn alerting other drivers that the bridge ahead has been washed out. These are the words of a father, scared for his teenage son, after discovering drugs in his backpack. This is the voice of God pleading with men who have all but inoculated themselves against the gospel. The Pharisees were missing out on the kingdom of God (v. 13), and Jesus was trying to get their attention before it was too late. But these words are not only for the Pharisees of Jesus' time—they're just as necessary, and just as loving, for anyone who's fallen into the same trap today.

"Clean the inside of the cup, and the outside will be clean as well!" shouts Jesus. The call to holiness is an invitation to draw near to God, to be made truly and deeply new so that there is no longer a need to manage sin, to hide brokenness, or to protect the deep wounds. All will be healed. All will be made well.

The gospel is a declaration of salvation—not just from the punishment our sins deserve but also from the struggle with those sins in our everyday lives. This transformation may not happen quickly, but it can happen. Holiness and the freedom that comes with it are available when we open ourselves up to Jesus completely and we stop playing games.

YOUR LIFE IN THE STORY OF GOD

Like the Pharisees of Jesus' day, we can carefully follow those biblical rules that make us look good outwardly—to "play the game" spiritually. But God is concerned with the spirit of the law, the condition of our hearts toward Him and others. As we play our parts in God's story, we don't ever have to pretend to be good. Our thoughts, attitudes, and actions will all flow in the right direction if our hearts are cleaned and maintained by God.

1. Why was Jesus so unhappy with the Pharisees (Matthew 23:25–28)? How common is the Pharisees' mind-set today?

2. How did Jesus expand upon the Old Testament's rule against murder (Matthew 5:21–22)? What does His teaching indicate about what we might call "big sins" and "little sins"?

3. Where does holiness begin (Matthew 23:26)? What kind of freedom does holiness bring?

Set Up to Win

ROMANS 6

The Christian life is rigged.

Have you ever felt this way? Be honest.

Think about the Bible. The Old and New Testaments are full of commandments about our behavior, our words, even our thoughts. But we're sinful people. No matter how hard we try, we seem inevitably to stumble and fall. Jesus offers us eternal life, but what about some help right here and now?

The cycle of sin, confession, repentance, and trying again brings with it shame, guilt, and condemnation. And it seems no matter how hard we try, the same sin patterns dog us month after month and year after year. Our efforts to turn over a new leaf are sincere—as sincere as we can make them—but with each new failure, we wonder if it's worth the effort. None of this makes us happy and, worse than that, the routine tends to make us wary of drawing near to God, since we know we've let Him down so often.

It seems like we've been set up to fail.

Bent the Wrong Way

Automatic doors parted to welcome me inside the Home Depot, and I proudly made my way to the lawn care section. Having just bought my first house (the worst one in town, remember?), I needed some yard equipment.

I looked carefully at every lawnmower on display, though I'd already done my research and came to the store knowing which one I'd buy. For the first time in my life I had reason to buy a lawnmower—a proud day and a rite of passage in the suburbs—and I wanted to enjoy the moment.

Savoring complete, I found a box that contained the mower of my choice, loaded it on a flatbed shopping cart, and made my way to the checkout. "Nice mower," the cashier said. Of course he did—as I mentioned, I'd done my research. This was the best little self-propelled beauty for the money.

Back home, I pulled the box out of my trunk, cleared some space in the garage, and began the task of putting the mower together. It looked pretty simple. Mainly, the handle had to be assembled. It ships in pieces, disconnected from the body of the machine, to save space. A few screws and wingnuts, and I'd be ready to add gas and start mowing.

At first, I tried to put things together without help. I knew what the mower was supposed to look like. For some reason, though, I couldn't get the last piece in place. So I gave in and pulled out the instructions, which confirmed that I'd done everything I was supposed to do. I tried getting that last stubborn tube of metal into position once again, but it wouldn't budge. Then I took the whole thing apart and reassembled it, thinking maybe I'd put a part in backwards or upside down by mistake. Nope. Still no good.

I called my brother, trying to explain the problem over the phone, but since he wasn't there to see it for himself, he was little help. Finally, after a few unsuccessful hours, I took the lawnmower back to the store. It felt like I was returning my self-respect with it.

When I showed the mower to the clerk, he smiled, shook his head, and laughed slightly. I was livid—and more than a little embarrassed. *How dare he laugh!* But he spoke before I could say anything in my own defense. "This thing was never going to get put together," he said.

"You're telling me," I said in the most affable tone I could muster.

"No, what I mean is, it's broken. You see this piece here?" He held up a section of the handle. "It's bent in the wrong direction. Manufacturing defect. It's impossible to assemble this mower."

We grabbed another lawnmower off the shelf, and I opened the box this time to make sure everything was as it should be. When I got home, I put the thing together in ten minutes. But I had wasted hours trying to assemble that first lawnmower. I had been set up to fail. No matter how much effort I might have exerted, no matter how much time I might have spent, I never would have been successful.

Sadly, I've talked with many people who feel this way about holiness. It just seems out of reach, impossible even. After all, we're born sinful, "prone to wander," as the old hymn says. We all have something deep inside of us that is—like that lawn-mower part—bent in the wrong direction. (Though, to be clear, the defect in us came not from our Manufacturer, but from our choosing to ignore His instructions.) Instead of consistently doing the right that we know to do, we often feel compelled to do wrong.

The apostle Paul struggled in this same way. In the book of Romans, he wrote, "I do not do the good I want to do, but the evil I do not want to do—this I keep on doing" (7:19 NIV). And that seems to settle the issue for many believers: living a life of holiness is simply out of reach. The answer is to do your best, be thankful that God forgives sin, and try to remember to show grace to others when they fail. They're in the same boat too.

But what if that's a lie?

Free Not to Sin

Earlier in Romans, Paul wrote, "Sin shall no longer be your master, because you are not under the law, but under grace" (6:14 NIV). In other words, we were once slaves to sin, unable to escape, forced to obey our master. But that is no longer the case. Because of Christ, we have been set free. Here's how Eugene Peterson put it in his Bible paraphrase, *The Message*:

> *You must not give sin a vote in the way you conduct your lives. Don't give it the time of day. Don't even run*

little errands that are connected with that old way of life. Throw yourselves wholeheartedly and full-time—remember, you've been raised from the dead!—into God's way of doing things. Sin can't tell you how to live. After all, you're not living under that old tyranny any longer. You're living in the freedom of God (ROMANS 6:12–14).

Sin is not a foregone conclusion in the lives of God's children. We are free to be good once again. That's the good news of holiness in God's story.

But notice that there are two elements to this freedom we have been given. First, there's what God has done for us: "you've been raised from the dead!" (v. 13 MSG). Because Christ died and took our sins with Him, we are now dead to sin. And because Jesus rose from the dead, we have come back to life too! That bent and broken part deep within us, the one that made it impossible to live according to God's design, has been made new.

Second, there's what we need to do. Consider how much responsibility Paul places on his readers: "*You must not give* sin a vote. . . . *Don't give* it the time of day. . . . *Throw yourselves* wholeheartedly and full-time . . . into God's way of doing things" (vv. 12–13 MSG, emphasis added). Walking in step with God is a daily decision; it's not something that just happens. But it's also not something we accomplish through a sheer act of will, either. Holiness grows as we cooperate with the life of Christ at work within us.

When I couldn't get that lawnmower together—after hours of trying—I was more than just frustrated. The experience pressed sharply on a wound that runs deep inside me. My dad left when I was seven years old, so I missed out on seeing him fix things, on learning about tools and drywall and electrical wiring. As a result, I tend to fumble my way through home improvement projects and doubt my abilities at every turn. So while others might have been confident enough to conclude the problem was with the lawnmower itself, I assumed the problem was with *me*. I kept trying, which just compounded my frustration and chipped away even more at my self-confidence. I didn't believe I could do it.

A lot of people fall into this same trap spiritually. When temptation comes, they don't believe they can stand up to it—so they don't. Their failure is assumed from the start. They agree with the enemy when he tells them they're no good. And so what do they do? *No good.*

But Paul's words here in Romans are a command to remember the truth: "Consider yourselves dead to sin and alive to God in Christ Jesus" (6:11). Once we have faith enough to believe God's Word, we won't be taken out so easily. Instead, we can stand and invite Jesus into the battle with us.

In Paul's letter to the Galatians, we read, "I have been crucified with Christ. It is no longer I who live, but Christ who lives in me. And the life I now live in the flesh I live by faith in the Son of God, who loved me and gave himself for me" (2:20). Have you ever invited Jesus to live His life through you? I'm not talking about salvation. I mean each and every day, and especially when you are staring temptation square in the face. If you are a believer in Jesus Christ, His Spirit—the Holy Spirit— already lives inside you, but it's up to you to invite Him into your decisions, your struggles, and your spiritual battles.

Sin entered the world when Adam and Eve put themselves at the center of God's story, to decide for themselves what was good and what was evil. In doing so, they ate from the one tree in the garden that God had forbidden, setting themselves up as their own gods. But instead of gaining more control, they lost the authority they did have. They became slaves to sin—and so did we along with them.

The path of holiness is the daily act of choosing to leave the forbidden fruit on the tree, as God commanded. But we are only able to do this because the power of sin has been defeated. We can exercise our freedom, fittingly enough, not by seizing control but by yielding the control we do have to our rightful Master and Lord, something Adam and Eve should have done in the first place.

This is the power of the gospel at work in our lives. This is the freedom and joy of no longer being bound to sin. It is possible, if only we will believe every word of the good news and then stand up and fight.

YOUR LIFE IN THE STORY OF GOD

It's tempting to believe that the Christian life is rigged against us, that in the fight against sin we have been set up to fail. But that's not how God writes our stories. Having been "crucified with Christ," we can now live in the power of His resurrection (Galatians 2:20). Believers in Jesus have a new Master, who breaks the power that sin once held over us. But we still have to choose whether we will allow God to work in and through us to develop holiness.

1. Have you ever had a frustrating experience like the lawn-mower episode? How do even the daily, practical difficulties of our world point out the problem of sin?

2. In the apostle Paul's discussion of our freedom from sin in Romans 6:12–14, what is God's contribution? What is our responsibility?

3. How much does our mind-set affect our ability to accomplish difficult tasks? What can you do to improve your confidence in verses like Romans 6:14, which tells us "sin shall no longer be your master"?

RESTORATION
God Offers Peace and Rest

*"Most of the things we need
in order to be most fully alive
never come from pushing.
They grow in rest."*
—MARK BUCHANAN

The Rest of the Adventure

GENESIS 2:2

At the end of the greatest stories, there's usually a note of, "And they lived happily ever after." Peace is restored to the galaxy. There's no place like home. The hero rides off into the sunset. There is rest for our favorite characters and the assurance that their stories will continue past the back cover of the book (and maybe the promise that no animals were harmed during the making of the film).

Happy endings are satisfying, and not just because they're happy; there is something inside us that looks for these endings. God has etched eternity onto our hearts (Ecclesiastes 3:11), and along with it, a desire for the life that is to come. That life, just like the endings of our favorite stories, will bring peace and rest but also continuing adventure.

The life we live now is exhausting, full of striving and conflict, so our longing for peace is not surprising. But we also want our stories to go on. No one relishes the idea of heaven as one long, never-ending church service in the clouds, do they? We want good to triumph over evil, but then we want to see what adventures await us once those old foes are no more.

In the interest of full disclosure, there are some people who find books and films without happy endings to be edgier, somehow more true to life. These tales seem to echo our own stories; rarely do the chapters in our lives wrap up neatly. But it's these broken endings that remind us something is not right. They resonate precisely because they give voice to our feeling that things are not as they should be. And the catharsis they bring is short-lived. We *are* out of place in the tragedies we experience. We were meant for a happy ending.

The Business of Rest

In the beginning, God rested.

Well, not at the very beginning. "On the seventh day God finished his work that he had done, and he rested on the seventh day" (Genesis 2:2). After the first six days of creation, God took a day off.

The Lord wasn't tired, of course. He didn't need a lazy Saturday to recharge after a busy week. Instead, He was sewing into the fabric of time a model for us to follow. We who bear His image would have a day of rest each week—one in seven to pause, to go softly and quietly or not at all. And God didn't stop there.

He gave us the seasons to bring rhythm and celebration to life, holidays to interrupt the unrelenting tyranny of the immediate. And to His people, He gave Sabbath years during which the land was not to be tilled or harvested (Leviticus 25:1–7), a mandatory vacation for a society based largely on agriculture.

The need for rest is in our DNA. It's required for life, just like food and water are. If you've ever gone a few days without sleep, you know that rest isn't simply a comfort issue. Our bodies and our minds need rest to function properly—things start to go a little haywire without it. That God wrote rest into the cycle of days, weeks, and years is therefore a gift.

Some might be tempted to conclude that our need for rest is a deficiency of design, akin to a low-end laptop computer with a battery that needs recharging far too often. God could have created men and women who operate like wind-up toys, running down over the course of a lifetime with no breaks required. But think about how satisfying a good night's sleep can be. Consider what it would be like to plow through a busy workweek that doesn't ever find its way to a weekend. Imagine going through life without natural timeouts to reset and start over. Required rest is not a deficiency; it is instead a luxury bestowed equally upon all members of the human race. Yet the gift of Sabbath rest has a deeper purpose still.

Imagine it's Christmas morning, and there's a large flat present, with your name on it, propped up against the fireplace mantle. The package is too big to fit under the tree. You examine it and think to yourself, *It could be a TV.*

When you pick up the gift, though, you discover it's not nearly heavy enough to be a television, and the shape your fingers meet through the wrapping paper tells you it's not an electronic screen. As you tear at the paper, you discover a beautiful framed canvas, an original painting by a famous artist you have long admired. The scene is of a breathtaking beach somewhere, perhaps in the Mediterranean.

The colors seem almost too vibrant for an oil painting. It's exquisite. You wonder if it's even a real place. You instantly know that once this gift is hung in a place of honor in your home, you will never grow tired of looking at it.

But then you notice a card, nearly hidden in the pile of discarded paper on the floor. And that's when you discover that the gift you've received is more than the painting itself: you have been given the actual Mediterranean beach.

This is the kind of gift-giver God is. As wonderful as a moment of unspoiled rest can be, it is merely a picture of something far more spectacular. Sabbaths in this life are a preview of the happy ending for which we were created.

If you've ever read the book *The Lion, the Witch, and the Wardrobe* or seen the film version of it, you know that the White Witch placed the land of Narnia under a terrible curse so that it would be "always winter but never Christmas." For a hundred years, there's been nothing but snow and ice, which never thaws to make way for spring. Christmas morning never comes either. But then, midway through the story, the sound of sleigh bells can be heard. Father Christmas has arrived, and it's a time for celebration. Winter still looms across Narnia, but joy has broken through: if Christmas can come, then maybe springtime can too.

This is the heart of God in our Sabbaths from the ordinary,

in our times of rest from the everyday struggles of life. *If relief can come—at least in part, at least temporarily—then maybe someday,* our hearts hope, *joy will come in its fullness.*

There's something else about the Narnian curse that echoes the situation in our own world. The entire land of Narnia suffered in the cold. It wasn't just certain characters or merely the children and talking beasts. All of Narnia—the rivers, lakes, rocks, and trees included—needed Christmas and then spring. So too does all of our world need rest:

> *The creation was subjected to futility, not willingly, but because of him who subjected it, in hope that the creation itself will be set free from its bondage to corruption and obtain the freedom of the glory of the children of God. For we know that the whole creation has been groaning together in the pains of childbirth until now* (ROMANS 8:20–22).

We've already seen how sin affects every aspect of life on our planet, how there is no corner where its infection has not spread. But the cure is more potent than the disease. God's story is not merely the tale of a loving Father who sets His children free from slavery. It is that, but it's so much more. It's an epic about a powerful and gracious King who sets everything free. No stone is left unturned, as Jesus spoke about "the renewal of *all* things" (Matthew 19:28 NIV, emphasis added), not just the renewal of souls.

The divine rest at the end of God's story—the one to which all the Sabbaths in this life point—is a time of unending joy and refreshment for the entire universe. On the seventh day of creation, God stepped into that rest, and He bids us to come and join Him there.

■ ■ ■

The invitation to join God in His Sabbath rest can be traced through the Bible. As the people of Israel traversed the wilderness under Moses, they were headed for God's rest—in the form of the Promised Land (Deuteronomy 12:9). But they did not trust the Lord, and they disobeyed Him over and over. So God declared that the entire generation would not enter His rest (Psalm 95:11).

David took up God's invitation and found rest in the Lord (2 Samuel 7:1, 11), and the people over whom he reigned enjoyed the same. A thousand years after David, the offer was still valid, as Jesus told the world, "Come to me, all who labor and are heavy laden, and I will give you rest" (Matthew 11:28). And in Hebrews, we find that God still holds the door wide open for believers today (Hebrews 4:1–14).

There is rest in God's presence, and one day, that rest will cover the mountains and fill the seas. It will be the happiest of happily ever afters.

YOUR LIFE IN THE STORY OF GOD

Many, if not most, people enjoy a story with a happy ending. For Christians, the story of this life ends with good triumphing over evil, followed by the continuing adventure of a perfect eternity in a restored world. God calls this His "rest," and we are all invited to take part. Even now, in a stressful, broken world, moments of rest—a good night's sleep, a well-deserved weekend—show us hints of the full joy God has planned for His people.

1. When you're tired and stressed, what would "the perfect rest" look like? How might that hint at "the perfect rest" God has planned for His people?

2. Why did the Israelites under Moses miss out on God's rest (Hebrews 4:1–8)? How can we take advantage of the offer of God's rest (Hebrews 4:9–14)?

3. How is our physical world groaning and struggling as it awaits its rest (Romans 8:20–22)? How can we bring "good news" to more than just people?

The Family Reunion
That Saved the World

GENESIS 45:4–5

Though he had eleven brothers and a sister, Joseph found himself in the privileged position of being his father's favorite child. As a sign of his affection for his son, Jacob gave Joseph a special robe. You may have heard that it was a coat of "many colors" (Genesis 37:3), but the meaning of the Hebrew in that verse is uncertain, and scholars debate the proper translation.

It may be that the garment was multi-colored as traditionally thought, or it could be that it was delicately embroidered—"ornate" as the NIV puts it. Some translators have suggested that what made the robe special was that it had long sleeves (NRSV), while the sleeves of Joseph's brothers' coats were short. In those days, only men who didn't work in the fields wore long sleeves—because these people didn't have to worry about getting the sleeves dirty. Therefore, wearing a long-sleeved robe was a sign of privilege and status.

Whatever made Joseph's coat special, it set him above his older brothers—and angered them to no end.

I know a bit of what those brothers went through. I am my father's oldest son, but my parents divorced when I was just seven years old. My father remarried a few years later and had three children with my stepmother—all boys—and it hurt me every time my dad shared something with one of his new sons that I had missed out on: baseball games, homework assignments, birthday parties. No one gets to redo their childhood, but it seems my dad got to redo fatherhood. He never gave one of my younger siblings a fancy jacket like Jacob gave Joseph, but he did give them something I didn't have much of growing up: himself.

Joseph's coat of many colors (or robe with long sleeves) was about much more than outerwear. It was an indication of a father's love for his child. It was a sign that Joseph, more than any of his brothers, had a special place in Jacob's heart. And while the gesture was sweet to Joseph, it was bitter to Reuben, Simeon, Levi, and the rest of Jacob's older sons.

Unfortunately, Joseph didn't help matters. He had dreams that suggested his brothers would one day bow down to him, but rather than keep those dreams to himself to see what God would do with them, Joseph shared them with his siblings. That made the brothers hate him even more. After the second dream, even his father Jacob pushed back: "What is this dream that you have dreamed? Shall I and your mother and your brothers indeed come to bow ourselves to the ground before you?" (Genesis 37:10).

Bitterness is like a weed. If not pulled out at the root, it will continue to grow until it takes over an entire garden. That's what happened in the hearts of Joseph's older brothers. Their hatred grew and grew until it consumed them, and there was just one thing to do: get rid of Joseph.

The brothers' first idea was to kill him, but Judah persuaded the others not to. Instead, they stripped Joseph of his coat and threw him into a pit, and when a caravan of traders came by, they sold their brother for twenty pieces of silver.

Joseph's Small Story in God's Big Story

Joseph's story unfolds like a serial TV drama designed for binge watching. Sold into slavery, he finds himself in a strange land all by himself—separated from everyone and everything he's ever known. Except for God.

While a slave in Egypt, Joseph rises to a place of honor in the home of an important official named Potiphar, and is put in charge of just about everything. Though he's still a slave, Joseph is living the good life. God, it seems, has come through.

But, as happens in any compelling drama, an unexpected plot twist changes things in an instant. Potiphar's wife tries to seduce Joseph, and when he refuses, she accuses him of attempted rape. Joseph is locked up.

God does not abandon Joseph, even in prison. There, he once again rises to a position of authority—as much authority as one can have while serving time in an Egyptian dungeon. He also takes on a new vocation: dream interpreter.

In prison with Joseph are Pharaoh's baker and cupbearer. Both men have dreams, and God gives Joseph the meaning of each. The baker's dream turns out to be a nightmare; he will soon be executed. The cupbearer's dream, on the other hand, means freedom. In short order, both interpretations come to pass. The baker is impaled, and the cupbearer is reinstated. But Joseph is forgotten. Two years go by with his situation unchanged.

Until one day, when the storyline takes a dramatic turn.

Pharaoh begins having strange dreams of his own, and no one on his payroll can interpret them. The cupbearer, though, remembering his stint in prison, recommends Joseph's services to the king.

Once again, God is with Joseph, giving him understanding of Pharaoh's dreams. The verdict? There will be seven years of prosperity for Egypt, followed by seven years of famine. But after he's explained the dream, Joseph doesn't stop talking. There before Pharaoh, he takes the opportunity to provide solutions. Joseph suggests that some of the grain from the seven years of good harvests be set aside to feed the people when times get tough.

Joseph's roller coaster life is about to find a new high point. Pharaoh is pleased with Joseph's plan, and puts him in charge of seeing it through. Not only that—right then and there, Pharaoh makes Joseph his right-hand man. If Joseph's story were a television show, this would be the scene to get people talking the next day. In one short meeting, Joseph goes from jailed slave to the second most powerful person in the world, with all the resources of the Egyptian Empire at his disposal.

As encouraging as Joseph's story is, God's plans are always much bigger than a single person. Of course, He often chooses to work through individuals, but His story is about the redemption and restoration of the entire cosmos. As Dutch statesman and theologian Abraham Kuyper famously put it, "There is not a square inch in the whole domain of our human existence over which Christ, who is Sovereign over all, does not cry, Mine!"[1] Through Joseph, God was not merely saving a man or a nation; He was saving the entire world.

The famine that plagued Egypt affected people near and far. When word got out that Egypt had plenty of food, the hungry came from miles away to buy it, whatever the cost. And among the weary and desperate travelers seeking an audience with Egypt's prime minister were Joseph's brothers.

Here we get to the place in Joseph's story toward which the various ups and downs were aiming all along. From the pit to Potiphar's house, from wrongfully accused to royally commended, Joseph—at God's direction—was coming to a place of reconciliation with his family.

In the beginning, Joseph was haughty and puffed up. He focused on the fact that his dreams showed him in a position of authority over his brothers. Joseph didn't stop to think what God's purpose might be in raising him up.

Now, though, standing before the men who had sold him into slavery, he knew the purpose. In that instant, power wasn't as important to him as his family: "And he kissed all his brothers and wept upon them" (Genesis 45:15).

For their part, the brothers were relieved to see Joseph alive—especially after he assured them he wasn't holding a grudge. And now they were eager to bow down to Joseph, fulfilling his dreams, since it meant their lives would be spared. No longer was Joseph wearing the "coat of many colors" their father had given him; instead, he was adorned with the finest garments Egypt had to offer. But in that room, there was no mention of "I told you so" or "That's not fair." There were only the sighs of relief that come from knowing the story God is writing turns out to be more wonderful than anyone could have guessed.

As I've said, God's story is bigger than any one family. It's bigger, even, than the nation that Joseph's family would one day become. God saved the world that day when Joseph and his brothers embraced and old resentments were laid to rest. How? In that moment of reconciliation, the seed was planted for the greatest reunion of all time.

Through Joseph's brother Judah, a special strand of the family line would weave its way across the centuries until Jesus was born to a virgin in the small village of Bethlehem. In His perfect life, sacrificial death, and glorious resurrection, Jesus would make a way for people to be reconciled to God, reconciled to one another, and reconciled to creation.

The gospel sets right all that is wrong. In God's kingdom, everyone and everything breathes with the rhythm of the Creator. Enemies become friends. Rivals set aside their complaints. Walls once erected to keep people out crumble to dust. God's story is still being written, so the kingdom has not yet come in its fullness. But wherever the kingdom is preached and hearts and minds are changed, reunions like the one between Joseph and his brothers are a regular occurrence—at least they can be.

As characters in the chapter God is writing today, it's our job to live out the gospel in every area of life, but especially in our relationships. Jesus said, "Love your enemies, do good to those who hate you, bless those who curse you, pray for those who abuse you" (Luke 6:27–28). If anyone else were issuing such commands, we'd be reasonably justified in rolling our eyes and politely disengaging. But Jesus doesn't merely offer ethical teaching—He gives us His Spirit so we can actually live as He says. When we walk day by day, hour by hour, and minute by minute with the Holy Spirit as our constant companion, we'll find there's no other way to live.

Jesus' goal is not to create a handful of really nice people. That's far too small a goal for the Son of God. His plan is to restore the entire world. Think about it: What might life be like if we all lived with the reality of the kingdom, here and now, always before us? What if we, like Joseph, trusted God? What if we looked for ways to bless others, even when our own lives could use some blessing at the moment? What if we were slow to anger, quick to forgive, and ready to embrace? What if we used our authority and influence to help a hurting world?

This is God's desire for us. It's only possible because of the gospel—and because God saved a young man who was stuck in a pit without his coat.

YOUR LIFE IN THE STORY OF GOD

Reconciliation is a beautiful thing. For thousands of years, the story of Joseph and his brothers has shown how forgiveness restored a family—even paving the way for the birth of Jesus, who offers restoration to everyone who follows Him. There will be a day when all creation is restored to its original glory, but until that time, we can advance God's story by being slow to anger, quick to forgive, and ready to embrace the hurting world around us.

1. Why were Joseph's brothers so angry with him? How did Joseph overcome the tensions within his family?

2. What are the ingredients of reconciliation? How do we know that Joseph and his brothers' reconciliation was real?

3. Have you ever been in a situation like Joseph's, either treated badly or having treated someone else badly? What steps did you take (or could you take) toward reconciliation?

Coming Clean

2 KINGS 5:1–14

For many years, one of my favorite songs has been "The Frozen Man" by James Taylor. It tells the story of a man who has just woken up from the dead, having been buried in ice for more than a hundred years. He discovers that in his frozen state, he had become something of a science project for practitioners of modern medicine.

Doctors were able to restart the man's heart, replace damaged limbs, and repair organs that no longer functioned properly. In short, they were able to bring him back to life to experience our modern world—though none of them had stopped to wonder whether he'd want to see it (through his new artificial eye) or not.

It's a resurrection, but as the song goes on, we discover it's a resurrection of the Frankenstein variety. The Frozen Man laments that everyone he ever knew is long dead. From his perspective, he is all alone in a busy, overpopulated world. Worse still is his realization that, because of his unnatural appearance, children cry when they see him coming down the street. By the end of the song, he is looking forward to dying again—and this time, he wants nothing left behind for the scientists and doctors to tinker with.

The story is pure fiction, but it still contains truth. By that, I mean that we can put ourselves into the shoes of the Frozen Man and feel his pain. Imagine being "saved," only to discover that the world you've come back to is unfamiliar, your loved ones are all gone, and you look like a monster, which only increases your isolation. Life has been restored, but at what cost?

God's story is one of restoration, of life returning to places where there was once only death. There is a cost to this new life, but Jesus paid the bill at Calvary. And unlike the case of the Frozen Man, there are no unforeseen consequences. Life, in God's kingdom, is restored to its complete goodness—no catches, no regrets, no strings attached. In fact, it is life "to the full" (John 10:10 NIV).

It is not strange, then, in anticipation of the kingdom God is bringing, that His people are called to pray for healing and wholeness (James 5:13–16). Nor is it surprising that the great moves of God in history are often accompanied by miracles of restoration.

Of Water and Dirt

Naaman was used to being in charge. As commander of Syria's army, he told soldiers what to do, and they obeyed. He was successful in his military campaigns, and he had earned the respect of his king. He even had a reputation among the people for being "a mighty man of valor" (2 Kings 5:1).

But there was one enemy Naaman could not defeat: a merciless skin disease. Though the word translated "leprosy" in our Bibles could be used to describe many conditions in the ancient world, Naaman appears to have been plagued by a deadly strain that was without a known cure (v. 7). And like the Frozen Man in our song, Naaman's appearance probably caused people to turn away.

Pity came from an unlikely place: a young girl in Naaman's household. She had been taken during a raid on Israel and was now a servant to Naaman's wife. Though she could have seen Naaman as just one of her captors, an enemy of Israel and of God (and therefore deserving of any pain he had coming to him), she instead saw a man who was suffering under the shame and discomfort of a serious skin condition. She told his wife, "Would that my lord were with the prophet who is in Samaria! He would cure him of his leprosy" (v. 3).

It seems this slave girl had a knack for seeing things as they really are. Despite her situation, she knew that nothing was too difficult for God—and that He might choose to work through His prophet to bring healing to Naaman.

The prophet in Samaria was Elisha. During the tempestuous years of the divided kingdom, when wicked kings often outdid each other in leading the people to chase false gods, God raised up prophets to speak truth to power and call the people back to himself. Like Elijah before him, Elisha's words came with signs and wonders—divine power to show that he was God's messenger.

By this point in his ministry, Elisha had parted the Jordan River and purified the waters of Jericho (2 Kings 2:14, 19–22). He multiplied oil for a widow on one occasion (4:1–7), and twenty loaves of bread for a hundred men on another (4:42–44). He had even brought a dead child back to life (4:8–37). For this servant girl, who had apparently heard the stories, there was no doubt in her mind that God could use the prophet to heal poor Naaman's leprosy.

To the Syrian commander's credit, he believed the girl. Perhaps it was because he had nothing left to lose, but I think there was more to it than that. It's no small thing to approach your king and request permission to seek help from the God of your enemy. Though Naaman knew nothing about the God of Israel except his slave girl's report, his willingness to believe tells us something about his character.

Jesus, speaking about Naaman centuries later, said, "There were many lepers in Israel in the time of the prophet Elisha, and none of them was cleansed, but only Naaman the Syrian" (Luke 4:27). He said this to contrast the faith of Naaman with the faith He could not find among His fellow Nazarenes (v. 24).

When Naaman arrived at the home of the prophet, Elisha didn't come out to greet him. Nor did he accept the lavish gift that Naaman brought. Instead, Elisha sent a servant out to tell Naaman he would be healed if he would just bathe in the Jordan River seven times (2 Kings 5:10).

Naaman was insulted, not only because Elisha was a no-show, but also because washing in a river any number of times couldn't possibly cure his disease. In the end, though, after a word of encouragement from his own servants, Naaman followed the prophet's prescription "and his flesh was restored like the flesh of a little child, and he was clean" (v. 14).

There may well have been something about Naaman that found favor with God. The Lord had given him many victories on the battlefield long before he came to Samaria to seek Elisha's help (2 Kings 5:1). Maybe God saw compassion or generosity in his heart, or perhaps even a spark of faith. But the story of Naaman's healing isn't really about Naaman's heart; it's about God's heart, which beats for the restoration of everything good.

As I noted in an earlier chapter, Jesus promises that one day, there will be a "renewal of all things" (Matthew 19:28 NIV). And in the book of Revelation, He says, "Behold, I am making all things new" (Revelation 21:5). Naaman's experience—coming up out of the water that seventh time and seeing smooth skin, no longer irritated and discolored—was a preview of that day.

It's fitting that the author of Kings described Naaman's flesh in terms of a baby's perfect skin, for the word translated "renewal" in Matthew 19:28 is a Greek term that means "new beginning," or somewhat more literally, "Genesis again." God, in renewing our world, is bringing us back to the pure, unspoiled shade of the garden. He is giving us back the earth as it was meant to be enjoyed. And He is giving us back ourselves as He created us to be. Naaman's skin was still his own, but it was given a fresh start, a rebirth.

■ ■ ■

Every miracle of restoration foretells this part of God's story—that God loves this world so much that He paid the price to make it new again. And this good news is shouted no louder than when a person is born again.

God says that when someone comes under the lordship of Jesus Christ, she is made new (2 Corinthians 5:17). Obviously, her skin doesn't become baby soft like Naaman's; this newness involves the restoration of her heart and spirit. The prophet Ezekiel records this promise from the Lord: "I will give you a new heart, and a new spirit I will put within you. And I will remove the heart of stone from your flesh and give you a heart of flesh. And I will put my Spirit within you, and cause you to walk in my statutes and be careful to obey my rules" (Ezekiel 36:26–27).

But that's not to say that God's work of restoration stops the moment someone is born again. In fact, it's just the beginning. Jesus promised the renewal of *all* things, remember?

The story of Naaman is, in a sense, a picture *of a picture* of a gospel promise. And that promise is but a down payment on something so big, it can hardly be described. This is how interconnected God's story can be at times.

Long before the New Testament, Naaman washed in the Jordan River and rose out of the water that seventh time "clean" as a result (2 Kings 5:14). He was, in a sense, baptized. The water didn't make him clean; God did. In the same way, there is no magic in the water of baptism for believers in Jesus Christ. The water doesn't make a person clean; God does. Baptism is only a symbol of the true cleansing that takes place when someone trusts Jesus.

So Naaman's cleansing was a proto-baptism of sorts. And baptism itself is but a picture of the spiritual cleansing that takes place when a person is born again. That's the picture of a picture of a gospel promise that I mentioned. But the too-big-to-adequately-describe reality to which all of this points is the restoration Jesus will bring when He comes again. Like our hearts and our spirits, all of creation, with the exception of those who refuse the grace of God, will be made new.

While we await that day, the faith of Naaman is required. After he was healed, Naaman made a strange request of Elisha: he asked to load two of his mules with packs of dirt to take back with him to Syria. Naaman wanted to worship the one true God while standing on soil from the nation God had chosen as His own possession. He wanted to be connected to the land of his healing.

We connect with the land of our healing—heaven itself—by taking a little bit of it with us wherever we go. When we live out the kingdom of God with our lives, we exercise our faith in His promises. We show that we believe this world, all of us included, will be restored to the original beauty and purpose God intended.

YOUR LIFE IN THE STORY OF GOD

The kind of healing the Syrian commander Naaman enjoyed is entirely within God's power today, and the book of James encourages us to pray for it (5:13–16). But just as important is the spiritual healing God offers through Jesus Christ, the implanting of a new heart that the prophet Ezekiel described (36:26–27). Within God's story, we can enjoy our own spiritual rebirth, share it with the world, and await the ultimate renewal God has planned.

1. How was Naaman's healing a preview of the day that God makes "all things new" (Revelation 21:5)?

2. What are the benefits of physical healing? What are the benefits of spiritual renewal?

3. How was Naaman "connected to the land of his healing"? How can we do the same?

Coming Home

EZRA 3:8–13

Deep within all of us, there is a longing for home. For some, home may not be an actual place they can remember. For others, memories of a place once called *home* are not all good. Still, inside every human being, there is a desire for a genuine and good home, where love and joy surround, masks can be removed, and burdens can be let down from our aching backs.

God's story tells us there is such a place. Like many of the places we now call home, it will be familiar and comfortable. But unlike them, no matter how sweet our memories tell us they were, this home will never disappoint. It is where we were meant to live.

But until we get there, the longing remains.

As I write this, my family is in the middle of a new adventure. A few months back, we began building a new house. Each week after church, we drive out to the lot and check out what the construction crew has done during the past seven days. Some Sundays, we're amazed at how quickly the house is taking shape. Others, I search from framed room to framed room, looking for something new. I'm told this is normal with building projects like ours. Though the house is scheduled for completion in late spring, when I think about moving in, Christmas comes to mind.

I can picture our oldest son, Jonah, running down the stairs in his pajamas on Christmas morning, ready to unwrap presents that have been tucked under the tree. I imagine Laurin and me meeting Jonah there with his little brother, Jude, fresh from his crib, experiencing his first Christmas morning. After opening gifts and covering the floor with wrapping paper, I'll make my way to the kitchen to cook a big pancake breakfast for the family while our favorite Christmas albums play in the background.

Right now, as we pick out flooring, I do so with an image in my head of discarded wrapping paper collecting on top of it. As we look at ovens and refrigerators, I smell pancakes, bacon, and egg nog. And when we make our weekly pilgrimage to see our house in progress, I see our Christmas tree in the corner of the family room—and in my mind's eye, Jonah is clutching the staircase railing to keep his footed pajamas from slipping as he races toward Christmas morning.

This video, playing on a loop in my imagination, isn't really about a new house or even Christmas. It's that longing for home deep inside me, welling up to see if it can be satisfied on this side of Jesus' second coming. We all have some kind of longing, but no matter how wonderful certain moments of life may be—even Christmas in a beautiful, new house with small children—they will always disappoint. Let's face it: they don't stick around long enough. Just as surely as little Jonah will fly down those stairs on Christmas morning, there will come a day when he will stomp up them, upset and angry with the world. That warm feeling of home, this side of glory, does not last.

You Can't Go Home Again

When God allowed His people to be taken captive to Babylon, He did so with a promise not to forget them. In fact, He put a limit on the length of their exile: "This whole land shall become a ruin and a waste, and these nations [Judah and her neighbors] shall serve the king of Babylon seventy years" (Jeremiah 25:11). And God didn't only disclose the date when the Jewish people would be permitted to return home; He also gave the name of the king who would issue the edict at the appropriate time:

> "I am the LᴋN', who made all things, . . .
> who says of Cyrus, 'He is my shepherd,
> and he shall fulfill all my purpose';

saying of Jerusalem, 'She shall be built,'
and of the temple, 'Your foundation shall be laid'"

(ISAIAH 44:24, 28).

This prophecy was written some 150 years prior to Cyrus's birth. But God, who is sovereign over all history, can be that precise.

The Jewish historian Josephus tells us that when King Cyrus read this passage in Isaiah, he was impressed with God's ability to tell the future through His prophets—so much so that he eagerly took up the task of fulfilling what was said about him. This must have been one of the ways "the LORD stirred up the spirit of Cyrus king of Persia" (Ezra 1:1). The decree he issued allowed the Jewish people to return to their homeland and rebuild the temple of God.

This was the day the people of Judah had been waiting for. They had passed seventy years in a foreign land, stuck in another culture and way of life, surrounded by dark gods and the people who worshipped them. And though they had repeatedly failed to live out the life God had prescribed for them—oh, how they pined for the land they loved and another chance to walk with God and enjoy His blessings. Now, it seemed, thanks to Cyrus's edict, they were well on their way.

Tens of thousands of Jewish pilgrims plodded a path back to the Promised Land in the first wave of resettlement—a second exodus from captivity to freedom, or so it must have felt. But the people arrived to see charred ruins marking the spot where the presence of God once took up residence. The temple had been the center of life and worship in Judah, but it was gone. Going home again would not be easy.

Sometime later, work began on a new temple. The foundation was laid, and the people celebrated. But not everyone. "Many of the priests and Levites and heads of fathers' houses, old men who had seen the first house, wept with a loud voice when they saw the foundation of this house being laid" (Ezra 3:12).

Perhaps it was just renewed sadness over the loss of Solomon's temple, or it may have been, as some speculate, that these older men saw the foundation and realized the new temple to be built would never match the glory of the former. But that didn't stop the people from trying. They rebuilt the temple and dedicated it, and worship commenced much as it had before. The problem was, before long, much too much would go on as it had before.

The people were back in the land. A new temple had been constructed. There was even a new wall around the city of Jerusalem. The books of Ezra and Nehemiah chronicle the comeback of God's people and God's city. Yet Nehemiah, the second of the two books, closes with a troubling scene. Having been away in Babylon for some time, Nehemiah returns to Jerusalem to discover that the people are not walking with the Lord.

The last chapter of Nehemiah reads like a laundry list of sins: The people of Judah have stopped giving to the Lord. They are no longer providing an offering for the priests and Levites so they could devote themselves to maintaining the temple, instructing the people, and facilitating worship. As a result, the temple is being neglected and worship has all but ceased in Jerusalem.

Maybe because the people are no longer receiving instruction from the priests and Levites, who are now working their own fields, they are also neglecting the Sabbath, treating it like any other day. Worse still, they are marrying foreign women and beginning to lose their identity as God's people. In a single generation, it seems, the people of Judah forgot every lesson they were supposed to have learned from their time in captivity. Once again, they are breaking their covenant with the Lord at every turn.

Just when we ought to be hoping for a happy ending in God's story, things appear darkest. God had promised His people a return from exile, and even though they are back in the Promised Land, home is still a long way off. Maybe their captivity isn't over after all. Maybe their real enemy was never the

Persians, or the Babylonians, or the Egyptians. Maybe they still need new hearts like God promised. Maybe they still need a Deliverer.

■ ■ ■

Home, this side of glory, does not last. The people of Judah discovered this sad truth when they returned to Jerusalem but couldn't find the true home for which they longed. But that does not mean that God failed to keep His promises to His people.

Jesus came to set captives free, to take the homesick home—or, rather, to bring home to them. This work of homecoming stretches back into the garden, when God began writing the story of redemption in beautiful promises to His people. Every step toward Christ—the rescue of Noah, the call of Abraham, the dreams of Joseph, the plagues of Egypt, the selection of David, and on and on—brought us closer to home.

But the surprising twist in the story was that the Son of God left His home and came to us, "wrapped in swaddling cloths and lying in a manger" (Luke 2:12), to show us the way. He lived among us, died for us, and rose again. Then He ascended to the Father to prepare a place for us. And that place is home—the ending toward which God's story is headed:

> *I saw the Holy City, the new Jerusalem, coming down out of heaven from God, prepared as a bride beautifully dressed for her husband. And I heard a loud voice from the throne saying, "Look! God's dwelling place is now among the people, and he will dwell with them. They will be his people, and God himself will be with them and be their God. 'He will wipe every tear from their eyes. There will be no more death' or mourning or crying or pain, for the old order of things has passed away"* (REVELATION 21:2–4 NIV).

YOUR LIFE IN THE STORY OF GOD

A longing for home is common, whether we grew up in a good home or not. This feeling hints at the ultimate home God is preparing for those who choose to follow Jesus. He left His home in heaven to live for a time on earth, to die on the cross for sins, and become our way home. We look forward to the promised day when "God's dwelling place is now among the people, and he will dwell with them" (Revelation 21:3 NIV).

1. Where is "home" for you? What makes "home" home?

2. What does God promise about the home He has prepared for us (Revelation 21:2–4)?

3. How can we make our present home more like the eternal home that God has planned?

Restoration Is Resurrection

MATTHEW 27:45–54

Tucked within Matthew's account of Jesus' crucifixion is a rather strange event—or rather, it would be strange if it weren't part of the larger story of the Son of God's mission to earth. But this short description, which a casual reader could pass over as if it were merely the mention of scenery, tells a remarkable tale of its own. It is the tale of *another* resurrection that Passover weekend.

> *The tombs also were opened. And many bodies of the saints who had fallen asleep were raised, and coming out of the tombs after his resurrection they went into the holy city and appeared to many* (MATTHEW 27:52–53).

Graves opened, and the dead came back to life to stroll through Jerusalem and say hello to some old friends. This would seem like front-page news, but only Matthew mentions it; Mark, Luke, and John are all silent on the subject.

While Matthew doesn't say why he chose to incorporate this secondary resurrection into his retelling of Easter weekend events, it may be as simple as this: Details within Matthew's gospel, as well as early church tradition, tell us that he likely wrote for a primarily Jewish audience. It's possible that some of the men and women who originally received his gospel remembered what had happened. Perhaps some of them had been greeted by a formerly dead friend or relative in Jerusalem, and since that day had not been able to make sense of it. *Was it a dream? A hallucination? An elaborate joke?* Matthew puts the incident into its larger and even more spectacular context.

But there is another audience for whom Matthew wrote. It

includes the people, down through the centuries, covered by Jesus' command to His friends to "Go . . . and make disciples" (Matthew 28:19). Since the early days of the Christian movement, the gospel of Matthew has been used to share the story of Jesus—and these few verses, about an appearance by no-longer-dead residents of Judea, have been a part of it.

There is nothing new in this idea of the dead rising to life in connection with Jesus. The Gospels record that He raised the widow of Nain's son (Luke 7:11–17), Jairus's daughter (Luke 8:40–56), and most famously his friend Lazarus (John 11). But this mass resurrection in Matthew is different. It wasn't brought about by the ministry of Jesus. He didn't place His hands on anyone or speak a word. Instead, the miracle came immediately after His death (Matthew 27:50), as if it were an unstoppable reflex of creation.

And this wasn't the only strange event recorded in that moment: "The curtain of the temple was torn in two, from top to bottom. And the earth shook, and the rocks were split" (v. 51).

The "curtain of the temple" was the dividing veil between the Holy Place and the Most Holy Place. It marked a line that was not to be crossed. Like no other bit of territory in all the world, God's presence filled the temple's Most Holy Place. Apart from the high priest, no one could enter that space and come close to God. And even the high priest was only permitted to do so once a year, on the Day of Atonement.

But with the penalty for sin paid by Jesus on the cross, that curtain—four inches thick, according to tradition—was torn from top to bottom, allowing everyone to enter God's presence by the blood of Jesus. He is the Lamb of God to whom all the Passover lambs through history have pointed.

The loud, shredding sound that must have accompanied the tearing of the curtain was a declaration that every broken thing was being made whole. Something similar was taking place with those saints who rose from the dead.

Just as the veil barring the Most Holy Place was largely symbolic of the separation between God and humanity, the grave is a symbol of another kind of separation, nearly as diabolical. Death separates us from one another, and from the world in which God placed us to live and reign with Him. When Jesus breathed His last from the cross, the curtain was torn and the dead were raised. Jesus' death and resurrection were undoing every terrible thing that had gone wrong in God's story.

"The wages of sin is death, but the free gift of God is eternal life in Christ Jesus our Lord" (Romans 6:23). It makes sense, then, that when Jesus received those wages for our sin, the gift of life was immediately bestowed upon "saints" (Matthew 27:52), those who were among the first to follow Jesus.[2]

But the work of Christ is about more than a moment in time. It's about forever—about everything being made new (Revelation 21:5). In this Good Friday resurrection, we have an answer to the questions that rise from our deepest fears: Is anything too difficult for God? Is it ever too late to make things new? The no-longer-dead who walked the streets of Jerusalem say, "No."

A New Sort of New Thing

Mary owed everything to Jesus. Prior to meeting Him, she had been held captive by not one, but seven, demons (Mark 16:9; Luke 8:2). Jesus had set her free, and she had followed Him ever since.

In a world where a woman's testimony was considered less reliable than a man's, Mary was chosen to be the initial eyewitness to the resurrection (John 20:11–18). On Sunday morning, she became the first in an unbroken, centuries-long string of believers to receive the good news and pass it on. But something initially prevented Mary from recognizing Jesus—she thought He was the gardener.

It could have been something as basic as grief or the low light of early morning. Or it could have been nothing more than the fact that Mary wasn't expecting to see Jesus alive that morning.

But I don't think those explanations fully account for this case of mistaken identity. Jesus was the most important person in the world to Mary—her Savior, Messiah, Lord, and Friend.

Think of someone you have loved and lost. What if they suddenly showed up on your doorstep? Would you not, at the very least, remark, "That's incredible! You look just like someone I used to know"? Now imagine seeing that person while you are still mourning, just a few short days after his or her death, at their tomb.

It seems unlikely that Mary simply mistook Jesus for the gardener. She was, for a short time, *unable* to see Jesus for who He was. And she wasn't the only one. Luke records another episode in which two disciples on the road to Emmaus needed to have their eyes opened before they too could recognize their Savior (24:31). These are our first clues that something was different about Jesus after His resurrection. But there's more.

That evening, Jesus' disciples were all together in a house, and the doors were locked. But Jesus suddenly appeared before them (John 20:19). Did He walk through the wall? Dematerialize from one place and then rematerialize in their midst, like something out of *Star Trek*? This happened more than once, it seems. After Jesus had revealed himself to those disciples He met on the road to Emmaus, He "vanished from their sight" (Luke 24:31), only to reappear a short time later in Jerusalem (vv. 36–37).

The body that was nailed to a cross on Good Friday was the same body raised to new life on Easter Sunday. But it was also different, changed, set free. And someday, all who know Jesus will receive bodies like His resurrection body—glorious, imperishable, and powerful, not subject to age or disease (1 Corinthians 15:42–44; Philippians 3:21), perhaps able to pass through walls without a problem. This is what restoration looks like in God's story.

Those saints who walked out of their graves on Good Friday were, at some later date, laid back to rest. Their resurrection, while an incredible and indescribable gift, was but a sign of the final resurrection.

Except for those who are still alive when Jesus returns, we will all rise from our graves one day (Daniel 12:2; 1 Thessalonians 4:16–17). But our resurrection will not be like that of those no-longer-dead saints who toured Jerusalem. We—and they—will rise like Jesus, never to return to a tomb, never to succumb to death again. There will be no more loss, no more grief, no more regret. The restoration of God means more than just putting broken pieces back together. His fulfilled promises always exceed the limits of our imagination.

The restoration of all things will be, in a real sense, the *resurrection* of all things. Sin brings death, and God brings life. Everything with the spark of goodness in it will be made whole, infused with fullness of life so that it can be what it was always intended to be. And this extends beyond the organic: music, story, art, friendship, love, adventure—everything that reflects the beauty of God—will be resurrected as if it were a dead body come to life.

You think the sunset is beautiful now? Just wait until you see it from the earth made new.

YOUR LIFE IN THE STORY OF GOD

During His time on earth, Jesus brought several people back to life including, at the moment of His own death, numerous "saints who had fallen asleep" (Matthew 27:52). Jesus' own resurrection foreshadowed the resurrection of all believers and the rebirth of everything that reflects the beauty of God—like music, adventure, and love. In His great story, this renewal will be perfect and permanent.

1. How did the mass resurrection around Jerusalem differ from other instances of Jesus raising people to life? What was the common end for every individual who'd been brought back to life?

2. How was Jesus' resurrected body different from His former body? How does the apostle Paul describe all believers' future bodies (1 Corinthians 15:42–44, Philippians 3:21)?

3. What will our ultimate, resurrected bodies *not* do (Revelation 21:4)?

The Undoing of Babel

ACTS 2:4–7

As a teenager, Squanto was captured by European slave traders and taken to Spain. There, the young Pawtuxet brave was bought by kind Spanish monks, who shared the gospel with him.

After a few years, these friars helped Squanto take a first step toward getting back home; they got him to London. There, he experienced the city of Shakespeare, learned the English language, and grew in his faith.

After a few more years, Squanto found passage on a ship headed for America. Sadly, when he arrived back home, he discovered that his entire tribe had been wiped out by disease. He was the last of the Pawtuxet.

Years passed with Squanto living by himself and no tribe to call his own. He was lonely. Very lonely. Until one day, when a friend from another tribe brought word that a ship from Europe had come and a group of settlers was attempting to farm the land nearby—the same land where Squanto had grown up. Squanto went to investigate, and seeing that the report was true, he walked out of the woods and in perfect English introduced himself to the Pilgrims.

Imagine the joy and relief in the hearts of those weary travelers. Here they were in a strange land, far from home in the harshest of circumstances, and they met a Native American who was not only a Christian but could even speak their language. In fact, Squanto had been in London more recently than the Pilgrims had!

Their new friend taught them how to farm the land and fish

the nearby waters. But it was God who took care of the Pilgrims, by preparing Squanto in the first place.[3]

Dividing Walls and Language Barriers

In the early pages of the Bible, God appears to stack the deck against humanity. First, He bars the way back to the garden of Eden so that Adam can't "reach out his hand and take also of the tree of life and eat, and live forever" (Genesis 3:22). Then, just before the flood, He limits to 120 years the incredibly long lives that men and women had enjoyed up until that time (Genesis 6:3). Finally, when people begin to work together to build a grand city, He confuses their language so they can no longer talk with one another (Genesis 11:7). His reasoning? With a single language, "nothing that they propose to do will now be impossible for them," He says (11:6).

To live forever and achieve our impossible dreams may be the stuff of Disney movies, but isn't it also God's desire for us? After all, didn't Jesus say, "For God so loved the world that he gave his one and only Son, that whoever believes in him shall not perish but have eternal life" (John 3:16 NIV)? And didn't He also say, "Nothing will be impossible for you" (Matthew 17:20)?

Yes, Jesus came so that we might live forever with Him. He wants us to have everlasting life. And He also promises that with faith, we can move mountains (Matthew 17:20); He wants us to do amazing things *with Him*.

In each of these passages from Genesis, God put the brakes on human life and power because, apart from Him, they will only bring more sin and pain into the world. Adam and Eve weren't allowed back in the garden because, without new hearts, everlasting life gained from the tree of life would amount to a permanent sentence in sin's prison. And prior to the great flood, God limited human lifespans to roughly 120 years because the less time wicked people have on this earth, the less evil they can do to one another. When people were building the tower of Babel, God gave them multiple languages so they couldn't finish the job; He knew that if human beings began to do the seemingly impossible without Him, they would start to believe they didn't need Him at all.

But these limitations were placed on people long before Jesus came. In Christ, we gain both eternal life and the power of the Holy Spirit. That's why, when God first sent His Spirit to baptize Jesus' friends and disciples, He also undid that whole tower of Babel incident, the confusing of our language.

When the day of Pentecost came, they were all together in one place. Suddenly a sound like the blowing of a violent wind came from heaven and filled the whole house where they were sitting. They saw what seemed to be tongues of fire that separated and came to rest on each of them. All of them were filled with the Holy Spirit and began to speak in other tongues as the Spirit enabled them (ACTS 2:1–4 NIV).

At first, God's Spirit appeared to bring more confusion to language. But in short order God revealed the purpose behind this miracle of speech:

Now there were staying in Jerusalem God-fearing Jews from every nation under heaven. When they heard this sound, a crowd came together in bewilderment, because each one heard their own language being spoken (ACTS 2:5–6 NIV).

Rather than driving people apart, this gift of the Spirit allowed Jesus' disciples, who were gathered in the upper room that day, to bring the world together by sharing the good news of Christ. At Babel, language had divided people, breaking up humanity into an ever expanding variety of tribes and nations. At Pentecost, God used the gift of tongues to bring people together under the banner of Jesus Christ, and "about three thousand were added to their number that day" (Acts 2:41 NIV).

Nearly sixteen hundred years after Pentecost, God used another miracle of language to direct the course of human history. The world's last Pawtuxet brave stepped out of the trees near Plymouth, Massachusetts, and said hello to a band of religious refugees trying to make their way in a strange new place. Because Squanto spoke English, he was able to help the Pilgrims survive. And because of the strong influence of Plymouth, and later the Massachusetts Bay Colony, America became a land of religious freedom, fertile ground for the good news of Jesus Christ.

Taken together, the miracle of tongues in Acts 2 and the amazing tale of Squanto illustrate the importance of communication and the hand of God at work in our world. But that's not the real reason I wrapped the true story of the Pilgrims and a Pawtuxet around Pentecost.

What happened at Pentecost was the undoing of Babel—and a major step toward the restoration of humanity. Through His Spirit, God is making one new people out of all the nations of earth, and the effort began in earnest that day in Jerusalem when tongues of fire alighted on the disciples and gave them the ability to speak other languages. Peter preached the gospel to men and women from all over the world, and thousands accepted it.

These people were Jews, but soon the gospel was also embraced by Samaritans (Acts 8:11–17), people who were essentially half-Hebrew but with whom "respectable" Jews had no dealings. After that, Gentiles of all stripes came into the kingdom.[4] In Christ, every dividing wall is torn down.

This was God's plan all along. Remember how He told Abraham that all nations on earth would be blessed through his offspring (Genesis 22:18)? In Christ, this promise became a reality. The good news of God's story—that He loves us and sent His Son to live and die on our behalf so that we could be with Him forever, restored to the identity and purpose for which He created us—is for *all* people. In the final chapters of the Bible, God gives us a view of His story's happy ending:

After this I looked, and behold, a great multitude that no one could number, from every nation, from all tribes and peoples and languages, standing before the throne and before the Lamb, clothed in white robes, with palm branches in their hands, and crying out with a loud voice, "Salvation belongs to our God who sits on the throne, and to the Lamb!" (REVELATION 7:9–10).

If you were to look carefully at that heavenly choir, you'd see one member, clothed in white, the sole representative of his tribe and native tongue—his name is Squanto. He is there because of the gift God bestowed upon His people at Pentecost, and because the Lord turned the evil actions of slave traders for good. But he's also there because he allowed God's story to inform His entire life after some Spanish monks introduced him to Jesus.

There was a day when Squanto peered through the trees at Plymouth Harbor and saw a ship much like the one that had once carried him off in chains. Then he saw men with white faces, from the same part of the world as his captors, occupying land that was rightfully his, land that his family had farmed for generations. But rather than finding fear and anger in his heart, he found the love of Christ. That moment was only possible because Babel has been undone.

YOUR LIFE IN THE STORY OF GOD

Pentecost was the undoing of Babel. Early in human history, God confused people's language to limit their prideful ambition; when He sent His Holy Spirit to live in believers, He used the languages of the nations to draw people to himself through His Son, Jesus Christ. God's story is open to all people, "from every tribe and language and people and nation" (Revelation 5:9).

1. What, besides language, are some of the "dividing walls" between people today (Ephesians 2:14–16)? How does Jesus break down those walls?

2. How did John describe the "multitude" praising God that he saw in a vision (Revelation 7:9–10)? What does that indicate about God?

3. What did God use to draw three thousand people into His story after the Holy Spirit's arrival (see Acts 2:38–41)? In what other ways can you help people find God?

THE STORY GOD IS STILL WRITING

"Traditions tell us where we have come from. Scripture itself is a better guide as to where we should now be going."
—N. T. WRIGHT

The Secret Weapon

PHILEMON

This final section could be called a "conclusion" or an "epilogue," but those titles suggest that we've reached the end of our journey—and the Christian life is one of new beginnings. There is no arriving. There is no point at which we'll have it all figured out. God is making all things new, and you and I are being remade as well. Every day is New Year's Day, every moment an opportunity to grow deeper with Christ, to grow nearer to God.

This may sound to some as if nothing will ever again be familiar. And many people live as if this should be the case. They wonder why God doesn't step in immediately to change their circumstances, to bring blessing where there is hardship, and prosperity where there is lack. They want God to solve all their problems in an instant—suddenly, the gospel has become all about them. God's story has become their story. And when their every wish is not granted, it may appear to them that Satan's original lie from the garden has some validity. "God is holding out on you," he whispers softly.

No Longer a Slave

It was the story Onesimus had wanted to be true, and now it was. He had finally escaped the house of Philemon, his master. The freedom he had dreamed about was his. But then, out on the run, he met the apostle Paul and was stopped in his tracks.

Paul knew about starting over. He had once been a Pharisee bent on destroying the nascent church in its cradle. He followed the law meticulously, and was quickly rising through the ranks of the religious ruling class in Jerusalem. Then one day, en route to Damascus to put more of Jesus' disciples in chains, he met the One he had been persecuting. A light from heaven blinded Paul (at that time called Saul), and a voice spoke to him—the voice of God's Son. Years earlier, the disciples who had known Jesus during His three-year ministry had become apostles, or "messengers," bearing witness to the resurrected Christ, whom they had seen with their own eyes. On that road to Damascus, Paul became, in his own words, as "one untimely born . . . the least of the apostles" (1 Corinthians 15:8–9). But an apostle he became nonetheless.

Onesimus was in Rome when he met Paul, who was in prison for the sake of the gospel. While we aren't privy to the exact circumstances surrounding that meeting, we have Paul's words to Philemon to fill in the gaps: "I appeal to you for my child, Onesimus, whose father I became in my imprisonment" (Philemon 10). Onesimus became like a son to Paul.

Yet, here's a strange thing: we know from this letter that Paul sent Onesimus, the runaway slave, back to his master. But that just can't be, can it? Runaway slaves could be killed under Roman law.[1] Wasn't Paul opposed to slavery? Didn't he want his "son" to be free? Isn't a new life in Christ just that—a new life? The answer to each of those questions, I believe, is a bold and confident "yes."

There isn't space here to adequately address the differences between Roman slavery and the human bondage that was part of life in Britain, the United States, and other Western nations in recent centuries. But those differences do not change the simple fact that people are not property. Every human being has been created in God's image and bears the dignity that such an origin demands. Paul's letter to Philemon isn't a treatise on the ethics of slavery, nor was it a political statement meant to goad the Roman senate into abolishing the practice. Debt slavery was a fact of life in Paul's day, and it was with this cruel reality in mind that Paul wrote his letter.

By sending Onesimus back to Philemon, Paul was subverting the very idea of slavery. Onesimus would live out Jesus' teaching in Matthew 5:41—"If anyone forces you to go one mile, go with him two miles." Many people believe Jesus was referring to Roman soldiers who forced Jews to carry their gear. Walking a mile with that soldier might mean you're his slave, but going the extra mile shows you're free. A slave is a slave against his will, so for Onesimus to return of his own accord would demonstrate his God-given freedom.

At the same time, Philemon, as a fellow believer, would be shamed when Onesimus showed up at his door with Paul's letter in hand. Slavery is not a practice that should exist in the kingdom of God, and Onesimus's contrite face would confront him with this truth. Paul fully expected Philemon to welcome the runaway, "no longer as a bondservant but more than a bondservant, as a beloved brother" (Philemon 16).

Regardless of what Philemon chose to do, Paul could send his beloved son back to his old life without a worry of him losing his true freedom. "For the one who was a slave when called to faith in the Lord is the Lord's freed person" (1 Corinthians 7:22 NIV). Paul, too, had willingly accepted hardship when he met Christ, stepping down from his privileged position among the religious elite in Jerusalem to embrace almost every imaginable bit of suffering a servant of Christ might face:

> *Five times I received at the hands of the Jews the forty lashes less one. Three times I was beaten with rods. Once I was stoned. Three times I was shipwrecked; a night and a day I was adrift at sea; on frequent journeys, in danger from rivers, danger from robbers, danger from my own people, danger from Gentiles, danger in the city, danger in the wilderness, danger at sea, danger from false brothers; in toil and hardship, through many a sleepless night, in hunger and thirst, often without food, in cold and exposure* (2 CORINTHIANS 11:24–27).

But it wasn't all bad.

"I know how to be brought low, and I know how to abound,"

Paul writes elsewhere. "In any and every circumstance, I have learned the secret of facing plenty and hunger, abundance and need" (Philippians 4:12). Paul's "secret" weapon? "I can do all things through [Christ] who strengthens me" (v. 13).

The same power that had sustained and protected Paul during his struggles would fortify Onesimus, no matter what awaited him in Colossae.

Personal Jesus

Jesus Christ living in and through His friends. It's what sets the Christian journey apart from every other religious path, world-view, or way of life. You may have heard it said that grace is what makes Christianity different than other religions. Grace is wonderful, and the sort of grace that God offered the world at Calvary is beyond comparison. But that grace becomes a part of our everyday lives because Christ lives within His followers. It's one of the ways we experience the gospel, here and now. We need power for living, day in and day out, so that we can be like Philemon and Paul—even like Jesus himself.

Paul called this reality of Christ living in us "the hope of glory," a "mystery" in which "glorious riches" are found (Colossians 1:27 NIV). No matter where you might go or what you might face, if you know Jesus, He is right there with you. This is how the story that God is writing can remain His story even as you and I play a vital role throughout our lives.

God doesn't promise to change our circumstances when life gets difficult. If you have any doubt about that, just go back and read Paul's description of his own suffering or, better yet, read the gospel accounts of Jesus' torture and crucifixion. In fact, it was because of the cross that Paul knew Christ's presence in His life would more than make up for any hardship he faced:

If God is for us, who can be against us? He who did not spare his own Son but gave him up for us all, how will he not also with him graciously give us all things? . . . Who shall separate us from the love of Christ? Shall tribulation, or distress, or persecution, or famine, or nakedness, or danger, or sword? As it is written,

> *"For your sake we are being killed all the day long; we are regarded as sheep to be slaughtered."*

No, in all these things we are more than conquerors through him who loved us. For I am sure that neither death nor life, nor angels nor rulers, nor things present nor things to come, nor powers, nor height nor depth, nor anything else in all creation, will be able to separate us from the love of God in Christ Jesus our Lord (ROMANS 8:31–32, 35–39).

No, God doesn't promise us soft, comfortable lives. He promises us something far better: himself. There will come a day when every bad situation crumbles, when every hardship is replaced with joy, and when every moment of pain is wiped away forever. That's the stuff of eternal life, but with Jesus living inside us, we have access to that life right now. In fact, Christ's presence in our lives is the very definition of eternal life. Take it from Jesus himself: "And this is eternal life, that they know you, the only true God, and Jesus Christ whom you have sent" (John 17:3).

One danger of a short chapter like this is that it can sound as if our response to suffering ought to be big smiles on our faces, and that we should never mourn our losses. But that's not real life. Walking through times of grief and weighing our heartbreaks allow us to appreciate just how wonderful God's promises are. If we never cry, there can nothing special about the Lord's promise to wipe away our tears one day (Revelation 21:4). Until then, He mourns with us.

I imagine that Onesimus was anxious during the long journey from Paul's prison cell to Philemon's house. Along the way, he may have prayed, again and again, through his decision to return. And in the moment of his arrival, when he knocked on the door and waited for an answer, I would be willing to bet that he was struck by the most terrible fear he had ever experienced.

But I know that through it all, Onesimus wasn't alone—because nothing "will be able to separate us from the love of God" (Romans 8:39). No streak of fear. No second-guessing of his decision. *Nothing* could get between Onesimus and the all-encompassing love of his Father. That's why he could keep going.

In the story God is still writing today, it's why you and I can keep going too. There's nothing that can separate us from God's love. Absolutely nothing.

YOUR LIFE IN THE STORY OF GOD

Christians possess a secret weapon in the battles of life—the actual presence of God in their lives. The apostle Paul said that nothing "will be able to separate us from the love of God in Christ Jesus our Lord" (Romans 8:39). This reality gives us strength to endure the kind of hardships Paul faced, or the stresses the runaway slave Onesimus must have felt while returning to his one-time owner. It's how we all keep going in the story God continues to write for our lives.

1. What is the hardest life event you've had to face—or are currently facing? Have you experienced God's love in it? How?

2. How did Jesus change the relationship between Onesimus and Philemon? What was Paul's role in their new status?

3. What does Paul say is "the hope of glory" (Colossians 1:27)? What did Jesus say is eternal life (John 17:3)?

What Jesus Says to Us at Breakfast

JOHN 21:15–19

Abraham believed God, but he was also so terrified of the Egyptians that he was willing to let Pharaoh have his wife (Genesis 12:10–20). Moses delivered the people of Israel across the Red Sea on dry land, but he was also a vigilante (Exodus 2:11–12). Solomon was the wisest man of his day, but he was led astray by his many wives (1 Kings 11:1–4). The Bible is God's story, and its greatest "heroes" help make that case—God is the only one in the Bible with nothing to apologize for.

Everyone else is broken in some way; each is in need of forgiveness and restoration. And that's not just true of the men and women of the Bible. Remember that God's story cannot be contained between two book covers. You and I are a part of the story today, and we, too, are in need of healing and a fresh start.

The children's song resounds, "Jesus loves me—this I know, for the Bible tells me so." But what would it be like to hear those words from Jesus himself? What would it be like to see that love in His eyes and hear it in His voice? One day, we'll stand face-to-face with our Savior, and we'll experience such a moment. But until then, the story of Peter gives us a taste of what such a meeting might be like.

Peter could be added to the list of less-than-perfect biblical figures. He's known for being impetuous and putting his foot in his mouth. For example, there was the time Jesus told His disciples plainly about His own coming death and resurrection, and Peter took Him aside to correct His theology (Mark 8:32). To his credit, Peter showed the same boldness when he asked to step out on the Sea of Galilee and walk on the water with Jesus—he was the only disciple willing to do so. But then his fear got the best of him, and he began to sink (Matthew 14:28–31). When soldiers came to arrest Jesus, it was Peter who took a swipe at one with his sword, still not understanding that a man who could turn water into wine, calm storms, and raise the dead could defend himself if He wanted to (John 18:10).

But Peter's greatest failure came when he denied knowing the Lord during Jesus' trial at the home of the high priest. Hours earlier, the Lord had actually told Peter he would do it, but Peter allowed fear to sway his heart. Three times he denied that he had any connection to Jesus, and so adamant was he that, according to Matthew, his second denial was accompanied by an oath and his third by curses (Matthew 26:72, 74). In other words, Peter appealed to God as his witness, asking for some terrible calamity to come upon him if he was lying—even though he knew he was!

When Jesus had warned Peter about his betrayal, He shared specific details. He said Peter would deny Him three times before the rooster crowed. (According to Mark, the Lord was even more specific, mentioning that the rooster would crow twice; see Mark 14:30.) When Peter's final betrayal fell from his lips, his ears were greeted by the bird's ominous early morning squawk, "and he went out and wept bitterly" (Matthew 26:75).

Peter remembered that Jesus had predicted his denials, but in that moment, I wonder if he also remembered something Jesus had said to him and the other disciples years earlier. The Lord was about to send the men out to minister on their own, so He wanted to give them words of preparation for their journey— not only that journey, but also for their ongoing ministry to the world. In that talk, Jesus had said, "Whoever denies me before men, I also will deny before my Father who is in heaven" (Matthew 10:33). Now Peter had done just that.

With God the Father as witness against him and Jesus having warned him of this very sin and its dire consequences, what hope could there be for Peter? If this were any other story, we'd have to admit there was none. Peter deserved no grace.

But grace is never deserved.

On the cross, Jesus accepted the penalty for Peter's lies of denial. And there, He received the curse Peter called down from God the Father. Jesus paid it all so Peter could be free—so that, a few days later, over an early morning breakfast on the beach, He could restore His friend (John 21:15–19). But this restoration did not come with a lecture or an "I told you so." Three times Jesus asked Peter if he loved Him, as if in answer to Peter's three denials. Each time, Peter assured Jesus that he did. And each time, Jesus told Peter to care for His sheep.

Son of Hope

"Well, you've got me beat," I admitted after Bridgette shared what she had done over the preceding weekend. It was a Sunday evening in November of 2002, and I was with a group of friends from church. Going around a table filled with snacks and drinks, each of us told the others what we had been up to lately. Bridgette had the best story: she had gone to Sullivan Correctional Facility in Fallsburg, New York, to visit an inmate serving a life sentence. But it wasn't just any inmate; it was David Berkowitz.

Between the summers of 1976 and 1977, New York City was the scene of a vicious crime wave. A serial killer was on the loose. Six women were killed, and though a police manhunt had been underway for some time, the murderer proved difficult to apprehend. The entire city lived in fear. When he was finally arrested on August 10, 1977, David Berkowitz admitted to the crimes and told the world that a demon spoke to him through the dog of his neighbor Sam, demanding the blood of young women. Years later in prison, Berkowitz—who became known as the "Son of Sam"—admitted that he had been a part of Satanic cult.

When Berkowitz had been in prison for about ten years,

another inmate named Rick approached him in the prison yard with a simple message: "Jesus Christ loves you and wants to forgive you." The two men became friends and Rick later gave Berkowitz a pocket New Testament with Psalms and Proverbs. He read it every night, and one evening he came to Psalm 34:6, which says, "This poor man cried, and the LORD heard him, and saved him out of all his troubles" (KJV). That night, David Berkowitz cried out too, and the Lord heard him and saved him as well.

Twenty-five years after David Berkowitz's arrest, my friend Bridgette went to visit the Son of Sam—though now he was going by another name, Son of Hope. She wanted to hear his story for herself, and as she relayed that story to me and the others that night, I couldn't shake the thought, *How can it be that someone who displayed so much evil in his life can deserve forgiveness?* I doubted Berkowitz's sincerity and convinced myself that his claims of being born again were just an attempt to gain sympathy and support—maybe even to sway a future parole board.

Later on, as we all got ready to leave, I jokingly told Bridgette not to make friends with any more famous serial killers. "Just this one," she said. I asked her if she really believed him. "That's why I went," she told me. "Because I didn't. I wanted to see for myself if God's grace was really that big."

"And?" I asked.

"Yeah, it's big enough. For even the worst killer."

My Name Is Peter

I am Peter. You are Peter. And David Berkowitz is Peter. God's story, from Genesis to Revelation and beyond, is the story of Him making a way for faithless people to become faithful. One of my favorite details from the night of Jesus' trial and Peter's abandonment is recorded in Luke's gospel. Just as Peter's tongue let loose its third denial of Jesus and the rooster crowed, Luke tells us that "the Lord turned and looked at Peter" (22:61). In the middle of a hostile, undeserved trial, full of slander, false accusations, and abuse, Jesus is unconcerned with His own well-being—He is focused on His friend. But isn't this the gospel? "God shows his love for us in that while we were still sinners, Christ died for us" (Romans 5:8).

Peter's story is the story of every disciple. Each of us in our sin, by our actions, through our words, and with our hearts, has denied knowing the Lord. Each of us has gone our own way, thinking it best. Each of us deserves to be denied by Christ and left to fend for ourselves.

Still, Jesus comes to us with a single question. He doesn't ask if we're sorry for what we've done; He already knows our hearts. He doesn't ask us to make up for our selfishness; there's nothing we could do anyway. And He doesn't withhold His affection so we might feel the weight of our crimes; He's already carried that weight. He wants to know just one thing: "Do you love Me?" How you answer that question will change your life.

To those who answer, as Peter did, "Yes, Lord; you know that I love You" (John 21:15–16), Jesus says, "Feed my sheep" (21:17). Though Peter's role as an apostle in the early church was unique, each of Christ's followers is called to serve God faithfully. That means loving everyone we meet, but especially those of Jesus' flock (Galatians 6:10). The restoration Jesus offered to Peter, and offers to all of us, is not just one of status but of position. It is not enough simply to be welcomed into God's family; in that family, we have a responsibility to look after our brothers and sisters. We are entrusted with loving those whom God himself loves, and that is no small thing.

Jesus was once asked which of the Old Testament's commands was the greatest. He chose two: "You shall love the Lord your God with all your heart and with all your soul and with all your mind. This is the great and first commandment. And a second is like it: You shall love your neighbor as yourself. On these two commandments depend all the Law and the Prophets" (Matthew 22:37–40; compare with Deuteronomy 6:5; Leviticus 19:18). In other words, Jesus was saying that if you can master these two commandments, you've got them all.

To Peter, on the shore of the Sea of Galilee that morning, Jesus offered a way back. His debt was paid, and though he was sad and sorry in that moment, there was now nothing standing between Peter and his fulfilling of these greatest of commandments. Peter could still be made whole. Jesus is God, so when He asked Peter, "Do you love Me?" He was really reminding Peter of the first and greatest commandment. And Jesus' command—"Feed My sheep"—was a call for Peter to love His neighbor.

In the first chapter of this book, we saw wisdom applied "under the sun" (Ecclesiastes 1:9). It's a way that seems right to us because it's what we've experienced. Under the sun, we expect that when we fail, we'll pay the cost, we'll lose opportunities, we'll have to settle for what can still be rather than what could have been. I imagine that's what Peter expected as he finished the last of his breakfast that morning. But Jesus did not come to Peter with the consolation prize of what can still be. He offered His friend life without limits, pleasing to God in every way—not because of any good thing Peter had done, but because Jesus had done every good thing.

The gospel here and now demands that we see past that night at the home of the high priest, where Peter sank to his lowest point. It demands that we see past Calvary, where Jesus paid the price so that Peter's sins could be washed clean. It even demands that we not stop with the empty tomb. To live out God's story in our everyday lives, we must find ourselves at breakfast with Jesus, hearing words of restoration and healing. In that conversation is our commission to live as God created us to live, whole and wholly loved.

"Follow me," Jesus told Peter (John 21:19). And to you and me, He issues the same invitation—into a deeper relationship with Him, into adventure, and into the story God is still writing, no matter what we may have done in the past. His grace is that big. Really.

YOUR LIFE IN THE STORY OF GOD

God's story, throughout the Bible and in our lives today, is the story of Him making a way for faithless people to become faithful. Peter failed miserably the night Jesus was tried, but the Lord restored him completely. God in His grace will forgive mass murderers who cry out for salvation; He will forgive *our* sins as well. Once we've been restored, our role in the story becomes one of caring for our fellow believers—as Jesus told Peter, "Feed my sheep" (John 21:17).

1. What did Jesus identify as the two greatest commandments (Matthew 22:37–40)? How did His restoration of Peter illustrate them?

2. Why do people sometimes struggle to accept God's forgiveness? What does the story of Jesus and Peter in John 21:15–19 say to those struggles?

3. What part of your life needs the gospel, here and now?

A Retelling
of God's Story

The Bible begins with God creating everything we know and love—and His creation is good. As the finishing touch to His wonder-filled universe, He forms a man from the dirt and a woman from the man's side, placing them in a garden. They bear His own image and are given the responsibility to rule over and care for the world. Walking in perfect step with their Creator and the good things He's made, these first two humans, Adam and Eve, have a life we can scarcely imagine.

One day, a serpent slithers toward Eve and strikes up a conversation. That Eve was not startled by a talking snake is a discussion for another time, but those few minutes change the world forever. The serpent deceives Eve, tempting her into tasting fruit from the tree of the knowledge of good and evil—the one bit of produce God had forbidden the first couple to eat. She then shares some with Adam and, in an instant, their eyes are opened, their innocence is shattered, and sin takes hold of our world.

God brings judgment on the man, the woman, and the serpent, whom we later discover is Satan in disguise. Satan is God's enemy, and though there are clues to his origins later in God's story, all we need to know at this stage is that he is a murderer, a liar, and a thief. He hates God and everything good that God made, especially human beings, who bear His image. In His pronouncement of judgment, God promises that one day Someone—a descendant of Eve—will destroy the works of Satan.

Adam and Eve make their way in the world outside the garden. Their life is not easy, but God is still good. Generations come and go until the sinfulness of mankind reaches a breaking point: God unleashes a flood to destroy everyone except a single family. Noah, along with his wife, sons, and their wives, are preserved on an ark. This ark also contains representatives from every animal species. God is not done with our planet, but He is, in a sense, starting over just as the story has gotten underway.

Years go by, and sin is still pressing down on everyone and everything God made. God speaks to a man named Abram and promises to make him into a great nation, even though Abram is old and his wife, Sarai, is past her childbearing years. God also promises to give Abram and his descendants the land of Canaan, a small corner of the Middle East about the size of New Jersey. And He promises to bless the whole world through Abram. When she's ninety years old, Sarai, now called Sarah, gives birth to a bouncing baby boy named Isaac. God leads Abram, now known as Abraham, as He will lead Isaac and Isaac's son Jacob, too. Each man follows God imperfectly, but God is patient and faithful.

Jacob goes on to have twelve sons. The nation God promised Abraham is beginning to take shape. But first, one of Jacob's sons must save the world.

A seven-year famine hits, and Joseph—Jacob's second-youngest boy—oversees Egypt's stores of grain. He had come to such a powerful position by a path of sibling rivalry, slavery, and imprisonment; God can use anything, even sin, to bring good things to pass. The region is saved, and along with it, Jacob and his extended family. The children of Abraham relocate to Egypt and settle in for four hundred years.

At some point in that span, the Egyptians begin to worry that with so many Hebrews in their land, they might just take over. The nation God is making is forced into slavery, building cities for Pharaoh, king of Egypt. To keep the slave population manageable, Pharaoh has all the newborn males of Israel thrown into the Nile. One Hebrew boy, however, is not tossed in. Instead, he is placed in a basket and set adrift on the river by his mother. This boy is then found and adopted by Pharaoh's daughter.

God raises up this unlikely hero, a child named Moses, to become the deliverer of His people. Through Moses, God challenges Pharaoh and the gods of Egypt, bringing ten plagues upon the land unlike anything the world has seen. The Nile runs red with blood, locusts and gnats bring pestilence, darkness blankets the sky, and death comes to every firstborn in Egypt. But God spares His own people by providing a means of escape: if they will place the blood of a spotless lamb on their doorframes, death will pass over their homes. It is a sign and a promise of things to come.

Once free of Pharaoh's grip, the Israelites are led through the desert by God. He makes a covenant with them, promising to be their God and to bless them if they will only follow Him and obey His commands. Almost immediately, the people fail. Judgment comes, grace abounds, and the people try (and fail) again. But God provides a system of sacrifices, administered by a priesthood led by Moses' brother, Aaron. The sins of the people can be covered over with the blood of animals, so that the covenant can continue despite Israel's failures. But the sacrifices do more than cover over sin; they point to a future Sacrifice that will *pay* for sin, once and for all.

Forty years after setting out from Egypt, the people's disobedience continues in their new home, the Promised Land of Canaan, under Joshua, Moses' successor. God continues to be faithful, though because of their sin, the people of Israel are surrounded by enemies on all sides. For the next few centuries, they repeat their mistakes; time and again, they sin, and God sends an enemy to oppress them. The people cry out to the Lord, and He brings a deliverer, also known as a judge. God works through that judge to bring a time of peace, but before long, the people forget God and rebel once again. This cycle finally stops, but not because Israel has learned to trust God. Instead, the people ask for a king just like the other nations have. God understands; they are rejecting Him as their true King.

God gives the people exactly what they want: a king like the kings of their neighbors. Saul is cowardly and, especially during the later years of his reign, faithless. He can be cruel and vindictive. He is the king the people of Israel deserve.

But God does not often give us what we deserve. He soon raises up a successor to Saul: David, a man after His own heart. David, though not perfect, loves the Lord and leads His people in righteousness. Under David, the borders of the nation are expanded, Jerusalem is made its capital, and plans are made for a house where God's presence will dwell. God promises that David's own house—his kingdom—will be established forever.

David's son, Solomon, builds God a temple in Jerusalem. Like the tabernacle that the Israelites carried with them in the desert under Moses and Joshua, Solomon's temple houses the ark of the covenant, the gold-covered box where God's presence dwells. Solomon is given supernatural wisdom, and the people of Israel enjoy an age of unrivaled prosperity and peace. But it doesn't last long. After Solomon's death, the kingdom splits in two: the nation of Israel (ten tribes in the north) and the nation of Judah (the tribes of Judah and Benjamin in the south).

In both kingdoms, God's people chase after false gods, bow down before idols, and commit the sins of their neighbors. The sin is more pronounced in the north, but the southern nation is not without its own evil. God raises up prophets, among whom are Elijah and Elisha, Isaiah and Jeremiah, to call the people back to the covenant He made with their ancestors and to remind them of His love and mercy.

These prophets speak on behalf of the Lord as wicked kings lead the nations of Israel and Judah deeper into sin. The prophets also speak about a new covenant and a Savior who will come to set the people free. But the people, for the most part, do not listen, and the Lord removes His hand of protection. First, the northern kingdom of Israel is conquered by Assyria, and the people are scattered across the world. Years later, Judah is crushed by Babylon, and her people are taken into captivity. The land God promised Abraham is taken away. But not forever.

Time in exile serves to shore up faithfulness where it can be found. Women like Esther and men like Daniel thrive in a far-away land full of foreign gods and evil practices. After seventy years, God raises up Cyrus as king of Persia. He allows the Jewish people to return to Judah and rebuild the temple. God's people go home, but they slowly realize that their biggest enemy still rules over them: sin weighs heavy on their hearts and in their hands. Even in the Promised Land, they need a Deliverer—a priest like Aaron, a king like David, and a prophet like Elijah—to show them the way. They remember the words of the prophets, and they long for the Messiah.

Four hundred years pass without a writing prophet among the people of God. Just as the people's ears have become attentive, heaven seems silent. But then the angel Gabriel visits a priest named Zechariah, promising that he and his wife, Elizabeth, will have a son in their old age. And there's another visit from Gabriel, this time to a teenage girl in Nazareth, a virgin pledged to be married to a righteous man named Joseph. Mary, too, is promised a Son. Zechariah and Elizabeth's boy will be a prophet. He will prepare the way for Mary's Son, Jesus.

Jesus is the Word of God, through whom all things were made. He is the promised seed of Eve that will crush the head of the serpent. He is the ark of safety in the flood. He is the world's blessing, come through Abraham's line. He is the Passover Lamb, who saves His people. He is the true King of Israel who takes up David's throne forever. He is the prophet who declares good news and pronounces righteous judgments. He is the Messiah who will deliver His people from the penalty and power of sin. He is God's only Son, who humbled himself to become one of us.

The Gospels provide us with four accounts of Jesus' life. They report many of the miracles He performed as signs of His identity and as glimpses into the Father's heart. They record His parables and His teachings on important subjects. And they tell us about His sinless life, His death on a Roman cross, and His resurrection from the dead in power.

On the cross, Jesus pays the penalty for our sins. His sacrifice, though foreshadowed by the sacrifices of the Old Testament, does more than cover over our sins for a year: Jesus, as our perfect representative, deals with sin once and forever. It is finished. The empty tomb serves as proof that the Father accepted the Son's sacrifice on our behalf. The good news of the gospel is true because Jesus is alive, the firstfruits of a resurrection harvest that all who know Him will one day experience for themselves.

Jesus returns to the Father, but He does not leave His friends. He sends His Holy Spirit to fill them with His presence and power. Just as God had taken up residence in the tabernacle and then the temple, He now takes up residence in every person who knows Jesus as Lord and Savior.

From Jerusalem, the gospel—the good news about Jesus and His kingdom—spreads throughout Judea, and then north to Samaria, and then to the larger Roman Empire. What started as a Jewish hope has become the world's hope. Men and women surrender to Jesus and are filled with His Spirit; some of them give their lives, as persecution follows the gospel wherever it is taken. Dividing lines are torn down between Jew and Gentile, slave and free, male and female. A man named Saul, later called Paul, meets Jesus on the road to Damascus and his life is turned upside-down; once a destroyer of the church and an opponent of the gospel, he becomes a planter of churches and a defender of the faith.

This is where we find ourselves in God's story. We belong to this age—to the era of the church, made up of disciples who have been charged by Jesus to make more disciples, sharing the good news of salvation with every person who has yet to hear. God's kingdom came to earth with His Son, but it is not yet here in its fullness. As citizens of His kingdom, we have opportunities to facilitate its coming as God's Spirit works through us to bless our world.

The Bible does not leave God's story open-ended. The book of Revelation gives us a sneak peek at Jesus' return. Until the end, Satan will continue to deceive as many people as he can, and God will continue to invite into His kingdom everyone who has ears to hear and eyes to see. Jesus has always been and will continue to be our ark of safety. And an ark will be needed, for judgment is coming, just as it did in Noah's day.

When Jesus returns, He will come as conquering King. Satan and his legions will be thrown into the lake of fire, along with all those who have rejected Jesus as Lord. The kingdom of darkness will be laid waste. Sin will be no more. Everything broken will be made new. Everything that has gone wrong will be undone. Heaven and earth will be joined together as the New Jerusalem comes down to meet a renewed earth. And God will dwell with His people forever in a glorious adventure beyond our wildest dreams.

Notes

INTRODUCTION: THE GOSPEL HERE AND NOW

[1]A longer but still quite brief summation is included in the appendix, which begins on page 271.

WEEK ONE: CREATION: God Is Up to Something New

[1]*YouthWalk,* July 2009, 11.

[2]C. S. Lewis, *Miracles* (New York: HarperCollins, 2001), 92.

[3]The phrase, "from Dan even to Beersheba," is a way of saying, "from north to south," or "the entire nation." Dan was the northernmost city in Israel at the time, while Beersheba was the largest city in the southernmost region of Judah.

WEEK TWO: RELATION: God Draws Near

[1]For a more detailed explanation, see Jeffrey J. Niehaus, *God at Sinai* (Grand Rapids, MI: Zondervan, 1995), 155–59.

[2]By making a nation out of Moses, one of Abraham's descendants, God would still be keeping His promises to Abraham, Isaac, and Jacob.

[3]God's grace is all around us. "He makes his sun rise on the evil and on the good, and sends rain on the just and on the unjust" (Matthew 5:45). He is "merciful and gracious, slow to anger, and abounding in steadfast love and faithfulness" (Exodus 34:6). But He is also just—and there is no sin that will go unpunished, at least not in the end. Sin was dealt with by Jesus at Calvary, and now anyone who places trust in Christ has his or her sins paid for. Therefore, the cross has made a way for sin to be punished *and* for God to be merciful. That is why He is "patient . . . not wishing that any should perish, but that all should reach repentance" (2 Peter 3:9). In this account from Exodus, God's desire to pour out His wrath on His sinful people is a rare glimpse at what should happen apart from His lovingkindness.

[4]John Piper, *Let the Nations Be Glad: The Supremacy of God in Missions* (Grand Rapids, MI: Baker Academic, 2010), 15.

[5]Please recall the discussion of Genesis 3:8 on pp. 64–65 as well.

WEEK THREE: SALVATION: God Rescues His People

[1] Andrew Hough, "Frane Selak: 'world's luckiest man' gives away his lottery fortune," *The Telegraph*, May 14, 2010, http://www.telegraph.co.uk/news/newstopics/howaboutthat/7721985/Frane-Selak-worlds-luckiest-man-gives-away-his-lottery-fortune.html. (Accessed September 2, 2016.)

[2] Jonathan Edwards, "Sinners in the Hands of an Angry God. A Sermon Preached at Enfield, July 8th, 1741," ed. Reiner Smolinski, *Electronic Texts in American Studies*, 54. http://digitalcommons.unl.edu/etas/54. (Accessed September 2, 2016.)

[3] There exists some debate as to whether the Genesis flood was truly world-wide or only localized to the Middle East and parts of both Asia and Africa, where the early members of the human race were clustered at the time. In Hebrew, the word translated "earth" can also be rendered "land," so both options are viable in the text. Read Genesis 6, substituting "land" for "earth," and you'll see what I mean.

[4] Interestingly, the first thing Noah did after exiting the ark was to plant a garden—a "vineyard" (Genesis 9:20). But just as with Adam and Eve before him, the fruit of his garden became a snare (v. 21).

WEEK FOUR: NATION: God Brings His Kingdom

[1] While most of Moses' childhood is not recorded for us in the Bible, when we first see Moses as an adult, he is very much aware of his Hebrew roots (Exodus 2:11).

[2] Before a single plague had been leveled, God warned that the punishment for the enslavement of God's "firstborn son" Israel would be the death of Pharaoh's firstborn son (Exodus 4:22–23). Notice, too, that Exodus 11:1 records the final plague was being brought not just upon Egypt, but also upon Pharaoh specifically.

[3] Hundreds of years earlier, when God first brought the people of Israel into the Promised Land, He miraculously stopped the waters of the Jordan River so the people could cross over on dry ground. This short walk across the Jordan marked the end of their forty-year journey from Egypt to Canaan. It was a trip that began with a miraculous water crossing when God parted the Red Sea, and it ended in a similar manner. On the far side of the Jordan, the Lord had His people build a monument of twelve stones—one for each tribe—as a reminder of His faithfulness. But the people had forgotten how much God loves them, so Elijah built another monument.

[4] The Greek word used here in Acts for "Lord" is the same Greek word used in the Septuagint, the popular ancient Greek translation of the Old Testament, as a stand-in for *Yahweh*, God's covenant name (see Exodus 3:14).

[5]I believe Paul's submission to Christ was virtually instantaneous. Notice that when Ananias greeted Saul in verse 17, it was with "Brother," indicating his belief that Paul was already a Christian.

WEEK FIVE: FORMATION: God Makes Us More like Jesus

[1]Jesus' words in Matthew 5:48 may have come to your mind: "You therefore must be perfect, as your heavenly Father is perfect." Doesn't Jesus command us to be perfect? Yes, in a sense. That verse comes at the end of Jesus' teaching on the heart-level meaning of several Old Testament commandments (more on this in chapter 31), and specifically at the close of His instructions on loving our enemies just as much as we love our neighbors. God's love is perfect—complete, not leaving anyone out—and so must ours be.

[2]C. S. Lewis, *Mere Christianity* (San Francisco: HarperOne, 2001), 50.

[3]Jamie Stengle, "Comics trove found in closet fetches $3.5 million," Today.com, February 22, 2012, http://www.today.com/popculture/comics-trove-found -closet-fetches-3-5-million-266216. (Accessed Dec. 21, 2016.)

[4]The land of Uz, mentioned in Job 1:1, is near Midian. This has led some scholars to suggest that Moses wrote the book of Job, having perhaps heard the dramatic story during his forty years as a shepherd in Midian. Cultural clues in the text itself tell us that Job lived during the lifetimes of Abraham, Isaac, and Jacob, long before the law was given to Moses.

[5]First Samuel 21–31 chronicles David's life on the run from Saul.

[6]Buildings of ancient Israel were often flat-topped, and residents sometimes used their roofs as additional living space.

[7]Read the full story in 2 Samuel 11.

WEEK SIX: RESTORATION: God Offers Peace and Rest

[1]Abraham Kuyper, *A Centennial Reader*, ed. James D. Bratt (Grand Rapids, MI: Eerdmans, 1998), 488.

[2]Though Matthew doesn't tell us who these saints were, there are good reasons to believe they were people who had become disciples of Jesus during His three-year earthly ministry. First, whenever the Greek term translated "saints" is used in the New Testament, it invariably refers to Christians, rather than to the Old Testament faithful. Second, in a world without photography, only those who had been known by the living would have been recognizable. Since these resurrected saints appeared to people in Jerusalem, the implication is they were known as those who had previously died.

[3]A note to parents and the young at heart: the full story can be found in Eric Metaxas's wonderful children's book, *Squanto and the Miracle of Thanksgiving* (Nashville, TN: Thomas Nelson, 2012).

[4]See Acts 10 for the account of Cornelius, the first Gentile convert.

CONTINUATION: The Story God Is Still Writing

[1]In order to finance his journey, Onesimus may also have stolen from Philemon. Note that Paul tells Philemon, "If he has wronged you at all, or owes you anything, charge that to my account. . . . I will repay it" (18–19). The idea of a thieving, runaway slave willingly returning to his master was almost unthinkable.

Acknowledgments

As it is with most of my written words, my wife, Laurin, made these possible, for time spent in front of a computer screen must be purchased at the expense of time spent elsewhere. During a busy season that included an interstate move, the construction of a new house, and the birth of our second son, my bride helped me find minutes of margin in which to write. And she read these pages before anyone else, offering feedback, asking questions, and finding errant commas. Thank you, Laurin, for loving me well and for once again allowing me to neglect yardwork in order to write a book.

Thanks are due to my friends at Our Daily Bread Ministries— J.R. Hudberg, Miranda Gardner, and especially Andy Rogers, who first approached me about this project and kept the conversation going even after I suggested we take it in a different direction. I am also grateful to Ken Petersen for his patience during a couple of long phone calls, in which I rambled out a rough sketch of this book. Thank you, Ken, for believing that the church needed one more volume about the most important subject in the world—the gospel. Finally, thank you to Paul Muckley, the saint who edited and polished these chapters (and who probably fixed a misplaced modifier or split infinitive in the very paragraph you're reading).

About the Author

John Greco is a writer living just outside of Nashville, Tennessee, with his wife, Laurin, and their two boys, Jonah and Jude. A graduate of Gordon College and Gordon-Conwell Theological Seminary, John has served in a variety of local church positions and has been a staff writer for In Touch Ministries, Crown Financial Ministries, and the Billy Graham Evangelistic Association. He is the author of *Manger King: Meditations on Christmas and the Gospel of Hope* and *Broken Vows: Divorce and the Goodness of God*. You can follow John on Twitter @grex77 or you can find him at JohnGrecoWrites.com.

Enjoy this book? Help us get the word out!

Share a link to the book or
mention it on social media

Write a review on your blog, on a retailer site,
or on our website (dhp.org)

Pick up another copy to share with someone

Recommend this book for your
church, book club, or small group

Follow Discovery House on
social media and join the discussion

Contact us to share your thoughts:

 @discoveryhouse   @DiscoveryHouse

Discovery House
P.O. Box 3566
Grand Rapids, MI 49501 USA

Phone: 1-800-653-8333
Email: books@dhp.org
Web: dhp.org